Amazing accounts that challenge history —

> *There were giants in the earth in those days,*
> *say the old Hebrew compilers of Genesis, who*
> *drew on ancient and vanished sources of*
> *antediluvian age. . . .*

There is evidence, in the shape of skulls, bones, and artifacts, that giants ranged over the whole planet from the plains of Asia and the mountains of central Europe into every part of America. In the Western Hemisphere, evidence is found from the far south in what is now Patagonia up to the tundras of Alaska — once a far warmer region. In that far day there existed land bridges that were, thousands of years later, destroyed in a terrible cataclysm that is recorded in Genesis and in many American Indian myths.

— from "The Giants in the Earth," p. 60

OUT OF TIME AND PLACE

Amazing Accounts That Challenge
Our View of Human History

From the Files of FATE Magazine

Compiled and Edited by
Terry O'Neill

1999
Llewellyn Publications
St. Paul, Minnesota 55164-0383 U.S.A.

FIRST EDITION
First Printing, 1999

Book design, layout, and editing: Terry O'Neill
Cover design: Tom Grewe

Library of Congress Cataloging-in-Publication Data
Out of time and place: amazing accounts that challenge our view of human history: from the files of FATE magazine / compiled and edited by Terry O'Neill. —1st ed.
         p.   cm.
    ISBN 1-56718-261-5
      1. History — Miscellanea.   I. O'Neill, Terry, 1944–   . II.
FATE (Saint Paul, MN)
D62.098   1999   98–33309
900—dc21   CIP

Llewellyn Publications
A Division of Llewellyn Worldwide, Ltd.
P.O. Box 64383, Dept. K261-5
St. Paul MN 55164-0383

Printed in the United States of America

CONTENTS

Evidence suggests that Druids may have
frolicked in New England.
(See p. 199)

Introduction

The past has left a legacy of enigmas. All about us are sacred sites, symbolic landscapes, ancient cities, and lost lands, fascinating alike to scholars and adventurers, curiosity seekers, and tourists. Yet still they keep their secrets.

It is clear that many of these mysteries will never be resolved, essentially for lack of conclusive evidence . . . . Perhaps it is better that way.

— Jennifer Westwood, *The Atlas of Mysterious Places* (1987)

What is it about mysteries that fascinates us? It is an innate characteristic of human nature to want to know more. Adam and Eve are said to have thrown away Paradise for the sake of knowledge. Today, we humans follow in that tradition. The explorers of ancient mysteries have risked life, limb, sanity, and reputation to try to find answers.

Fortunately, perhaps, for humanity's future existence, most of us are content to do our exploring from an armchair. We can vicariously enjoy the thrill of perils—whether physical, mental, spiritual, or social—that others have confronted in their search for knowledge. This book, a collection of some of the best articles from FATE Magazine's first fifty years, takes the reader on unconventional explorations of things and places that are "out of time and place."

How do we explain the presence of first- or second-century Semitic writing at an American Indian burial site in Tennessee? The Bat Creek tablet, discovered in 1889, shows just that. How about hieroglyphics that appear to show modern helicopters and military tanks in an ancient Egyptian tomb? Some claim these hieroglyphs, found in Abydos, Egypt, in the 1970s prove that modern technology is not new, while others say the symbols are merely flukes caused by time and wear.

How do we explain the presence of a 9,300-year-old Caucasian skeleton found in 1996 near Kennewick, Washington? Historians had been certain that Caucasians did not appear in this part of the world until much, much later.

What about living creatures that have been entombed in solid rock for decades, only to come shakily to life when the stone is broken open? Frogs, insects, and worms have all been found in such circumstances.

The truth is, these mysteries have no clear-cut solutions. That's what makes them so intriguing. Some members of the scientific community might simply ignore such anomalies. Others may be convinced they have the answers: coincidence, fraud, or a geologic disruption such as an earthquake, perhaps. Nonscientists may believe they have the answers as well: Extraterrestrials, ancient gods, early humans much more sophisticated and much more widely traveled than science has ever thought possible may be responsible for these enigmas.

Francis Hitching, author of *The Mysterious World* (1978), writes,

> In many scientific disciplines, the more that is discovered, the farther the horizon of knowledge seems to recede.

In others, the underlying assumptions have become so shaky that they will soon be discarded and replaced. All contain mysterious and uncomfortable facts which cannot be explained by conventional reasoning .... Models of science and prehistory succeed each other with surprising rapidity.

That's why, despite the ridicule and dishonor often heaped upon proponents of unconventional interpretations, they hang in there. As more information comes to light and theories are revised, it is sometimes the unconventional theories that turn out to be true. Not so long ago, scientists laughed at the idea that the continents' locations changed over time as they moved over the Earth's surface. Now continental drift is accepted as fact. Not so long ago, the knowledgeable laughed at the idea that Mars could sustain life. Today we know it can and did. Not so long ago, historians weren't sure whether Troy was a real place or a figment of Homer's imagination. Then in 1870, Heinrich Schliemann discovered its site; a myth was proven to be a fact.

That's why we continue to explore the unknown and to look for unconventional solutions to the universe's mysteries. Time has shown that what was laughable yesterday may be taken as fact tomorrow. As Jennifer Westwood writes, history's enigmas

> ... challenge modern thinking and its ideas about the supremacy of twentieth-century technology and the 'foolproof' dogma of the scientific method. The riddles enshrined in the world's mysterious places undermine, time and again, any condescending assumptions about the so-called 'primitive' cultures of our ancestors.

The mysteries of objects and lands out of their "proper" time and place continue to stimulate and delight us, and will do so as long as they remain unsolved.

Is there such a thing as frog rains?
(See p. 3)

Mysteries Fall from the Sky

During August 1994, strange, transparent, gelatinous blobs about the size of half-grains of rice fell at least twice on a farm outside Oakville [Washington]. Sunny Barclift, resident of the farm, said that after the blobs fell, her mother, Dotty Hearn, had to go to the hospital to recover from dizziness and nausea. A kitten on the farm died of digestive problems attributed to the blobs . . . . A hospital technician stated that the blobs are an organic substance, containing something similar to human white blood cells.

— "I See by the Papers," FATE, March 1995

Gelatinous blobs falling from the sky? These are not, by far, the most unusual things people have reported "raining" down upon them. Anomalous ice falls are fairly common, but how about rains of blood, flesh and bones, money, frogs and fish, stones, grain, perplexing pieces of metal, turtles and alligators, coffins—and even cats and dogs? All of these have been reported as falling from the sky with no known explanation.

One of the greatest chroniclers of these anomalous rains was Charles Hoy Fort (1874–1932), a former New York newspaper writer who, after receiving a small inheritance, was able to quit work at the age of forty-two and devote the rest of his life to his greatest interest—the collecting of accounts of anomalies of all kinds. He scoured scientific journals and popular magazines and newspapers searching for what he called "damned" data, meaning that it was excluded from consideration by the scientific establishment.

Fort collected his findings, along with his often humorous comments and interpretations, in four books (*The Book of the Damned*, 1919; *New Lands*, 1923; *Lo!*, 1931; and *Wild Talents*, 1932). Besides strange falls, Fort chronicled bizarre appearances and disappearances, artifacts that did not belong to the time and place in which they were found, unexplainable astronomical occurrences, "impossible" animals, bleeding icons, and all manner of mysteries ignored by science.

The Book of the Damned opens with these words:

> A procession of the damned. By the damned, I mean the excluded. We shall have a procession of data that Science has excluded.
>
> Battalions of the accursed . . . . Some of them are corpses, skeletons, mummies, twitching, tottering, animated by companions that have been damed alive . . . . The little harlots will caper, and freaks will attract attention, and the clowns will break the rhythm of the whole with their buffooneries—but the solidity of the procession as a whole: the impressiveness of things that pass and pass and pass, and keep on and keep on and keep on coming.

Fort's delight in the world's anomalies has made his name synonymous with such enigmas. Today we call anomalous falling blobs, apported objects, and unexplained disappearances Fortean phenomena. The following chapter contains articles from FATE that give true accounts of the Fortean phenomena of anomalous falls.

Does It Rain Toads?

William W. Bathlot
June 1953

"The objects poured down on my wagon. I held out my hand and caught four fat, brown, baby toads."

In the question and answer department of a Sunday newspaper a while back a writer asked, "Does it ever rain toads, frogs, or fish?" The answer was dogmatic: "No! Toads, frogs, and fish never have fallen from the skies and never will, but a hard rain will cause toads to come forth from the ground so suddenly that folks believe it rains them."

Well, I admit—toads do come from the ground after a hard rain, for I have seen them come, but I know also to an absolute certainty that toads have other ways of appearing on old Mother Earth. Down in Beaver County, Oklahoma, from 1908 to 1916, I drove a team of broomtails on a mail wagon. One unusually sultry evening toward the last of October 1912, I was about a mile from the Floris post office on my return trip when a streak of lightning, followed closely by a crash of thunder, caused me to peer out of the open window of the mail wagon at the skies.

A black rain cloud filled the skys to the west, and the heaviest and darkest part of the cloud seemed to hover directly above me. In a few minutes small objects I took to be hail came thudding down upon the roof of my mail wagon. In amazement I gazed at the thousands of small objects spraying outward and downward from the roof of the wagon and from the backs of my horses. They bounced up from the sandy soil like little rubber balls, lay stunned upon the ground for a few seconds, and then flopped over on their stomachs as lively as you please.

Among this myriad of small creatures I failed to see one killed or crippled from the fall. For some unknown reason they all landed upon their backs, thus protecting their little, soft, white bellies. I could peer outward for perhaps 100 feet through the falling rain, and as far as I could see, the top of the Earth was alive with the little creatures.

I held my hand out of the wagon window and caught four, fat, brown little toads all about the size of my thumbnail. Each was perfect, with legs and no tail. I had heard of fish and frogs falling from the clouds, but I never had heard of a fall of toads. And these real honest-to-goodness baby toads were coming down upon the wagon top and upon the backs of my horses instead of coming upward out of the Earth.

The toads continued to fall for something like three minutes and then no more fell, but the rain continued in torrents. When I reached the post office, which was located in a general store, I found that the shower of baby toads had reached as far as the store and a little beyond it. As near as folks who had seen or been caught in this shower of toads could figure, it had covered a space of about a mile long and a quarter of a mile wide. There was no exact way of measuring, for the little creatures had disappeared completely within a short time after their fall. They must have worked down into the soft, wet, sandy soil.

Scientists claim lakes and pools are scooped dry by tornadoes, and fish and frogs are carried high into the air by the winds and suspended there to be dropped later somewhere else upon the Earth. This may be so of fish and frogs, but toads are an entirely different proposition. In our North Temperate Zone the toad is hatched from an egg, usually during the month of April. By the first of June it has grown four legs and has shed its tail. It then is ready to leave its watery home and live out its life on land. It hunts bugs and flies through the cool of the evening on through the night. Through the day, if the weather is warm, it hibernates under logs, leaves, or grass in some damp, cool place. It finds a moist spot somewhere in the shade and, using itself as a corkscrew, drills four or five inches down into the ground, out of sight of prowling enemies. It would be impossible for a cyclone to scoop up and carry very many toads at a time. The little toads my neighbors and I saw fell in October and should have been half as large as my fist. Why were they tiny babies when they should have been grown?

I doubt if there are a dozen places on the face of our globe where so many millions of toads can be found at one time as I saw in Oklahoma in 1912. Like the flying disks, one wonders where they came from.   ■

Cobwebs from the Sky

Cliff R. Towner
September 1955

The strange radioactive substance covered several city blocks. Was it cotton fiber, powdered milk— or something else?

The night of February 20, 1955, was still, cold, and quiet in the village of Horseheads, in southern New York State. The wind was from the south and of low velocity. Yet, during the hours of darkness a mystery developed that put the quiet little village in the world news.

Mr. Charles L. Shull, president of the Shull Electronic Corporation, reported a strange "cobwebby" substance, spread over his plant property early on the morning of February 21. At the same time, shortly after sunrise, other residents and workers in the area discovered more of the strange material covering trees, lawns, and buildings for an area of several blocks.

A news photographer from the Elmira, New York, *Star-Gazette* photographed the "web" and collected a specimen that was examined by Dr. Francis A. Richmond, Professor Emeritus at Elmira College. Dr. Richmond's preliminary inspection indicated that the "web" consisted of short, weak fibers that looked and felt like cotton or wool.

The specimen was passed on to the professor of chemistry at the local college, Dr. Charles B. Rutenber, who issued a statement that his findings, based on chemical analysis, showed the mystery substance was cotton, either waste or fibers, that "had been in an explosion and were heavily damaged."

Tests with the college geiger counter showed the material to be radioactive. The doctor's findings on the composition were supported both by Dr. Richmond and Mrs. Hans Bernt, assistant professor of art, who, as an expert in textiles, examined the specimen. Again, no explanation was offered as to the source of the material.

Other reports referred to a similar mysterious deposit found in London and in other major cities in 1954. It was generally agreed that the substance could have been carried great distances in the upper air and that the cobweb might have knit itself together and fallen in a small area, pulled down by its own weight.

By February 23, the local mystery had attracted the interest of the Atomic Energy Commission, which asked Dr. Rutenber for information on the results of his tests. The Associated Press carried the story on its wire services, and the New York correspondent of the London *Times* expressed an interest because of the similarity to the "web" found last year in London. Meantime, Mr. Shull, who first reported it, said the web was rapidly disintegrating and disappearing.

While the scientists continued their tests at the college, a new avenue of conjecture was presented by Mr. Lawrence Peer, plant manager of a local dairy. Mr. Peer, supported by Mr. John Stelmak, a chemical engineer at the Westinghouse

Electronic Tube Division plant at Horseheads, suggested the possibility that powdered milk, not cotton fibers, was the basis of the substance. Mr. Peer claimed it was possible that some powdered milk could have passed through a vent pipe and been converted to stringy casein fibers by the 300-degree temperature of the machine. He admitted, however, that a large quantity of milk powder would have been required to cover the half-mile area with fibers.

Too, the milk theory did not explain the radioactivity, the amount of which prompted the Westinghouse plant to conduct another investigation to discover why the "web" produced a higher count on the testing machines than matter usually taken from the local air. Spokespersons from the plant stated that a metallic content would be more likely to pick up radioactivity than organic matter would.

February 24 brought even more confusing and muddled reports. Dr. Rutenber, who had held to the cotton fibers "heavily damaged in an explosion" theory, suddenly reversed his decision. He announced that he now was convinced the material was a protein product created by the escape of a hot milk product at the local milk plant.

The manager of the chemistry section of the local Westinghouse plant, Mr. John B. Diffenderfer, also held to the milk theory. However, the Westinghouse tests showed the contents of the "web" to be only about 30 percent carbon, with quantities of calcium, silica, aluminum, iron, and about ten other traceable elements. In the interval, the radioactivity had dropped to almost nothing.

Directly opposing the milk theory were the findings at the milk plant where the theory first originated. Louis R. Hermann and Robert L. Mix, chemical technicians at the plant, reported after conducting their own tests that the material consisted of cotton and wool fibers with pieces of fine copper wire mixed in. "It looked like it might have come out of a carpet sweeper bag," they said. In the midst of this confusion all the investigators expressed complete satisfaction with their own findings. The tests were discontinued.

Was the mysterious web-like material really powdered milk? If so, why the variance of radioactivity compared with that usually found locally? If so, where did the metal elements, the aluminum and iron, come from? What about the vast quantity of powdered milk needed to make enough casein fibers to cover a half-mile area?

On the other hand, if the material was cotton fibers, why did it settle only in one solid area and not in scattered areas? Why the high radioactivity? Where was the explosion that "heavily damaged" the fibers?

Can either of the two theories explain the "webs" found in London, Philadelphia, and other parts of the world?

Perhaps some time during the night of February 20, 1955, a strange aerial object hovered over the village of Horseheads. Reports from other "web" sites say this was true before the appearance of similar material in their localities.

As things now stand, the mystery "cobweb" has disappeared and the explanation of the phenomenon of Horseheads, New York, may never be known. ■

Storms and Little Fishes

Fred H. Koch
August 1966

"Lightning-man," famed for his storm photos, catches something new this time.

On May 3, 1952, during the hot afternoon, I was out taking pictures of a storm that was moving in near the town of Bingham, New Mexico. A black cloud had appeared from the north, and ahead of it was a strong wind that seemed to move and roll the dirt from the ground high into the sky.

I was interested because of the lightning. Almost everyone within a 150-mile radius of my home in North Hollywood, California, called me the lightning-man because if a storm was forecast by the weather bureau I was there with my camera. I was a freelance photographer and newspaperman for many years, and I always had orders for lightning pictures. I could supply any kind of lightning photograph you wanted. I have seen lightning come from white rainless clouds when the sun was shining bright and hot.

If you want to see lightning a yard wide snapping and cracking like gunfire, just be in the region between Amarillo,

Texas, and Texico, New Mexico, before a storm. I have traveled with my camera in every state in the Union and in many foreign countries, but I never have seen lightning that could compare to it in force and power.

On this particular day fourteen years ago, I sat in my car watching the dirt storm as it moved toward me. It was hard to breathe in the dusty haze that had penetrated even my tightly closed automobile. After the dirt, the rains came. Usually it doesn't rain in that area in the spring and summer, and things were pretty dry. But now water poured down like a cloudburst for almost two hours. Then the sun came back out as bright and hot as before.

I walked out into the desert and watched the sand suck up the rain water. Almost within minutes the whole area was dry and beginning to drift again. Only the dry-bed arroyos still held small pools of water.

Some persons call this region, not far from Alamogordo, Black Water Draw, and parts of it have been excavated by archaeologists who have found huge dinosaur and dinotherium bones here.

I always look around for Indian arrowheads after a windstorm because the shifting, drifting sand sometimes leaves artifacts uncovered. But this day as I moved along I found instead hundreds of tiny dead fish.

They all appeared to be about the same size—one inch long—and they were scattered all over the area. In the arroyo where the small pools of water remained, I saw a few fish still alive and swimming—but not for long, because the sun soon drank up these pools, too.

I picked up one of the fish and it was very soft—the slightest pressure mashed it. Soon the air began to smell of fish; it was as if I were standing at the seashore.

Of course I took pictures of the fish, some of them at close range, and these were published in the local newspapers.

A biology group from Lubbock, Texas, came and picked up a great many of the fish and put them in jars of alcohol. They reported that the fish had prominent eyes, and one scientist said this indicated they were not of several species known to inhabit underground pools. The reason underground pools were mentioned is that one of the ranchers thought maybe the fish were pumped out of a 150-foot well nearby. It was the only well in the entire area, and it could not have accounted for fish scattered over miles of desert as these were, but the State Fish and Game Department stated that there were no traces of fish on the screen over the discharge pipe of the well, in the catch basin, or in the irrigation ditch into which the water from the well flowed. There were no lakes, rivers, or ponds anywhere near either.

Entomologists, biologists, ornithologists, botanists, and archaeologists from nearby colleges and universities converged on the area. Many questions were asked and many theories advanced, but no real explanation was found. Perhaps most logical was the claim that the sun had drawn water—and fish—up into the sky from some large body of water hundreds of miles to the north—which would mean Colorado—and when the storm moved south because of the low pressure over the hot sand desert, the clouds had emptied water and tiny fishes together onto a rain belt about two miles wide.

This theory often is advanced to explain falls of fish and frogs, but there never has been any evidence to back it up. In this case, after checking, I found the rain belt was more or less two miles wide where I had been and became wider farther south, but the tiny fish had fallen only within a one-square-mile area, in the location of the dry sandy bed of the arroyo. Where did the fish come from?

I cannot answer this, but I can tell you they didn't grow out of the waterless sand.   ∎

Money from Heaven

Larry E. Arnold
December 1978

We know how money slips through our fingers.
Can it slip through other dimensions as well?

An invigorating breeze blew through the intersection of Broad and Vine Streets in Philadelphia on July 27, 1977. Officer Jack Einhorn was busy directing early morning commuter traffic, when suddenly, at 7:50 A.M., pandemonium broke loose.

Motorists jumped from their cars to look up toward the sky. Pedestrians ran about like chickens. Traffic jammed for four blocks around the startled police officer. Passengers leaped from stalled buses and joined the frantic melee. Was it a UFO above Philadelphia? No. For many it was something even more exciting. It was money from heaven!

"It rained $20 bills here yesterday," read the Associated Press dispatch from Philadelphia for July 28. People "were on their hands and knees, grabbing money right and left," commented police officer Roland Elliott.

There were a lot of smiling faces in the City of Brotherly Love that morning as, for a few brief moments, Philadelphia's Broad Street was "papered with 20s"—an estimated $242,000 worth!

What caused this cache to fall suddenly, enriching this tiny area of southeastern Pennsylvania? Did the Broad and Vine intersection temporarily become what Charles Fort termed "an appearing-point" wherein objects—in this case $20 bills—mysteriously materialized into this physical reality?

The solution is more mundane. In this instance the "money from heaven" came from a Brooks Armored Car Service truck whose door opened unexpectedly and allowed one of eight bags containing some $1,238,000 to tumble onto the street where it burst.

Still, there was a baffling aspect to the case. "Neither police nor Brooks was able to explain why the truck door opened and how the bag fell out," reported *The Philadelphia Inquirer* on July 28, 1977.

Perhaps the most incredible aspect of the event is that almost all the money was returned to Brooks and the police.

But what if—unlike this case—money falls around you and it can't be determined where it's coming from? Is the windfall yours to keep? Consider, for instance, the precipitation of valuable coins that fell upon London's Trafalgar Square in the early part of the twentieth century. The crowd went for the money; the bobbies went looking for the rich litterers. But unlike the Philadelphia case, no explanation was to be found.

Consider the astonishment of Mr. and Mrs. Basil McGee when, as they tended their lawn in Gastonia, North Carolina, one fine October afternoon in 1958, a glittering something fell into the pile of wet leaves near Mrs. McGee's rake.

She stooped and retrieved a shiny two-franc coin. No one was nearby, nor was an airplane visible overhead.

The McGees kept their treasure, which had little monetary value but great worth as a memorial to an unknown French person's loss and to the Unknown itself.

Consider also the perplexity of the shoppers at Ramsgate, Kent, England, on the weekend of December 7 and 8, 1968, when pennies began bouncing onto the pavement. "Between forty and fifty of them came down in short, scattered bursts for about fifteen minutes," Mrs. Jean Clements told the London *Daily Mirror*. "You could not see them falling—all you heard was the sound of them hitting the ground." There were "no tall buildings nearby, and no one heard a plane go overhead." Yet the coins were dented from the impact.

Certainly these airborne (or air-dropped) bonanzas don't rival the shower of $20 bills in Philadelphia, but in this instance, the finders could keep their windfall with a clear conscience, for no one could determine where the money came from.

Mysterious rains of money are perhaps the rarest form of Fortean precipitation. We believe there are more cases of falling alligators than of plummeting pennies.

Yet if you're lucky enough—or unlucky, depending on accompanying circumstances—your financial nest egg will get a boost courtesy of the Unknown.

One such person was a Mr. Steward. In January and February 1901 a cascade of copper coins fell inside his London home. This lucrative deluge was accompanied by what Steward called "showers of the most varied missiles descending as if from the ceiling." Stones, nuts and screws, gas pipes, pieces of quartz, old nails, and other things fell with the more desirable coins. All witnesses were "mystified as to how this miscellany had got into the room." Where could one expect to find these diverse objects in the first place, that they should somehow fall together? Only one plausible source comes to mind: a hardware store!

We can offer a theory, which remains, for lack of documentation, a romantic fantasy: Somewhere in a British hardware store a careless clerk, his customer's money in hand, trips and knocks over several stacks of merchandise. Instead of the expected deafening crash, however, the clerk is dumbfounded as the mass of tumbling objects (including the money) suddenly and silently disappears into a warp in what Fort called the supergeography of time and space. The distraught clerk finds himself confronting an unexplainable inventory-and-cash loss, while elsewhere—specifically, in Mr. Steward's house—the forces of nature that demand balance rematerialized these "lost" goods back into another (but slower moving) timespace framework in the form of a mass of mostly unwelcome debris.

Then there was the poor lad Harry Boddington mentions in *Materialisations, A Critical Analysis of Physical Phenomena.* The youth wasn't poor in the financial sense, mind you, because he was unable to prevent coins from suddenly clattering down in his vicinity. Not only should this have made him rich monetarily but one would expect him to be wealthy in friendships, too!

But alas, not so. Like Midas' golden touch, the lad's seeming good fortune was also a curse: "In the midst of friends he was at one time smothered with an inexplicable shower of pins," writes Boddington. With things like this likely to descend upon one's head, it's easy to see why the youth suffered not only "considerable embarrassment," but lack of close companionship as well.

Wild talents there are indeed, to borrow a phrase from Charles Fort.

In Boswell's *The Life of Samuel Johnson,* Johnson quips that "there are few ways in which a man can be more innocently employed than in getting money." These words certainly are true of Mr. and Mrs. R. A. Beatty and their fifteen lodgers at the Ohiro Lodge in a suburb of Wellington, New Zealand. During late March 1963 they were innocently standing around when a New Zealand penny (a large coin weighing almost as much as a United States half-dollar) crashed through a veranda window. This was at 9:30 P.M. For the next seven-and-a-half hours the lodge was bombarded with coins and, less enriching, stones!

Twelve police officers and a score of civilians searched the area, but they could find only thirty stones and four pennies by the time the fall ended, despite the boarders being forced to huddle in the kitchen at the height of the assault, according to the *Evening Post*.

To everyone's consternation, the mysterious attack of coins began again the next evening and lasted until 1:00 A.M. And again, detectives and police dogs failed to find a strong-armed joker with a catapult.

The third night about 600 people showed up, and as the strange shower began at 6:30 P.M., the crowd cheered as each penny and stone descended upon the house. The police caught some persons in the crowd tossing coins, but they couldn't capture the unseen force that continued the freakish bombardment.

New Zealand isn't the only part of the British Commonwealth to experience mysterious monetary deluges. In January 1928 the Robinson household in Battersea, London, suffered a bombardment of copper coins accompanied by chunks of coal. "The Robinsons are educated people," reported the New York *Evening World*, "and scout the idea of a supernatural agency. However, they are completely baffled and declare the phenomena take place in closed rooms, thus precluding the possibility of objects being thrown from outside."

The Beattys and the Robinsons had become, for some unknown reason, recipients of money from heaven.

Rains of riches are not always the welcome gift one would expect in this dollar-dominated day. Unfortunately, sometimes they are accompanied by disquieting, even dangerous forces. The "Great Amherst Mystery" is a good case in point.

Walter Hubbell's best-selling little book *The Haunted House* (1879) described the nightmarish events of the diabolical affair. It began in the summer of 1878 and for a full year continued to plague the David Teed family of Amherst, Nova Scotia. "Ghosts" ripped sheets, kindled fires, threw knives and utensils, and caused objects to disappear.

Amid these mixed horrors one almost overlooks the fact that coins were among the objects that "continually vanished and suddenly turned up, or rather fell down, mysteriously, from ceilings," writes Hubbell.

When the mystery that haunted the Teeds finally left them it did not leave Canada. A similar case, equally horrific, began fourteen months later for the George Dagg family of Clarendon, Quebec. On September 16, 1889, it was discovered that a five- and a two-dollar bill had been mysteriously teleported. This movement of money heralded a two-month reign of terror in which a "demon" unleashed a plethora of poltergeist-type phenomena.

Famous psychologists of the nineteenth and twentieth centuries have asserted that, under the watchful eyes of parents and police, a young girl or boy can secretly overturn sofas, kindle "spontaneous" fires by tossing matches, and make money "appear" by flipping it about when no one is looking! This blame-the-child mentality was invoked in both the Teed and Dagg episodes. Yet one member of the prestigious Royal Canadian Academy did not agree. "I have no theory to offer. The mystery still remains," wrote investigator Percy Woodcock.

The evidence leads me to agree with Woodcock. The above poltergeist cases (with their materializing money) were not caused by trickery. I suggest instead that discarnate beings intervened in human financial affairs. Seeking company in this belief, I note that Everard Feilding, an extremely cautious secretary of the Society for Psychical Research, was not so skeptical that he couldn't believe in the "jinn—a most desirable imp" that accompanied his Hungarian lawyer.

Feilding described the jinn's activities in a letter written in 1914: "This creature first started operations at a time when, for lack of pence, the lawyer wanted to commit suicide. He suddenly found money in his pocket which he knew wasn't there before. . . . Then money began to drop on the table."

The jinn continued to meet what it thought were the lawyer's needs. The Emperor's cigars appeared "out of the air," as did screws, pipes, toys, marble slabs, and many other articles.

It's fun to fantasize an unseen genie who showers you with riches. In some cases, however, humans have ended up on the debit side of the ledger because they received money from heaven.

For an incredible three years, beginning in late 1829, the John McDonald family at Baldoon, Ontario, suffered "most mysterious and extraordinary happenings" which included falling money.

One astounding incident involved Patrick Tobin, a peddler who stayed overnight at McDonald's farm. Tobin awoke to find twenty half-dollar pieces had vanished from his wallet during the night. He was even more startled when during breakfast nineteen of them flew, one by one, against a windowpane and plunked onto his plate. The twentieth piece never did return.

The cosmic jokesters must have laughed even harder as they watched perplexed humans respond to the showers of money in Poona, India. From June 1928 to January 1930 Miss H. Kohn, a well-educated British lady, kept a careful diary of the bizarre manifestations that plagued her home in western India.

"On several occasions in broad daylight we now saw coins fall among us from above," she wrote in one entry. "At first we . . . merely saw them fall," she wrote. Soon however, she and her entire family" actually saw the money appear in the air." In some cases the coins were known to belong to individuals.

Miss Kohn also described how her momentarily unguarded handbag suddenly "lost" its purse. Furious, she yelled, "Purse, please!" Whereupon the purse fell at her feet, but without "a sign of the two rupees, nor were they returned to me subsequently." At other times paper money disappeared from locked safe boxes. Sometimes it was never recovered, but on other occasions an equivalent amount reappeared in the form of small change.

After reading some of these cases of money from heaven one begins to wonder just how solid our money is—intrinsically, economically, or materially—if it can vanish before our eyes only to reappear elsewhere. Apparently money which so easily slips through one's fingers can also slip through multiple dimensions.   ■

Glob of Glass from the Sky

Vernon E. Koenig, Jr.
February 1981

"We hadn't seen anything like it before, and we soon learned that someone didn't want us to see it."

In 1961 I was assigned to the meteorological department at the U.S. Naval Air Station in Corpus Christi, Texas. My ambition was to become an air traffic controller, but because all the navy training schools were filled to capacity, I was forced to take my second choice for a military vocation.

Operating any weather office is a twenty-four-hour-a-day job. Our department was no exception. We had two shifts, called "watches." Day watch was from 7:00 A.M. to 4:00 P.M., night watch from 4:00 P.M. to 7:00 the following morning. I worked two-day watches, was off duty for two days, then took two night watches and got off for a day and a half. This rotating schedule afforded us much free time. I put this time to good use by taking flying lessons at our base aero club, and after ten hours of dual instruction I made my first solo flight. The plane, a Beechcraft T-34 Mentor trainer numbered N913 I R, was a dream to fly. It was white with

21

orange and silver trim and black numerals. Its home was the sky, and when I turned it onto a runway for takeoff, it acted as if it couldn't wait to get back into the blue.

At eighty miles an hour I would gently pull back on the control stick to aim the nose skyward. The runway slipped away beneath us, and the world we left behind became an immense tapestry of varying shades of green formed by the farms below.

Two doors down from our weather office was the base aviation safety department. The chief petty officer who worked there was soon to retire from active military service. I met him one day after delivering a weather report that was to be part of an investigation into a minor aircraft accident that had occurred at the base.

In his office there was a large collection of military aircraft recognition models. Each was a scale model once used by naval pilots to practice identifying the friendly or hostile aircraft by their shapes. One of those models was of a T-34. As soon as I laid eyes on it, I knew I wanted it as a memento of the airplane I had learned to fly in. I asked the chief if he would sell me the model for a few dollars. He declined, saying that it was part of his collection that he had acquired during his military career.

Whenever I passed by his office, I would always kid him about the T-34 model. I'd say, "Sure hope that model doesn't get stolen," or, "I've been seeing a lot of people looking at that model lately." He'd reply, "If it disappears, I'll know where to find it."

One day as I was walking through the hangar on my way to work, the chief called me over to his office. "Do you want to see something strange?" he said.

He removed an object from a filing cabinet and placed it in my hand. It appeared to be a lump of ordinary glass that might have fallen while in a molten state onto a waffle-shaped surface. It was oval in shape, approximately six inches in length by four inches in width. At the center its thickness measured about one inch. The top was a smooth convex curve crowning near the middle. The bottom seemed to be in total disagreement with the top. It was relatively flat and displayed a waffle or diamond pattern consisting of three-quarter-inch squares framed by one-eighth-inch ridges. The glass was clear and there was the usual diffraction of light when held near a bright source.

The chief told me this odd story. He said a sorghum farmer had been plowing his fields when the object fell from the sky, colliding with and breaking the hitch on his tractor before burying itself several feet into the ground. When he reached into the hole to retrieve the object, it was hot and burned his hand. Not knowing what the object was, he called the base, reported the incident, and waited for a naval investigation team to arrive. After several hours, it had cooled sufficiently and was taken to the base for identification.

At first the team theorized that it might be part of a satellite. Since none of ours had fallen, that left only the Russians, who only a few years earlier had launched their Sputniks. Of course the Russians would never admit that one of their satellites fell from orbit, especially if it fell over the United States.

"Watch this," the chief told me. He took the object from my hand and dropped it onto the hangar floor. After picking it up, he handed it back to me. The once-clear glass had developed what appeared to be lines of stress radiating from the point of impact throughout its shape in very soft rainbow colors.

The chief told me he had discovered the effect when he accidentally dropped the glass from his desk. He also said the lines would disappear after four or five minutes, and the glass would be clear again.

I asked the chief if he weren't afraid of breaking the object before the investigation was completed. In response he took the glass and threw it onto the floor. It bounced into the air and struck the side of a T-2V jet in the hangar. The cement floor was scarred white where the glass had made violent contact.

I rushed over and scooped up the glass, hoping no one had seen it hit the side of the airplane. The object now displayed new stress lines radiating from the point of impact in darker hues. Whatever material the object was composed of, it could not be broken or chipped.

Several weeks later I received my copy of the base newspaper. Each issue contained a photo of an object taken at very close range. The photos were usually of such things as tire treads, radiator cores, and so on. There were no prizes; yet everyone tried to guess what the pictures showed. In this issue, however, was a half-size picture of the unbreakable glass object.

I saw the chief later that day and laughingly told him his glass object had made it into print. He was upset. Word about the glass and its arrival in Texas had gotten to our newspaper staff. Since the investigation was not yet completed and there was little of substance to say about it, the news people had decided to photograph it for the "WHAT-IZ-IT?" feature. After the object had been photographed and the presses began to roll, the object was shipped to the Bureau of Weapons for analysis. The chief was distraught because the day our weekly newspaper was distributed to all the base personnel, he received a phone call from his division officer informing him that all information pertaining to the glass object was to be classified.

The division officer said the glass defied analysis. The scientists were unable to break or melt it. It also stood up to thermal-shock testing (rapid changes in temperature).

Nothing affected it. Because of these findings the navy wanted to put a lid on the entire matter. The chief, due to retire soon, now realized he had authorized the photo session and disclosure of a now classified object.

For the next few days the chief wasn't very talkative. One day I passed by the aviation safety office and all his model airplanes were gone. I never saw the chief again, nor did I find out where he went.

Whenever I read about UFO coverups I always think about that piece of glass and the events that took place twenty years ago. No one ever mentioned a possible UFO connection then.

Any first-year chemistry student knows that all compounds can be broken down into basic known elements with little difficulty. Yet one day an object fell from the sky and refused to yield the secrets of its chemistry to anyone.

I often wonder what became of that object. Even more often I wonder where it came from.   ■

When the Skies Rained Blood!

Harold T. Wilkins
April 1953

The early Romans ruled their world—the land and sea, anyway. But even their power could not stop the anomalous rains of blood, coins, milk, and flesh.

Ancient writers recorded many strange happenings which, because they are incapable of routine explanation, are denounced and thrust into oblivion by conventional scientists. This *terra incognita* has been left unexplored by even such chroniclers of the inexplicable as the late Charles Fort, who, with a few exceptions, confined himself to "damned" phenomena beginning with the nineteenth century.

Let us examine some of the numerous recorded observations about blood, flesh, oil, stones, and other remarkable things falling from the skies, or issuing from the Earth, which took place in the days during the rise, decline, and fall of the Roman Empire.

265 B.C.: Blood came from the Earth in Italy.

222 B.C.: In the consulates of C. Quintius Flaminius and P. Furius Philon the waters of the river Picenum turned to blood.

216 B.C.: At Antiuim, an old city on the seacoast, fifteen leagues from Ostium, bloody ears of corn fell into one of the baskets of the harvesters.

215 B.C.: Rains of much blood and many stones fell from the skies over Rome and on the Aventinus Mons, and hot water ran from a cold fountain.

213 B.C.: A rain of blood fell in the cattle market of Rieme. (*Julius Obsequens*).

The following reports of this phenomenon came from old writers after the day of Julius Obsequens, except for the first three:

A.D. 89: A rain of blood fell for three days in England.

A.D. 249: When the Roman emperor Decius ascended the Imperial throne it rained blood in Britain, and a terrible bloody sword was seen in the air for three nights and a little after sunset. (*N.B. It is easy to dismiss this story as imaginary, nor can it be said if the "sword" was an auroral display.*)

A.D. 324: There were six hours of rain of blood in Somerset, England.

A.D. 436, 535, and 540: Colored rain fell in England; and in A.D. 442, there was a rain of blood in York, England (*Stowe's Annales*).

A.D. 596: Flashes of lightning, and many drops of water the color of blood fell in Surrey, England; and at the same time there was a noise in the sky like armies in rout.

A.D. 684: Colored rain and rain like blood fell in England, and milk and butter turned to blood. In Ireland, Lake Nagh turned to blood. Bloody rain fell for seven days in Scotland and Britain. (*N.B. It seems doubtful if an eruption of the Italian volcanoes in faraway Vesuvius, or Etna, Italy, caused this phenomenon which is reported in the Irish Monk Tighernac's Annals, and in John Fordun's Chronica Gestis Scotorum, who adds that the rain of blood lasted seven days in Britain and Scotland.*)

A.D. 742: A rain of blood in York, England.

A.D. 766: Alcuin of York saw, in Lent, a shower of blood falling tremendously on the northern side of the great abbey at York, from the summit of the roof, though weather was fair.

A.D. 865 and 878: Says the Irish *Annals of Ulster*: "Lake Lebinn became the colour of blood and the blood coagulated like the inward parts of animals." The *Chronicon Scotorum* says: "It rained in Ireland, in 878, a shower of blood which was found in great lumps of gore of blood, in the plains of Connaught, especially at Dunha-na-n-Desi."

Volcanic eruptions will not explain this phenomenon in Ireland in A.D. 865 and thirteen years later.

In A.D. 541 the rain of blood that fell from the sky over England was "followed by dreadful mortality," says the monk, Roger of Wendover, who also records that the year before a great comet appeared in Gaul (France) "so vast that the whole sky seemed on fire." (*Was there any connection between the appearance of the vast comet and the bloody rain?*)

An independent Irish chronicler, Tighernac O'Braian, abbot of Clun, Ireland, says the mortality following the rain of blood was "very extensive" in both England and Ireland.

Then there are the mysterious rains of milk, which no one has ever explained. What was this substance and whence came it? There are sixteen recorded cases and they occurred on dates between 274 B.C. and 94 B.C. (a range of 180 years!):

274 B.C.: A rain of milk from the skies in Italy.

In 110 B.C., the rain of milk from the sky lasted for three days in Rome, at the time of the war with Jugurtha, and again for three days in Rome in the following year.

Twice there was a fall of milk from the sky on the quarter called the Graecostasis, or the location of the Greek and other foreign ambassadors, accredited to the Roman senate—phenomena occurring in 124 and 123 B.C.

In 103 B.C., milk rained from the sky in Lucania, Italy, and issued from the ground in Tarquinia.

Again, in 124 B.C., both milk and oil fell from the skies in Veii, Italy, and there is no suggestion of any waterspout.

Rains of wheat are recorded in Germany and Ireland:

A.D. 759: A shower of wheat fell in the kingdom of Muredoch, in Inis-egain. (*The Annals of Clanmacnoise*).

A.D. 828: In Wasgau a mass like corn fell from the sky (*Volckeren Chronik*: Zurich).

A.D. 1021: "A shower of wheat fell from the sky in Osraighi [Ossary]," says the *Chronocon Scotorum*.

Fort would have made great play about the monistic identity of the universe—a body responding to the call of one of its parts—in regard to the fall of wheat in A.D. 759; for the Irish *Annals of Clanmacnoise* say that in 759 there was a great famine, and when

> ...King Niall the Showery and seven bishops prayed there fell such an abundance of wheat from the skies that it poured like a river in flood and the like was never seen before. All the fields were covered, and it was estimated that this wheat, falling from the sky, was able to maintain many kingdoms.

The *Ulster Annals* say this phenomenon happened in A.D. 763.

Again, in A.D. 533, in the west of Kent, it rained both wheat and blood! The blood fell in great drops and caused extreme dearth.

In A.D. 788 wood fell from the skies over Freysingen, in Bavaria. There is no evidence that a waterspout was seen. (*Annales Boiorum*, Leipzig, 1710).

There are two recorded cases of silver falling from the Irish sky! A.D. 715: A shower of silver fell from the sky in the kingdom of Muredoch. Honey also fell, when Niall Frosach was king. It fell on Otham Mor, in A.D. 759, when wheat and honey fell from the heavens. (*Annales of Tighernac O'Bra-ian, abbot of Clun.*)

Flesh fell from the sky in 462 B.C., in and near Rome, says Julius Obsequens. "It was like snow and in pieces more or less thick." In the following year, 461 B.C., Titus Livius records:

> There was a rain of flesh from the skies in Italy, and numbers of birds flying about seized on the flesh, which fell into water, and when the flesh was thrown down and scattered about it lay for several days and emitted no odor.

What sort of substance was this odorless unputrescent flesh? It fell again in 59 B.C.:

> Flesh like snow fell from heaven over Italy, in great and small pieces. It was snapped up in the air as it was falling, and on the ground, by all sorts of birds, and the residue lay on the ground for a long time, in both cities and fields, and neither its colour nor taste changed, which is contrary to what happens to ordinary meat and flesh. Much fell in Rome (*Titus Livius*).

Fish fell from the skies of old Saxony, Germany, in A.D. 989, and there are recorded cases of this phenomenon at and near Worcester, England, in the nineteenth century of our own age, at places far inland from the sea where no waterspout was seen.

There are sixteen recorded cases of stones falling from the skies over Rome and Roman Italy between 644 and 101 B.C. and four cases of earth and chalk. In some cases the falls of stone and what looked like blood were simultaneous. In 644 B.C., during the reign of Tullus Hostilius, men were sent to verify the phenomenon on Mount Alban. They saw the stones falling in great numbers like hail. In B.C. 204 so great was the rain of stones that people were terrified and the Sybilline books were consulted. In 170 B.C. the clay suddenly became night, between the third and fourth hours (9 to 10 A.M.), and a rain of stones fell on the Aventinus Mons for the second time.

Three showers of earth and stones rained down on a place called Ameriternus, thirty-five miles north of Rome, in the years 193, 191, and 190 B.C. In 124 B.C. at another place, Arpi, some 180 miles east of Rome on the Adriatic, stones rained from the sky continuously for three days! In Etruria (Thusius) the rain of stones from the sky lasted four to nine days, and the badly frightened people marched, with magistrates at their head, to offer sacrifices to the gods. In B.C. 305 earth rained down from the sky and many soldiers in the army of Appius Claudius were killed by thunderbolts.

Even honey is twice recorded to have rained down! In A.D. 715 a rain of honey showered down on Ofham Bec, Ireland, in a year when, on midsummer day,

> A dark cloud spread over the sky and then withdrew and all the air seemed on fire and armies and monstrous creatures appeared as fearful sights in the air, upon which followed a great storm that broke many ships to pieces in the havens, rent up mighty oaks, and overturned houses (John Seller's *History of England*, 1696).

One meteorological annalist called this very mysterious phenomena "probably mythical." The "air on fire" could hardly have been an aurora on midsummer day!

Honey again fell in a shower in A.D. 759 in the kingdom of Muredoch, in Inis-egain, Ireland. (*Ulster Annals* say the honey fell in A.D. 763; the *Clanmacnoise Annals* say A.D. 759).

There is one recorded fall from the skies over the splendid old Etruscan town of Veii of oil and milk simultaneously—it is not recorded whether they mixed nor what flavor resulted: "Year 629 after the foundation of Rome (that is, 124 B.C.), 'Oleo et lacte in Vejente pluit': Oil and milk showered down from, the sky over Veii." (*Julius Obsequens*).

A shower that fell in Connaught, Ireland, in A.D. 224, say the *Annals of the Four Masters*, caused death and terrible diseases to anyone who drank milk from cattle on pastures where the shower fell. The shower extended over many miles of country. What was the cause or origin of this pathogenic shower from the skies?

The mysterious falls of ice from the sky in Somerset, Essex, London, and Scotland in 1950, which killed sheep and were officially and absurdly attributed to defective de-icing equipment on planes—planes not visible to anyone nearby at the time, are not new.

In A.D. 207, ice chunks bigger than ducks' eggs fell from the sky in England.

A.D. 459: Many people and cattle were killed in the British Isles by ice falling from the sky.

A.D. 586: Men in Constantinople were killed by ice from the sky.

A.D. 1022: Ice in the summer, as big as crab apples, fell from the sky and killed an infinite number of cattle in Ireland. (*Annals of Clanmacnoise*).

In A.D. 1726, in the canton of Orne, France, ice fell in sunny weather in May, and ice as big as a man's fist fell from the sky in England and killed people.

No meteorologist has the ghost of an idea of the meaning of the following curious passage: "A.D. 1501-03: Cross-rains (*Kreuz-regen*) fell in almost all Europe, and in Nurnberg they were especially severe on 26 January." (*Duisburger Kronik*, and *Dortmunder Kronik*).

A well-known Prussian meteorologist, Dr. R. Hennig, calls these *Kreuz-regen* "most puzzling phenomena." Others, in spite of the fact that reports of these phenomena could hardly exist without some basis in reality, will dismiss them as "probably mythical." ∎

The Pulsing Honeycomb from Space

Faustin Gallegos
September 1958

*What was this football-shaped object that landed in
a Miami yard? It pulsated, was translucent—and
was weirdly intangible.*

Friday, February 28, was a special day for the Gallegos family.
It was payday for the Miami Police Department, and since I
am a detective, my wife had aroused me from my sleep at
approximately 9:15 A.M. so she could get an early start on her
shopping. I dragged myself reluctantly out of bed, and after
washing and dressing, I walked into our living room to speak
to my wife and mother about shopping matters and other
dreadful problems that confront men when payday arrives.

I was standing approximately in the middle of our living
room, looking through two large double windows into our
backyard, when suddenly a white ball about the size of a
large medicine ball drifted from the sky and made a landing.

My mother, Thelma, was sitting in a rocking chair facing
the front of the house and was not in a position to see the
white ball descend. My wife, Dorothy, however, was sitting

on the couch and had a clear view of our backyard. I asked her if she had seen anything fall from the sky and land in our yard, and she said that a large piece of paper or some white object had fallen and come to rest near the two large windows. My mother said that she had seen a white reflection on the right lens of her glasses.

I asked my wife to go out into the yard and see what it was. She stepped out and immediately called mother and me to come to see the strange-looking object that had come down. I ran out and there at my feet was the strangest looking substance that I have ever seen.

What I had thought was round had changed its shape and was now about the shape of a football. It was approximately twenty inches long and eight or ten inches high. The strangest thing about it was its body, which seemed to be made up of thousands of minute cells resembling those of a honeycomb. It was not white as it had appeared when it fell, but was clear like glass. Amazingly, this translucent object was pulsating over its entire body.

We could see the inner as well as the surface body, and the entire thing was pulsating. It is very difficult for me to describe the pulsation of the inner and surface body of the material. Although it moved its body, it did not leave the spot where it had landed.

We stood over the object for five or ten minutes, discussing it and its fall from the sky, and I finally made up my mind to touch it. My mother objected strongly. She was afraid it might have something to do with guided missiles or perhaps that I would get radiation poisoning.

At any rate, I was very curious and felt I had to touch the substance. I slowly shoved my right index finger into the pulsating material. To my amazement I could feel nothing. I withdrew my finger at once and saw that I had left a hole in the material the size and length of my finger. This was the first time in my life that I had been able to see and touch an object yet been unable to feel it.

Then I got down on my hands and knees and made an attempt to smell the substance. It had no odor. Then I touched it again, pulling my finger from stem to stern along its "body." Again I had no sensation of touch, but my finger gouged a furrow its entire length. I noticed that nothing clung to my finger—it was as if what I saw before my eyes actually wasn't there.

By this time my wife had reached the point where she, too, could not resist the temptation to touch it. As Mother and I watched, Dorothy seized the pulsating substance with her right hand. Her results were the same as mine. She made a hole in the material but could feel nothing. My wife then went to our next door neighbor, Mrs. Peggy Townsend, and invited her into our yard to see the strange object. Mrs. Townsend, too, was dumbfounded.

While we were discussing this strange event, the four of us noticed that our glob of material had begun to shrink from all sides—as if it were collapsing in upon itself. I quickly asked my wife to get a jar so that we could trap part of it. She brought me a pickle jar and I succeeded in filling the jar with part of the material that was left.

The rest of the object remained upon the ground for a short while, but we saw that it was "melting" away very rapidly. Soon there was nothing left to show where it had been— not a single trace. We looked over the ground and grass carefully for signs of moisture, imprint, burns, or anything that would show it ever had existed. We could find nothing.

Meanwhile I noticed that the material I had trapped in the jar had stopped pulsating, although it still retained its bodily structure. I sealed the jar with a lid. I then shook it vigorously to see if shaking would have any effect on it, but I could see none.

As you can imagine, thoughts were racing through my mind as to what this odd stuff might be. I decided finally that it must be the result of some kind of weather phenomena. I called the United States Weather Bureau and told the weather man what had happened and described the material to him. He told me that he never had seen nor heard of any weather phenomenon that produced this kind of thing. After my conversation with him and with another man in the weather office, we headed for the police station. Material remained in the jar when we left home. The drive to the police station took us approximately twenty minutes.

We noticed soon after leaving for the station that the substance had begun to shrink. We hoped it would last until we arrived so that we could have both proper photographs taken of it. But we arrived too late. All the material in the jar had disappeared before we arrived. I would estimate that from the time I saw the white ball in the sky to the time it vanished, forty-five minutes to an hour elapsed.

At the police station we uncapped the jar for inspection but could find no trace of moisture or anything else to establish that anything but pickles had ever been in the jar. When I returned home I received a call from a local newspaper, the *Miami Herald*. They printed a story about what had happened, and as a result we had many inquiries and visits to the place where the object landed. One man tested the ground for radioactivity, but the reading was negative. Another took samples of the earth where the substance had lain.

I was an invited guest on a radio program that discussed UFOs. As a result of this publicity I learned that many other people had seen a similar substance in the past. A woman from Arkansas called and told me that in 1955 she had witnessed a falling object that behaved exactly as the one we had in our back yard. A captain of detectives of the Miami

Police Department told me, in the presence of an inspector of police, that on the same day the material landed in my yard, an unknown substance also landed in his. Our homes are several miles apart. I believe firmly that both substances are related in body and in origin. I have no idea what the material might be, but I do know it comes from the sky. ■

Catfish from Heaven

Rose B. McCalmont
March 1959

The proof of the pudding is in the eating, they say.
That was true of the fish that fell in our yard.

In the Spring of 1918 we were living in the 800 block on Kentucky Avenue in Lawrence, Kansas. That was the year we ate a catfish from the sky.

There had been a mid-afternoon rainstorm with a great deal of wind from the southwest. The storm, as I remember it, was unusually severe. The water in the street overflowed the curbing and lay an inch deep or more over the yard. We stood at the front door watching it, Mother, Dad, and I. My father, the Rev. Joseph Barricklow, ran out across the porch to measure the water in the yard. Stooping off the low porch, he put his thumb at water level on the yardstick. While he was stooping there, Mother and I saw something fairly large land out in the yard. We both shouted in the same breath, "What's that?"

Dad looked up and asked, "Where?" We pointed toward something floundering several feet out in the yard. Dad shouted, "It's a fish!" and went after it. Mother warned him, "You'll be wet to the skin!" but he replied, "I'm wet already," and went on after the fish.

He grabbed for it, but the fish flopped out of his reach and he waded on. Realizing it would be next to impossible for him to capture and hold it with his hands, Mother told me to go after the big kettle and be sure to bring the lid.

When I returned with the kettle and lid Dad had chased the fish toward the porch. He reached up and took the kettle from me. Holding it on edge, he let the fish flop into it, then he quickly righted the kettle and popped the lid on.

Dad handed the kettle to Mother, and she and I went to the kitchen while he waded around to the back porch, where he took off most of his wet clothes before coming into the house. Mother held the kettle under the tap and I ran water enough to cover the fish. It was a catfish such as I have caught in Kansas waters more than once—a big catfish measuring more than twenty inches and weighing two and a half pounds.

In our excitement we forgot about the rain and tried to explain to each other this fish-from-heaven. Dad suggested that a draft of wind must have taken the fish up from the Kaw River, which ran through the north end of town, and carried it into the air, whence it had landed in our front yard.

However, there was no report of a tornado in the area that afternoon, and the wind was blowing toward the river instead of away from it. We were all of a mile and a half from the river at its nearest point, which was beyond Mt. Oread, so the fish would not only have had to travel a mile and a half through the air but would have had to be carried several hundred feet upward to have reached our front yard from the Kaw River.

And on this day it would have traveled against surface winds.

Yet it landed in our yard alive and with a good deal of fight in it. It must have taken Dad at least ten minutes to land it in our kettle.

At any rate, we ate it and it tasted just like a good catfish should taste, neither more nor less heavenly.   ∎

The Rocks from Nowhere

Alson J. Smith
December 1952

*Out of the night the limestone rocks came falling
with a dull plop onto the Chattin's garage roof.*

On the morning of Thursday, August 7, 1952, the Associated Press carried into the city rooms of its member newspapers an odd little story datelined Evansville, Indiana. It was headed: ROCKS FROM "NOWHERE" STILL FALLING, and was an account of a strange and apparently inexplicable shower of small rocks on a garage outside of Evansville.

The rocks had been falling for six nights and nobody could figure out where they were coming from. The AP gave the story a tongue-in-cheek treatment, coupling it with alleged sightings of flying saucers and other forms of "midsummer madness." It was good hot-weather filler for the papers, and apparently that was all the AP intended it to be.

When the editor of FATE saw the AP story in the Chicago papers, he knew that it was the kind of thing a magazine like FATE should investigate and report fairly. He called me—and that was how I found myself on a sweltering Friday morning, the next day, in the old railroad station at Evansville.

When the *Courier* office opened at nine o'clock, I interviewed the day city editor. He didn't think much of the story and was surprised that the AP had picked it up. Just a lot of damn foolishness, he said. The "rocks" were limestone pebbles ranging from a half inch to an inch and a half or two inches in diameter. They were of a type indigenous to the neighborhood; nothing unusual about them except that when they landed they were warm.

They had been falling for a week on and about the garage of a family by the name of Chattin, who lived seven miles north of Evansville, at the intersection of U. S. Route 41 and Old State Road. The rocks had seemed to come right out of the sky. Two deputy sheriffs had been stationed out there by Vanderburgh County authorities, but the thing had them baffled. A lot of people gathered around out there nights to see the stones fall, but neither the deputies nor the Chattin family nor the onlookers had been able to figure out where the stones came from. It was an odd thing, but the editor had no doubt but what some boys had rigged up a sling-shot or something and were lobbing the pebbles from out in the woods.

The editor wasn't very helpful. But a cab driver, whom I hired to take me out to the Chattin place, was able to provide some interesting background information. When told the nature of the errand, he nodded gravely.

"This heah's Dutch country," he said. "Anything can happen heah." He went on to say that several years ago an old woman in nearby Madisonville had died and that after her death a tree in the yard of her home twisted itself into a shape that reminded people very much of the deceased. Picture postcards had been made of the tree, and thousands had been sold to the curious who came from miles around to see the "miracle." He was not at all surprised at the "rocks from nowhere" and had no doubt that the phenomenon had a supernatural explanation.

Dutch country. I recalled immediately the fat red barns with the curious anti-hex symbols of York and Lancaster counties, Pennsylvania, where I had gone to college. I recalled, too, the "hex" murders—one as recent as last year—in which Palatinate Germans had sought to evade a spell by killing the hexer and driving a stake through his heart.

"Dutch country" was indeed an eerie land full of Old World superstitions and customs where anything could happen. *Poltergeist* would not be an unfamiliar word to the Pennsylvania Dutch. And Evansville, in Vanderburgh County, Indiana, was the westernmost outpost of the great Palatinate German Migrations that had settled eastern and central Pennsylvania and southern Ohio and Indiana.

At a little filling station and restaurant at the intersection of U.S. Route 41 and Old State Road, I found the Chattins. Or rather, I found Mrs. Chattin, who operated the restaurant and filling station, and her seventeen-year-old son, John, who helped her. Louis Chattin, the husband and father, was at work at the Schnacke Manufacturing Corporation in Evansville, where he was employed in the machine shop.

Mrs. Chattin was a rather shy, pleasant woman of forty-six or forty-seven who was pretty much fed up with the "rocks from nowhere." Reporters had been swarming around, she said, and photographers from *Life* magazine. They had been taking pictures of the silly little stones. (She gave me one.) The family had picked up several buckets of them and she guessed they could have sold them if they'd been of a mind to. People were such fools. No, she wouldn't be photographed holding the stone and she didn't want to talk about the matter. However, she had no objections to my taking pictures, and she asked her son John to show me around and answer questions.

John Chattin was a big seventeen-year-old boy, shy like his mother, but affable and willing to help. Most of the story of the rocks from nowhere came from John and his married sister, Betty Niethammer, who lives with her husband and two small sons, Kenneth Robert and Carl Louis, in a little white frame house about a hundred feet south of the garage that was the target for the rocks. There is a Chattin daughter, also married, who lives away from home.

The physical set-up is as follows: The restaurant and filling station is at the intersection, fronting on Route 41. Just behind it is the white frame house, considerably larger than the Niethammer dwelling, where the elder Chattins and John live. About thirty feet to the south of the house and twelve or fifteen feet from the southeast corner of the restaurant is the square, stucco-block garage, dingy and rather unkempt-looking, where the rocks have been falling. Several windows in the garage have been broken by the falling stones.

A hundred feet due south of the house is the Niethammer house. A small dirt road, plentifully sprinkled with limestone rocks, runs from Old State Road down past the Chattin house, the garage, and the Niethammer house. Due east and slightly north of the Chattin house, across the dirt road, is a white frame dwelling occupied by a family named Costello. These are the only people living in the immediate vicinity—the Chattins, the Niethammers, and the Costellos. The Chattins and the Niethammers are of Pennsylvania German extraction, and the Costellos are of Irish ancestry. All are pleasant, unassuming, middle-class people.

The rocks first began falling on the evening of July 30, 1952. From then on they continued to fall sporadically, beginning usually about dusk and continuing until one or two in the morning. (They are still falling as this is being written.) They seem to come directly out of the sky and it is impossible to trace their trajectory. Sometimes only one or two rocks an hour will come down, and at other times the fall is large enough to awaken the family as the stones rattle off the sides and roof of the garage. The garage is definitely the target; none of the stones fall outside an area within a few feet of it.

For the first couple of evenings, only the Chattins and the Niethammers witnessed the fall of the rocks. By the third evening, however, word had gotten around and a crowd of about fifty persons gathered about the garage. When windows were broken and the stones kept coming down, the Vanderburgh County Sheriff's office was notified, and two deputies, Raymond Umfried and Leonard Denton, were assigned to the case. Their job was to apprehend the culprits and protect the Chattin's property. From the third night on, the deputies stationed themselves before the Chattin garage.

At first the deputies were sure that mischievous boys were responsible. With Mr. Chattin, Mr. Niethammer, Mr. Costello, and John Chattin cooperating, plus several volunteers from the crowd, they scouted the neighboring woods, hid in the high weeds near the garage, fired into the treetops, and tried in various other ways to capture or frighten the "vandals" who were responsible for the rockfall.

They found no trace of any human agency, although they and their volunteer posse searched diligently both night and day over an area a half-mile in diameter. The woods to the east of the Chattin residence and parallel to U.S. 41 were the most likely site for some sort of a homemade bazooka or slingshot capable of hurling the stones, and these were scoured without success.

The deputies agreed that it was almost inconceivable that boys or even men with some ulterior motive could rig up a device capable of shooting the stones over such a long distance with the accuracy that the "rocks from nowhere" displayed. They fell into such a small area that it would almost require a Norden bombsight to pin-point the target so accurately.

From about the fourth night on, the rocks began coming in at different speeds, sometimes smashing against the stucco bricks of the garage like fired missiles and at other times dropping limply and rattling down the roof. At first they had come at about fifteen-minute intervals, but as time went on they spaced out to half-hour intervals, coming either singly or in showers. On the fifth night the deputies' car was included in the target area, and the stones began banging down on its steel top. The deputies jumped out and blazed away at the treetops, with no effect other than riddled branches.

Meanwhile, Mr. Chattin and the neighbors were secreting themselves throughout the woods and weeds in an attempt to trap the miscreants. Neither they nor the deputies were able to uncover the smallest clue that might indicate a human agency.

Although the rocks did not usually begin coming in until dusk, the crowd began gathering about eight o'clock the night I visited the house. The restaurant and filling station both did a flourishing business, with Mr. Chattin manning the gas pump and Mrs. Chattin frying hamburgers and pouring coffee. By eight o'clock there were already some ten cars parked around the filling station and along the dirt road that led down past the Niethammer place. About 8:10 the deputy sheriffs, Denton and Umfried, drove up and parked their car in the garage driveway. They came into the restaurant and I sat down at a table with them. Other people in the restaurant gazed at us curiously. We ordered coffee.

I said: "What do you boys make of this?"

Denton didn't say anything, but Umfried said: "I can't see how it can be anything but kids. But then again, I don't see how it can be kids either. We've gone over the woods with a fine-tooth comb."

A tanned old farmer in well-worn overalls, who was sitting on a stool at the counter, horned in on the conversation.

"Chattin there [nodding towards Louis Chattin, busy at the gas pump] thinks them rocks comes right out of the sky. He believes ghost'r throwin' 'em."

Umfried laughed. "Do you believe in ghosts, Fred?"

"Hell, yes," said the farmer. "I seen too many not to b'lieve in 'em."

Everybody laughed. Umfried looked at the clock. "Let's go, Len." He and Denton went out to their car. The crowd followed them. It was 8:20 now and beginning to get quite dark.

Mrs. Chattin stayed in the restaurant, but Mr. Chattin, a middle-aged, well-built, weather-beaten man with bright blue eyes, left the gas pump and went over to the deputies' car for a conference. Young John Chattin joined them. Soon Louis Chattin called to some other men and they all clustered around the car. About 8:30 the whole group, led by Umfried, fanned out across the dirt road and disappeared into the woods.

By now about thirty cars were parked along the dirt road and around the filling station. Some of them had turned their headlights on the garage. Thirty or forty persons, men, women, and children, had gotten out of the cars and were standing or sitting in a semicircle about thirty-five feet back from the garage. I was leaning against the door of the police car when the first rock came in, at about 8:40.

It dropped with a soft 'plink' on the roof of the garage and bounced off into the driveway. Nobody made a move to get it.

Umfried said: "Go pick it up. It'll be warm."

The rock had rolled to within four feet of the front bumper of the car. I walked over and picked it up. It was a small white limestone rock, little larger than a pebble, easily distinguished from the other limestone in the driveway by its lighter color. It was quite warm, about as warm as the bowl of a pipe after a few minutes puffing.

Seconds later another rock fell. This one came in out of the dark with more velocity; it cracked sharply against the stucco brick of the garage and rolled out toward the crowd. A little girl darted out, picked it up, and ran back.

Almost immediately, another stone came down, hitting the deputies' car roof. Denton said: "Weve been in the target area for three nights, now. At first every stone hit the garage."

From the woods there was the sound of a pistol shot. The crowd turned in the direction of the shot and a buzz of conversation ensued. I looked inquiringly at Denton.

He shook his head. "Just Ray, shooting up into the tree-tops," he said. "We do that every once in awhile, just to scare 'em. Only they don't seem to scare."

For a half hour no more stones fell. Some of the crowd got restless and left. As one car drove off the driver leaned out and hollered, "The goblins will get you if you don't watch out!" People smiled but nobody laughed.

I talked with a young couple by the name of Gerhardt, who had driven out from Evansville. They belonged to the Church of the Brethren and were very serious. The rocks were a sign, Gerhardt said. Of what? He didn't know. But he was sure the rocks came from heaven and were a sign. Only God knew what they were a sign of.

The Evansville *Courier*, which hadn't taken much notice of the story, had finally come to life after the AP dispatch had gone out, and the paper had a photographer out at the Chattin place taking flash pictures. He shot everything—the garage, the deputies' car, the Chattin house, the rocks. He was a young fellow whose name I didn't bother to ascertain, completely cynical.

"Some clever kid has rigged up a mortar or something out of an old stovepipe and is making asses out of all of you," he said, generously including me among the asses. He stayed about fifteen minutes and then hopped back to town.

Umfried, Chattin, and the group that had been searching the woods came back for coffee before crossing U.S. 41 and beginning the search among the weeds and brush over there. They hadn't found anything.

As they sat in the restaurant drinking coffee, the rocks began coming in again, in little showers this time. Smaller in size than the first rocks, they rained softly down on the roof of the garage and bounced or rolled off into the driveway or the grass. I noted that every man who had gone out had come back, including the two Chattins, Louis and John.

They finished their coffee and went across the road, fanning out again to take in as much territory as possible. Back at the deputies' car, Denton was talking with Evansville police headquarters on his two-way radio. "Nope, nothing. Rocks are still coming in. Ray has just left the woods and is going through the weeds across 41 now."

I looked at my watch, 9:47. My train left at 10:40, and Evansville was seven miles away. Regretfully, I left. My friend, the taxidriver, shook his head. "Well," he said, "I seen it. I seen it with my own eyes." He took a little limestone rock out of his pocket. "Rock," he said, "if I knowed where you come from, I'd know everything there is to know."

Previous to my arrival on the scene, "experts" were called in and gave varying opinions. David M. Bigelow, Director of Education at the Evansville Public Museum, announced that the limestone layers under incinerators often explode when the heat expands the air pockets in the stones, and that the "rocks from nowhere" were probably the result of such an explosion.

This explanation had to be discarded when it was pointed out that the Chattins, the Niethammers, and the Costellos did not have one incinerator among them, although the fact that the rocks were warm when first picked up seemed to lend credence to this explanation.

Another "expert" opined that the rocks were meteorites, but Evansville's leading astronomer, circuit court judge Ollie Reeves, examined the stones and stated that they could not possibly be meteorites. Besides, he said, the rotation of the Earth would make it impossible for meteorites to hit the same target night after night. Evansville weatherman Stanley Rampy agreed with the judge.

Most non-experts agreed with Deputy Umfried who said: "There's probably a simple explanation to it, but we haven't found it yet."

Both deputies were very sure that the most obvious explanation—mischievous small boys—could not possibly hold water. "We were expecting to find someone in the shadows throwing the rocks when we first went out there," said Deputy Umfried, "but we searched for two nights, and it would have been impossible for anyone to be out there at those times."

What children were in the vicinity? John Chattin was an observer of the phenomenon and an eager assistant to the deputies in their attempts to uncover a human agency. The two Niethammer boys were little more than infants, and both were securely in bed from seven o'clock on. The Costellos had a teen-age boy, Fred, but he was sick in bed and had been for a week. The Costellos also had a girl, Frankie, but she, like John Chattin, had been a wide-eyed observer of the happenings and could not possibly have thrown the stones. There were no other near neighbors, and the Chattins had no enemies that they knew of.

If boys or men were throwing the stones they would have had to come from a distance of several miles to do it, and it was inconceivable that anyone would be concerned enough with pelting the Chattin's garage to make a trip of several miles each night and stay up until the small hours of the morning to do it.

Of all the people I interviewed, only the cab driver and Louis Chattin himself considered the possibility that the stones were the product of a poltergeist. Mr. Chattin insisted that the stones were coming "out of the sky" and that the whole thing smacked of the supernatural. He had received several crank letters, he said, telling him the stones were divine retribution for his family's not attending church regularly.

Besides me, only one other person had mentioned the word *poltergeist*. That had been a reporter for the Indianapolis *Star*, who had phoned in for information and had given his opinion that here was a clear case of telekinesis caused by a poltergeist. The Chattins had not been sure just what he was talking about.

After a considerable amount of digging, I unearthed a fact that had not hitherto been disclosed and that other reporters had not considered significant. The Costello girl, Frankie, was fourteen years old. As every student of psychical phenomena knows, the presence of a girl just entered upon puberty is a common condition for the activity of a genuine poltergeist, or "mischievous spirit." In some mysterious way, an adolescent child becomes a catalyst for poltergeist phenomena.

Carl Carmer, a student of psychics, once wrote a book called *Stars Fell on Alabama*. Perhaps someday someone will write one titled *Stones Fell on Indiana*. What are they and where are they coming from? It is hard to say, and since they are still falling as these words are written, it is dangerous to hazard an opinion. But at the risk of being made a fool of by tomorrow's papers, and having examined all the evidence and being of sound mind (I think), I would be inclined to state that here is a classic case of poltergeist activity.

They are still prowling the woods back of U.S. 41 for a human agency down in Vanderburgh County, Indiana, but the bet here is that they will never find one because there never was one.   ∎

An ancient astronaut from Japan?
(*See p. 122*)

Gods and Humans

Nazca, Peru. Site of one of the most magnificent pieces of earth-art in the world. Ancient geometric figures, spiders, hummingbirds, whales, and flowers. Who created this art, and why?

After decades of study, archaeologists believe they know *how* the designs were created, but their purpose is still open to question. James Moseley wrote in a 1955 FATE article that the "unprejudiced student of the Nazca ruins is forced to consider the possibility that these ancient people . . . . constructed their huge markings as signals to interplanetary visitors or to some advanced Earth race." In 1970, Swiss researcher Erich von Däniken wrote his unforgettable *Chariots of the Gods?* that forever popularized the idea that gods or "ancient anstronauts" must have been the reason for Nazca. Von Däniken's latest book, *Arrival of the Gods* (1998), continues this theme.

Kosovo, Yugoslavia. The fourteenth-century fresco of the Cruxifixion at the Visoki Dechany Monastery of the Serbian Orthodox Church is a medieval masterpiece. On both top corners are strange little images that clearly depict human-like beings that appear to be riding in flying vessels with jet streams shooting out behind.

The Great Plains, 1870. Omaha Indians unearth the skeletons of eight men—but these are no ordinary skeletons. The living creatures supported by these bones were giants. Their skulls were two feet long.

Do these diverse pieces of evidence, and many more like them, prove that gods—or a long-lost super race—once roamed the Earth? The articles in the following chapter explore nine examples of anomalous evidence that challenge our beliefs about human history.

The Mysterious Circles of Shasta

Johnny Noble
November 1951

Anthropologists say they aren't made by humans; geologists say they are not natural. Where did these mysterious mounds come from?

November darkness was closing over the lonely plain as the first snowflakes slanted silently down from Mount Shasta. The farm boy, bringing his cows from the far pasture, glanced uneasily at the brooding white mountain, barely visible now in the swirling night. No other human should be abroad this stormy evening, and yet the boy was positive he heard voices.

The cows seemed uneasy too. Picking their deliberate way between the rolling hummocks, they stopped frequently to look back and listen. The boy had to pelt them with rough lava clods to hurry them along, and once they veered away from a low-crowned mound, as if turned by invisible hands, and stampeded halfway across the field. Then the boy looked back, shrieked with terror, and fled to the yellow lights of the farmhouse, a mile away.

"There were lots of them," he sobbed to his father an hour afterward, "maybe a hundred of them tiny little men in funny hats standing in a big circle. You know the Circles . . ."

"Aye," said the bearded homesteader, "the circles I know, but I've never seen them. "'Tis the 'Little People' abroad again."

For more than a century, the story of the "Little People" on Mount Shasta has persisted. Their hoary legends cling to the icy slopes of the old volcano, and there are strange tales of unmortal men descended from the Lost Continent of Atlantis. Occult clans have formed and flourished about Shasta city—and died away. But debunkers never have been able to laugh off one incontestable phenomenon, evident to every eye—the mysterious Siskiyou Stone Circles. Nor has science been able to explain them.

These odd earth formations protrude like swelling grass-covered nipples over six hundred acres of the flat prairie near the northwestern foot of the peak. Each concentric mound is the same, sixty feet in diameter with the dirt rising in an almost perfect circle to a crest approximately two feet above the level of the surrounding terrain. Each ring is surrounded by a stone path, or mosaic, the rocks obviously gathered from the millions of volcanic stones tumbled over all the neighborhood. One curious thing to scientists who have investigated is the manner in which these rocks have been set in circular trenches, with gravel and smaller rocks at the bottom graduating upward to boulder size at the surface.

"Nothing in geology explains this," asserts Burton J. Westman, B.Sc., of Etna in Siskiyou County. "The mounds are not natural. They must be human. The trenches and mound soil indicate they may have been used for agricultural purposes less than two hundred years ago."

The mounds themselves, he noted, are pure dirt down to the clay hardpan that underlies this whole area. There, on the hardpan, investigators find the scattered volcanic stones resuming, just as they are found on the ground surface above the mounds. And they show signs of weathering, as if they hadn't always been covered with dirt.

The rock rings around the humps appear to be smooth pathways of steppingstones, carefully laid, it would appear, to make easier walking between the mounds or around them, far easier than striking off across the rock-strewn fields where only sagebrush and weedy grass will grow. Even the yellow pine that thrives in the area seems to shun the field of mounds.

"I can't believe these are natural," confessed Franklin Fenenga, University of California anthropologist, "but neither can I find any function for which they would be built."

Fenenga, an expert on all the early peoples who inhabited California—all the scientifically recognized peoples, that is—was the latest expert called into a mystery that was buzzed in low-voiced speculation for decades. Local folk spoke of the mounds in tones not likely to carry to tiny unseen ears, until 1946, when the phenomenon came to official attention.

A field of the strange humps appeared on an aerial photograph taken by the United States Forest Service that year, and non-superstitious people demanded, "What are they?"

Ground parties of skilled woodsmen and geographers looked; they couldn't find an answer. Old Indians of the region shrugged; nothing in their lore explained the circles, and they seemed unwilling to think too closely. Geologists had their day and went away puzzled. Hundreds of practical people, in fact, have looked and given up during these four years. To this day no one has a logical explanation.

Fenenga and C. E. Smith, a fellow anthropologist, were willing to grant that the stone circles certainly look like the organized effort of many people—and definitely unlike the work of nature. But they could find no relic, no tool, no evidence of a human hand, to indicate that mortal beings had been around the mounds. A single arrowhead was picked up by a child, but it had been chipped from Glass Mountain, the obsidian peak northwest of the area, and apparently was lost by an Indian while hunting.

Fenenga and Smith proved that these were not burial mounds of earthly people. Acid poured on the soil would have caused a violent reaction if there had been bones or other limey substance mixed in the dirt. There would have been artifacts, for the known natives of this area buried people's wealth with them.

"We have found nothing—not a single thing but that arrowhead," says George Schrader, assistant supervisor of the Shasta National Forest and officer of the Siskiyou County Historical Society. Schrader, a studious man whose whole working life has been in the outdoors, personally took over the mystery when others admitted defeat. And he still has no solution.

One theory, unsubstantiated by geologists, is that lava "bubbles" burst and left the mounds inside their rock circles. This fails to explain why the lightest stones are at the bottom of the trenches and the heaviest on top.

Another theory is that the mounds are Indian works, built for ceremonial purposes during the annual big game hunt of early days. "Why, then, aren't there artifacts?" demand Fenenga and Smith. "That many people working over the years would have left a large quantity of material behind. People of later years might have carried away arrowheads, tools, and household relics—but they certainly would not have carted off all the bone or flint chips that would mark an Indian activity." The anthropologists, who have investigated Indian works throughout California, admitted they have never encountered any puzzle such as the stone circles.

Westman, the geologist on the scene—still convinced that living persons built the mounds—concludes his report with the observation, "What made the aboriginal Indians choose this area for these mounds, what was the exact use of these mounds, what was the culture of the inhabitants, and what caused them to abandon the mounds are questions that await reply."

The reply of the experts is that no Indians chose the site or used the mounds. Then who did?

Four years of scientific searching and examination has given no answer that can be backed with proof. Local inhabitants who watched the cults come and go and pondered the legend of the "Little People" and the Lost Continent of Atlantis are not so sure.

Certain oldsters, who spend hours in presumably tranquil meditation on the slopes of old Shasta, smile with open composure at the hubbub.

Schrader, most constant of the objective searchers, is ready to shake his head in frank puzzlement, quickly turning an oblique glance up at Mount Shasta, as if seeking still to find the answer in the mountain's snowy aloofness.

"The Egyptians," he murmurs, "didn't have the only Sphinx with a riddle." ■

The Giants in the Earth

Harold T. Wilkins
January 1952

Human skulls two feet long suggest that a super race existed long before humans.

There were giants in the Earth in those days," say the old Hebrew compilers of Genesis, who drew on ancient and vanished sources of antediluvian age.

Evidence, in the shape of skulls, bones, and artifacts, suggests that giants ranged over the whole planet from the plains of Asia and the mountains of central Europe into every part of America. In the Western Hemisphere, evidence is found from the far south in what is now Patagonia up to the tundras of Alaska—once a far warmer region. In that distant day, land bridges existed, which, thousands of years later, were destroyed in a terrible cataclysm that is recorded in Genesis and in many American Indian myths. The Iroquois, the Osage, the Tuscaroras, the Hurons, the Omahas, and many other North American Indians all speak of giant men who once lived and roamed in the territories of their forefathers. All over what is now the U.S. are traditions of these ancient giants.

In addition, evidence in the form of bones, skulls, and artifacts lend credence to the existence of giant men in North America. This evidence justifies the theory that these giant men were contemporaries and even adversaries of monstrous animals and dinosaurs, which palaeontologists assume vanished in an epoch preceding by many thousands of years the appearance of either human or any anthropoid ape or mammal.

The weight of this evidence would justify the theory that civilized societies must have existed in the Tertiary Age in what is now the United States!

What is also remarkable is that these giants had six toes and, in some cases, a double row of teeth in their tremendous jaws! I have space here for only a small selection of the evidence that would fill a pretty long book. It is sure to shake many preconceived notions of evolution and the age of ancient human civilization in America.

About 1810 there were found near Braystown, at the headwaters of the Tennessee river, footprints of immense age impressed in the solid rock. They included six-toed feet of giant people. One such track is the print of a human heel ball actually thirteen inches wide! Close to it are prints of the hoofs of ancient horses—those horses that fallacious history asserts never existed in the America of pre-Columbian times. One of these horses slipped for several feet and then recovered its footing. The prints suggest that an army of giants was traveling in the same direction and that a giant led his horse when passing the mountain with his army! The track of the horse is eight by ten inches.

Sixty years later (about 1870), Frank la Flèche of the Indian Bureau in Washington, D.C., reported that the Omahas, digging a grave near the house of their former chief Two Grizzly Bears, unearthed the skeletons of eight giant men lying in a row. The skulls of these giants were two feet long—

staggering dimensions when compared with the skull of the average modern man!

These discoveries seem to bear out the ancient traditions of the Omahas that in the land of their forefathers lived giants called *Pasnu-ta,* who abducted men and women of lesser stature. Whether the giants enslaved these lesser breeds or ate them is a moot point, but it may be noted that down south in ancient Peru, a similar race of giants landed in rafts from the Pacific, invaded South America's shores from what is now Puerto Viejo, ascended the highlands, killed the small Indians, and raped and ruined their women. These giants sank fine wells and lined them with stone and built megalithic cities. The myths charge them with the perversions of Sodom and Gomorrah—but the point to be noted is that they were skilled engineers and architects.

It is significant that the Osage called these ancient giants of North America *Mu-a-lu-shka*—a name that points straight to their possible origin in the vanished Pacific continent of Mu, land of ferocious giants who had also developed a megalithic culture. Moreover, the Osage said these giants had amazing skulls with a vertical diameter of more than two feet.

I stress this histological characteristic for a reason that will soon become clear. In 1924, the Dohenny Scientific Expedition to the Havai Supai Canyon of Arizona came upon startling evidence in the shape of astounding petroglyphs that indicate that these giants were contemporaries of the fearsome dinosaur tyrannosaurus. Cut in the hard sandstone rock of the Supai canyon is a petroglyph in which the dinosaur tyrannosaurus stands erect on tail and hind legs as if to challenge an enemy. The picture must have been carved by an eyewitness. Indians in the area have a tradition that the glyph was cut by a "big feller" in a very ancient day.

The immense age of this petroglyph, and of others close to it, is attested by the iron patina that very slowly accumulates on the face of the rock; some of it is found in the furrows of the glyph and also around it. This indicates that aeons must have passed since the glyph was made.

There is geological reason to suppose that, as is the case of plutonic regions in central Brazil, the high plateaus of Nevada, Arizona, and Utah are among the oldest parts of the Earth and have not been under water since the azoic ages, more than 40,000,000 years ago. How old then must this amazing petroglyph be if the dinosaur became extinct in America more than 12,000,000 years ago?

How long were these giants denizens of this weird region of ancient North America?

The vivid answer is another petroglyph in the same Arizona canyon that depicts a giant man either attacking or being attacked by a mammoth. And yet this carving seems to have been made ages later than the image of the tyrannosaurus.

Be it also noted that this same ancient picture gallery, whose canvas is a granitic stone on which wind and weather have little erosive effect, has additional glyphs of unknown monsters with goatlike feet and an ancient hieroglyph resembling the old Greek sign of Mars.

Here too, attesting its antiquity, iron scale has formed in the furrows of the glyph.

Another mysterious discovery was made in Arizona in the township of Crittenden in 1891. Workers were removing earth in order to make the foundation for a hotel. Eight feet down, their picks struck soft masses of stone that seemed to have been well-worked masonry at one time. Excavating deeper still, the workers came on an ancient tomb of large square blocks of rose granite, most skillfully cemented so that the whole construction looked solid. An architect named Hendrickson was summoned and took charge of the work. Hendrickson forbade the use of gunpowder on these amazing remains.

Inside this granite tomb the men came upon an amazing sarcophagus of Egyptian type. But, of course, it was not the work of the ancient Egyptians. It took the form of the image of a giant man lying at full length, and it was made of some strange material like clay, but brightly colored blue. The giant was naked but had a girdle at the waist. Close-fitting sandals were on his feet, and on his head was a crown shaped like a bishop's mitre, but topped with what looked like either a hawk's or an eagle's head.

The face of this giant was as imperious as those of the colossal portrait images on Easter Island. The nose and mouth were large, but the low cheekbones were not those of an Indian. His hands were as small and delicate as those of a woman. They were crossed on the breast, and the image of a hawk or an eagle was stamped on their backs.

The feet were also crossed—and had six toes! The sandals had been cut so as to bring the sixth toe into prominence, as if the giant were proud of the distinction! The hair was shown as thick and bushy, reaching to the shoulders.

Inside the sarcophagus were handfuls of dust—all that was left of bones and skull. No more amazing evidence of antiquity could be found, for of all parts of the human anatomy, the very last to disintegrate is the human skull.

There was one more notable feature of the image on the sarcophagus—in the giant's hand was clasped the queer image of a squatting figure, which might have been that of a god. The image was male, squatted on a pedestal, and squinted and grinned in hideous fashion. Both hands were clasped over the ears as if to shut out sound. (A type of ancient image resembling this old Arizona image has been found in an extremely old Peruvian huaca or grave.) Its hair hung down its back in plaits.

The crown worn by the giant, and also the girdle, was of thick red gold finely carved with minute and delicate designs

and drawings depicting battle scenes, a triumphal proces-
sion, marches, and other scenes whose meaning is unknown.
On the girdle were carved unknown hieroglyphs. Along with
the sarcophagus image—probably a portrait of the giant
within—was a large battle axe whose blade was of some
hard, glassy substance like obsidian, but the handle was of
petrified wood, more evidence of immense antiquity. Magnificent green stones or *chalcuithes*—emblems of immortal-
ity—were in the giant's mouth.

Amazing finds were also made in California about 1810
and in Montana in 1924. One was that of a six-toed giant,
the other was the skull of a man found 130 feet deep in a
lava-covered mine. A human molar embedded in an eocene
coal measure was found in November 1926 in No. 3 Eagle
Coal Mine at Bearcreek, Montana, and in strata anywhere
between thirty and seventy-five million years old. An amazing skull—there is no other word for it!—of a giant man
with double rows of teeth all round the massive jaws was
found on Santa Rosa Island in the Santa Barbara Channel,
California. It has a singular tie-in with the statement in the
old Babylonian *Talmud*, called the *Berakthoth*, that the giants
before the Great Deluge had double rows of teeth!

Many of these discoveries were made early in the nineteenth century, and in one case where a giant man's skeleton
was exhumed by soldiers at Lampock Rancho, California, the
Roman Catholic padre ordered the skeleton to be reburied
because the local folk swore it was the skeleton of a god.

These remains were often discovered accompanied by
cemented gravel six feet thick lying under volcanic ash—the
sign of and ancient cataclysm—ancient metal skillets, beautifully made plummets of syenite, strange inscriptions on
ancient artifacts, sea shells lined on the inside with gold and
worked with unknown inscriptions, carved blocks of por-
phyry engraved with hieroglyphs, hieroglyphs on hard

rocks covered with iron scale, queer slate tubes and cylinders, and well-made pestles and mortars. All of these, of course, are evidence of ancient civilizations.

And now for one of the most interesting of these accounts. This story comes from an eyewitness who was a disgusted observer, helpless to make any protest at what was done under his eyes.

In the spring of 1943 a volunteer detachment of the U.S. Army Engineers (Branch of the Alaska Defense Command) was sent to work on the Alcan Highway. While they were at Fort Lewis, they were put into another outfit and sent across the Pacific to a little island right at the western end of the Aleutians. Its name is Shemya, and it lies close to the volcanic island of Attu but will be found on none but U.S. military charts.

On Shemya the men's job was to build an airstrip for landing purposes. One day in May 1943, a remarkable discovery was made. At the northeast end of this tiny island is a bluff of sedimentary rock, and below it, on the beach, are strewn igneous and sedimentary boulders. When these beach boulders were shifted, the bulldozers started to work and turned up layer on layer of fossils, each layer differing from that below it.

In one of these layers were huge human bones and skulls of giants, lying near fossil ivory and mammoth and mastodon bones. Some of these giant human skulls lacked the lower jaw. The skulls were from one foot ten inches to two feet long! They were emphatically human and not animals. The bones of the animals lay far enough apart for them to be clearly perceptible.

The height of these giants measured no fewer than twenty-four feet! I questioned my informant and he was positive in his affirmation of the astounding height of these men—a height that tallies with that asserted in ancient

Hindu lore about the giants of old, and the height of the famous Bamian statues in Central Asia at the foot of the Hindu Kush mountains.

My informant went on: "I was in the 92nd battalion and must ask you not to give my name, as I am under draft orders in connection with this war in Korea and might be victimized if Army brass knew what I am telling you. The officers in charge in Shemya ordered strict secrecy about this discovery. Not a man was allowed take any souvenirs, whether of the giant skulls and jaws or of the fossil ivory and mammoth bones. One soldier, who knew something about paleontology and anthropology realized that here was a priceless discovery that any scientist would almost give his head to be allowed to examine.

"A day later the officers found that one soldier had made a cache of some of the bones. They threatened him with a court martial if he did not at once give up the cache. He surrendered his cache and the threat was dropped."

I may tell the reader that the editor of FATE Magazine has been given, in strict confidence, the name and address of this ex-G.I. who lives in a western state.

His story goes on: "These giant remains in the Shemya beach were found about six feet below the surface. The ground where the skulls and bones were found is swampy and sandy, and the beach was just muck and deteriorated rock. Mixed in with the big bones were smaller ones. They might have been deposited there in a cataclysm, but there is evidence that this may have been also an ancient graveyard of the giants. It is curious that all these skulls of giant men had holes in them two inches in diameter. Maybe that was in accord with the notion of ancient folk that you could let the soul out of the head by trephining the crania. It may have been done with clubs or arrows, but as all the skulls were perforated, I reckon it is more likely that an ancient ritual was followed."

I asked my informant if any artifacts were found with these giant human bones and skulls. His answer is remarkable: "Yes, in this graveyard of the giants there were also found little carved ivory toys such as dolls, boats, arrowheads, [and] spear heads, the latter made of some chipped and ground stone. The stone, too, was not of a kind found on Shemya Island. The skulls of these giants were, except as to their Brobdingnagian size, like those of modern man and with a high forehead.

"It is odd that I saw no lower jaw in any of these skulls. These carved ivory artifacts were found among the giant remains and were of a style much more advanced than would be found among primitive or modern Indians.

"There is no sign of any recent vulcanism on tiny Shemya Island. The tusks of mammoths were also found, but broken, close to the giant human skulls and bones.

"No, I sure never heard, nor did any other soldiers, that any of these remains reached a U.S. museum. Scientists got a chance to investigate in Shemya. Yes, one of us measured these giant men. They were eighteen feet, six inches high!

"I prefer not to give the name of my unit on Shemya when this happened in May 1943. If I get called up on draft, as I expect I shall be shortly, it might mean trouble for me. But I'd take an oath before any public notary the truth of these facts of which I was an eyewitness right on the spot." ■

America's Giants

Frank Joseph
June 1993

*Astounding prehistoric findings among
Wisconsin's Aztalan mounds.*

For the past several years, I have been investigating the
remains of a lost North American civilization known as Aztalan. Actually, that is just the name of its capital, once a 175-acre
ceremonial city about half-way between Madison and Milwaukee in southern Wisconsin.

Three mighty walls with watchtowers every twenty feet
encircled a trio of earthen pyramids oriented to the movements of the sun and moon. A colossal irrigation system
connected the city with Rock Lake, three miles away, where
the enigmatic leaders of Aztalan society interred their honored dead under stone pyramids on small islets.

Behind their forbidding walls, the ancient aristocrats lived
in fine houses, traded great quantities of raw copper, farmed
gourmet crops, and conducted their grisly rituals of human
sacrifice and cannibalism. Then, in the early years of the fourteenth century A.D., they suddenly and inexplicably abandoned Aztalan, burning its walls and vanishing forever into
the American wilderness. Why they abruptly relinquished

their empire, which spread throughout Wisconsin and into neighboring Minnesota, Iowa, and Illinois, continues to baffle researchers.

Since their unaccountable disappearance seven centuries ago, the Rock Lake necropolis has sunk beneath the waves and into legend. All that remains of Aztalan itself are two pyramids and a modern reconstruction of part of a wall, together with broken artifacts in several Wisconsin museums.

In conducting my own investigation of this little-known chapter in ancient American history, I have called upon many old and original sources, but none more startling than the work of Theodore Hayes Lewis. He is a genuine, almost forgotten American hero, a surveyor who, alone and with little money, personally explored and documented the prehistoric cities and effigy mounds of lost Aztalan and beyond, throughout the Midwest.

Beginning in 1881, he covered 54,000 miles, more than 10,000 of them on foot, sometimes foraging through the most hostile terrain. He was often the first discoverer of mysterious geoglyphs, regularly finding them in difficult, remote areas.

Twentieth-century analysis of his drawings proves that all the sites he documented were authentically ancient, indigenous creations, not the work of white settlers or early explorers. The fragile remains of pre-Columbian America were being obliterated by advancing settlements. Lewis felt he was working against time to preserve their memory, if not their physical existence. He was particularly interested in prehistoric rock art and the often enormous effigy mounds —mostly animal representations, but some abstract designs skillfully sculpted from the Earth itself.

Lewis meticulously surveyed thousands of these prehistoric artifacts for fourteen years, dying in obscurity about 1930. But his life's work is preserved in dozens of large folders at St. Paul's Minnesota History Center.

There I read Lewis's original field notebooks written in his own hand, and I gingerly unfolded his drawings, which almost crumbled to dust on their 100-year-old paper. Happily, this perishable material is now being transferred to microfilm for the benefit of future researchers.

From the first to the fifth centuries A.D., the ancient civilizers raised some 10,000 effigy mounds, 90 percent of them in Wisconsin, and Lewis succeeded in surveying most before they were destroyed. His accuracy in reproducing each one shows not only his dedication, but his professional expertise.

He drew what he saw, bequeathing new generations an exact picture of a vanished world of gargantuan earth sculpture, mostly of giant creatures beautifully and precisely molded according to some lost standardized system of lengths and measures. Many are so realistically configured that the species of the animal portrayed can readily be determined. Others are bizarre, unfathomable abstracts.

As I paged through Lewis's drawings, I felt I was literally turning back the pages of time to the nineteenth century, seeing these wondrous things through his eyes and far beyond into a distant past. Clearly, the majority of the effigy mounds were accurate re-creations of what the ancient Americans saw on a daily basis. There were obvious figures of buffalo and deer, birds and fish, cats and dogs.

Every so often I came upon a figure that riveted my attention in disbelief. Between the numerous representations of eagles and spiders appeared—elephants! At first I doubted my own interpretation of the renderings. But there were others even more unmistakably elephantine. Nor were they the images of mastodons, who did indeed inhabit North America until about 12,000 years ago. No, the ancient earth mounds represented modern elephants. Altogether, I counted six elephant effigies formerly located in Rock and Vernon Counties, Wisconsin, and Iowa's Allamakee and Lansing Counties.

But the Lewis drawings held more surprises. At Dodge County, Wisconsin, he surveyed the 176-foot-long image of an ocean-going seal from the Arctic Circle. On the north side of Lake Wingra, he found the effigy of a Peruvian llama, 127 feet long and three feet high. How a people living at least a thousand years ago and inhabiting the upper Midwest could have been familiar enough with creatures from Africa, the Arctic, and South America to accurately portray them in colossal effigy mounds is no small mystery.

Do these ancient images imply an Old World or extraterrestrial connection for ancient midwesterners? Left: "Impossible" elephant drawing from Wisconsin mounds. Right: Celestial-themed drawing from Iowa cave.

At Pipestone Mountain, Wisconsin, Lewis reproduced a cave drawing of a naked figure with a club raised in its right hand. It is the usual representation of Hercules seen throughout the ancient European world, but found most commonly along the Atlantic shores of Morocco. Near the American Hercules appears an unusual design, a triangle within a circle, a symbol recurring among the Guanche, the original, pre-Spanish inhabitants of the Canary Islands off the Moroccan coast. Is the Wisconsin figure an example of cultural coincidence, or was it left behind by visitors from far over the sea centuries ago?

The most perplexing image appeared in Rock County near one of the elephant mounds. There Lewis discovered the 98.5-foot-long effigy of a wheeled animal.

Historians are unanimously agreed that Native Americans had no knowledge of the wheel before the sixteenth-century arrival of European discoverers. To many observers, the earthwork resembles a horse, a no less anomalous feature, because the animal was first introduced by the same modern Europeans. Moreover, why memorialize a geoglyph of this kind?

Interestingly, the most famous wheeled horse in history was invented by Bronze Age Greeks as a seige-weapon in their war against Ilios: the Trojan Horse.

Were the ancient creators of the Rock County effigy familiar somehow with the story of the fall of Troy?

The mound is absolutely unique, with no other parallel among the many thousands of earth works in North America. Together with the elephant and Hercules images, it at least suggests contact with Old World culture bearers, perhaps 3,000 years ago.

The atypical effigies surveyed by Lewis are not the only disquieting images in the American landscape he documented. I should mention that I am not a devotee of so-called "ancient astronaut" theories. Von Däniken-like explanations of the past have never appealed to me very much. However, some examples of the cave art Lewis reproduced must give every honest skeptic pause.

These individual drawings may portray a shaman's drug-induced hallucinations, or they may represent something else.

Deep inside a large cave in Allamakee County, Iowa, near the Mississippi River, among more elephant mounds, appeared a unique figure. At a West Salem cave, in La Crosse County, Wisconsin, Lewis copied another drawing. Interestingly, the walls of both caves were decorated with hundreds of images of stars, suns, and crescent moons, all implying a heavenly setting.

Concerning the anomalous animal effigies and Herculean figure, a clue may once have existed in another set of geoglyphs surrounding Aztalan itself. They were gigantic mounds shaped to represent oars, often in excess of 160 feet long; their very size suggested naval power. Perhaps they were the emblems of a people proficient in seamanship, who traveled farther than present-day scholars give them credit for, and who saw many strange animals never indigenous to the Midwest.

This interpretation of the oar-mounds as symbols of sea power is underscored by the numerous drawings of turtles and tridents, both signs for sea travel, in the cave containing the Hercules figure.

Regarding those otherworldly cave drawings of creatures and possible interstellar vehicles, maybe the answers lie beyond the stars depicted on their walls.   ∎

America's Lost Race

John Thomas
August-September 1951

*Silver crosses and undeciphered inscriptions
make up a mystery that archaeologists
haven't even begun to solve.*

Historians agree that Columbus did not discover America.
The Vikings were certainly here before he was, and maybe
the Portuguese, and there is pretty good evidence about the
Welsh. But the people I am talking about go back a long way
before this.

Evidence is gradually accumulating that America was
inhabited by a civilized race long before it was inhabited by
Indians. There is a clue here, a hint there, a relic somewhere
else. There are coins or coin-shaped objects dug from great
depths. There are inscribed stones, written in a strange lan-
guage.There are tablets, undecipherable writings in what is
evidently an alphabet and not pictographic forms. It may be
years before definite proof is in; perhaps some people will
never be convinced, but here are some of the bits of evidence
that have been dug up.

Take the case of the Georgia crosses. In the *Report of the Smithsonian Institution*, 1881–619, Charles C. Jones tells of a pair of tiny silver crosses found in Georgia. They were skillfully made and, unlike the usual kind, all arms had equal length.

Jones, being a scientific fellow, suggested that De Soto had halted at the "precise" spot where the crosses were found. The engraving on the crosses, however, does not suggest Spanish origin.

The inscription, according to Jones, consisted of the letters IYNKICIDU. This, he tells us, must have been the name of some nearby Indian tribe, but no Indans known in the Americas ever bore the name. And even if there were such a tribe, how would one account for the fact that the "C" and "D" were turned backward in the original?

It is cases like this that make archaeologists unhappy. Nevertheless, this type of evidence is constantly turning up.

What about the copper mines of Lake Superior? These extensive and remarkable mines, extending for many miles, were evidently worked by highly skilled hands. Says the *American Antiquarian*, 25–258, there is no indication of any permanent settlement near these mines, "not a vestige of a dwelling, skeleton, or a bone has been found." The Indians of the region have no traditions relating to these mines.

Unknown coins have been found in some diggings. During September 1833, workers boring for water near Norfolk, Virginia, came upon a strange coin thirty feet down. It was described as being the size of an English shilling, but oval in shape. W. S. Forest, in *Historical Sketches of Norfolk, Virginia*, describes the coin as stamped with figures resembling "a warrior or hunter and other characters, apparently of human origin."

Another coin, this time copper and the size of an old two-cent piece, was unearthed in a Michigan mound. Another strange coin, over which controversy raged for some years, was found by Jacob W. Mort of Chillicothe, Illinois. Mort discovered the coin while boring at a depth of 120 feet! Writing in the *Proceedings of the American Philosophical Society*, 12–224, Moffit describes the coin as uniform in thickness, never hammered out by savages. He added, "There are other tokens of the machine shop."

But Professor Leslie couldn't see it that way. He insisted on referring to the coin as an astrological talisman. "There are upon it the signs of Pisces and Leo," said Professor Leslie. "The coin was placed there as a practical joke, though not by its present owner, and is probably a modern fabrication, perhaps of the sixteenth century, possibly Hispano-American or French-American in origin."

The legend about it suggests it is "somewhere between Arabic and Phoenician without being either." Evidently Professor Leslie was not too sure of the thing himself.

Professor Winchell, in *Sparks From a Geologist's Hammer*, p. 170, says that the signs were neither stamped nor engraved, but "looked as if etched with acid."

Inscribed stones and tablets also bear mute witness to an unknown past. Take the stone found by the Rev. Mr. Grass, who opened several mounds near Davenport, Illinois. In these mounds he found a large number of tablets, one of them bearing the legend TFTOWNS.

Ah, but there was no mystery about this! The tablet was of Mormon origin. Why? Because the characters were similar to those on a brass plate found in Mendon, Illinois. And why was the brass plate of Mormon origin? Because it was discovered "near a house once occupied by a Mormon." There is no need to make comment on that.

Probably the most famous of all inscribed tablets is the Grave Creek stone. In 1838, A. B. Tomlinson, owner of a mound at Grave Creek, West Virginia, excavated and found a stone tablet that was small, flat, and oval, and upon which were engraved alphabetic characters. Avebury, in *Prehistoric Times*, p. 271, calls it a fraud, and claims that the inscription is modern Hebrew. Colonel Whittlesey, in his *Western Reserve Historical Tracts*, says that Wilson, Squires, and Davis (whoever they may be) also believed it to be false.

But Colonel Whittlesey was in for a blow. The Congress of Archaeologists, meeting at Nancy, France, in 1875, endorsed the find.

Not one to let such an affront go unheeded, Colonel Whittlesey moaned that Tomlinson had "so imposed his views" upon the convention that they were forced to that decision. Shortly after the meeting was closed, Schoolcraft announced that the stone was genuine. Now several philologists got on the validity bandwagon, while a few volunteered to translate the inscription. Here is a sample of their efforts:

Translation by M. Jombard: *Thy orders are laws: thou shinest in impetuous élan and rapid chamois.*

M. Maurice Schwab: *The chief of emigration who reached these places (or this island) has fixed these characters forever.*

M. Oppert: *The grave of one who was assassinated here. May God, to revenge him, strike his murderer, cutting off the hand of his existence.*

Personally, I like the first one best. The beautiful picture of someone briskly polishing away at a brass rail is so clear! Of course the last one is much more dramatic, but how can a mere "hand of existence" compete with a "rapid chamois"?

These inspired translations ended the career of the Grave Creek stone. In a parting shot, Colonel Whittlesey quotes the words of Major De Helward at the Congress of Luxembourg in 1877: "If Professor Read and I are right in the conclusion that the figures are neither of the Runic, Phoenician, Canaanite, Hebrew, Libyan, Celtic, or any other alphabet language, its importance has been greatly overrated."

And that is probably the most asinine statement in the history of archeology. Without opinions or interpretations, without trying to slant the facts one way or another, we are led to accept only one conclusion. We are not given any alternative.

The evidence is real and we must take cognizance of it. Perhaps some of the above cases were frauds. One can hardly conceive, however, of some giggling practical joker secretly making a strange coin and burying it 120 feet underground. He must have been quite optimistic to hope that anyone would find it.

Facts are facts, and that is all there is to it. It appears that America has not always been the home of uncivilized peoples. Somewhere in the dim past there lived a Lost Race.

Having accepted that idea, we are naturally led to ask, "Who were they?" Actually, there is no way of knowing. They may have been North American counterparts of the Incas, or colonists from Donnelly's Atlantis. Or a lost expedition from Somewhere. . . .

Whoever—or whatever—they were, it is certain that they were not the usual type of primitive civilization. Those "other tokens of the machine shop" suggest something beyond all present knowledge—as do these last two cases:

A ritual mask was found in Sullivan County, Missouri, in 1879. It was made of iron and silver.

J. H. Hooper, of Bradley County, Tennessee, found a curious stone on his farm. Digging near the same spot, he found a long wall. On it were inscribed numerous alphabetic characters. "Eight hundred and seventy-two characters have been examined, many of them duplicates, and a few of them imitations of animal forms, the moon, and other objects. Accidental imitations of oriental alphabets are numerous." (Trans. *N. Y. Acad. of Sciences*, 11–27.)

And all this would not be quite so startling except for one fact: The inscription was hidden under a layer of cement. ■

Lost World of the Bible's Giants

Barry Chamish
November 1997

*Did an ancient Middle Eastern race build
its own Stonehenge?*

Sitting atop the Israeli-controlled Golan Heights is a
monument that, despite its relative obscurity, ranks as one
of the remaining wonders of the ancient world. This Stone-
henge-like structure is called *Gilgal Refaim* (the Circle of the
Refaim) in Hebrew and *Rujum Al-Hiri* in Arabic. It consists
of five concentric stone rings with a total diameter of about
five hundred feet. Researchers believe the monument's
builders used it for astronomical purposes. But the builders'
identities may be the biggest surprise of all, for evidence
hints that they were a race of giants mentioned in the Bible.

Because the stones used to build Gilgal Refaim are enor-
mously large and heavy, constructing the monument was
not an easy task. The monument's best preserved ring is the
outermost, which contains stones measuring more than six
feet tall and eleven feet thick. Some weigh as much as twenty tons. Standing in the center of the monument is a tumu-

lus, or grave mound, that measures about sixty-five feet across. Only recently have researchers begun studying the rings, which remained hidden from archaeological study while the Syrian regimes held the Golan Heights. But after Israel took control of the area following the 1967 Six Day War, it opened the site for scientific inspection. Even now, however, only a few people have studied the rings.

Researchers are particularly fascinated by two large openings in the rings—somewhat like doorways—one facing northeast, the other southeast. In 1968, Professor Yonathan Mizrahi of the Department of Anthropology at Harvard University and Professor Anthony Aveni of Colgate University discovered that in 3000 B.C. the first rays of sunlight on the summer solstice shined directly through the northeast opening—as seen from the central tumulus. At the same time, the southeast opening provided a direct view of Sirius. These discoveries strongly suggest that the circle's builders used it as an astronomical observatory and stellar calendar.

Lichenometric tests and carbon dating of potsherds found at the site confirm that Gilgal Refaim was constructed before 3000 B.C. In fact, Mizrahi and Aveni erred on the side of conservatism. The shards have been dated to 6,000 years ago. If this age is correct, the circles pre-date the pyramids and Babylonian temples, making them the oldest astronomical complex in the Middle East.

Dozens of dolmens, similar in appearance to those found in northern Britain and France, stand in the same region as the rings. One is outstanding. It is powerfully magnetic: Compasses placed on it spin wildly. Geology department researchers from Tel Aviv University in 1996 used aerial sonar technology to peer into the ground surrounding the site. They found a complex of walls and buildings buried under two to three feet of earth. They conducted a preliminary dig based on the aerial map and discovered two remarkably preserved corpses, their clothing almost intact.

The researchers who studied the bodies concluded that the two were nomadic, unhealthy, and badly clothed. The Mount Golan Field School reported that the state of the bodies, as well as Chalcolithic potsherds found nearby, suggests that the corpses are of a primitive people incapable of building the circles, let alone understanding its astronomical functions.

If the local nomads who inhabited the region didn't build the rings, who did? Surprisingly, there is strong evidence that the biblical giants, or Refaim, were the architects and engineers who constructed the monument. Consider the following biblical clues, written in modern terminology (*The Book*, Ken Taylor, Tyndale House Publishers):

Genesis 14:5 tells us that the Refaim inhabited the place called Ashtherot-Karnaim. Ashtherot was an ancient Canaanite city ten miles from the rings. Its inhabitants named the city after the Canaanite goddess of war and love. Ashterot was the Canaanite name for Sirius, from which the Hebrew name Esther was derived.

Joshua 12:4 says that "King Og of Bashan, the last of the Refaim, who lived at Ashtarot . . . ruled a territory stretching from Mount Hermon in the north."

In 1 Chronicles 6:71, the Bible tells us that the half-tribe of Manasseh later inhabited "Golan," in Bashan.

Deuteronomy 3 contains the most explicit description of the size of the people of Bashan. This passage describes how King Og was attacked and defeated: "King Og of Bashan was the last of the great Refaim. His iron bedstead is kept at Rabbah . . . and measures thirteen and a half feet long and six feet wide." Enticingly, in the same chapter we are informed that "the Sidonians called Mount Hermon 'Sirion.'" This again implies that Gilgal Refaim was used to view Sirius.

Deuteronomy also tells us that the Refaim "were a large and powerful tribe, as tall as the Anakim (giants)."

Chronicles 20 describes how the last of the Anakim was killed: "A giant with six fingers on each hand and six toes on each foot, whose father was also a giant . . . was killed by David's nephew Jonathan. These giants were descendants of the giants of Gath and were killed by David and his soldiers."

A 1993 study by Bruce Curtis goes beyond biblical clues and delves into the apocryphal work *The Book of Knowledge: The Keys of Enoch* to unravel the mystery of the Rings of the Refaim. Curtis concludes that "Enoch reveals that these stone timepieces are connected with those scriptures which contain the codes for 'specific events on Earth and in space that man must key into.'"

His report also says, "Enoch is telling us that symbols such as this are part of a greater communication system, namely one coming from higher intelligence." These intelligences "periodically come into the Earth dimension to assist in the transformation of humanity."

The respected Jerusalem biblical author Rabbi Yisrael Herczeg rejects Curtis's thesis, but he inadvertently confirms part of it.

He begins, "The Jewish tradition rejects the apocryphal books, though they have been adopted in Christianity. Enoch predates Noah and the flood, so how would his works have survived? The Jewish oral tradition says Og, the King of Bashan, stowed away on Noah's ark and was the only survivor of the flood aside from Noah's family. Og was descended from the Nefilim, deities who fell from the heavens."

Herczeg rejects claims that the Nefilim were aliens. "No, [they were] more like fallen angels. Og had children with Noah's daughters, and they were hybrid giants called the Anakim or Refaim," he added. "These were the most likely builders of the Circles of the Refaim."

More research needs to be done at Gilgal Refaim, but this mysterious stone monument already has revealed tantalizing evidence supporting biblical stories that giant races once walked the Earth. ∎

Solving the Mystery of Nazca

William H. Isbell
October 1980

"Airfields" on remote Peruvian plains set off endless speculation about ancient space voyageurs. The facts are more exciting.

Visitors to Lima, Peru, find that it is a huge, modern city, distinctly European in flavor. It *should* seem European, for it was the symbol of Spain's hold on South America for 300 years. But the Inca language is still heard in the markets and in the crowded suburbs, and vertically layered terraces on stepped mountains clearly reflect an indigenous spatial organization.

Taxis and buses leave on regular schedules for the 300-mile trip south to Nazca on the Pan American highway, a narrow asphalt ribbon stretching across endless desert. To the west, the barren sand and stone drop sharply to the sea, and bleached shacks of fishermen dot the sheltered coves. Sea life is bountiful, but there is no fresh water. To the east, the Andes Mountains rise, and here, high above the coast, mountain chills turn the sea breezes to rain. Streams rush to form small rivers and tumble back toward the ocean through steep-sided canyons.

When our car noses steeply down into one of these oasis canyons, the landscape turns from stark desert to emerald green, and we are surrounded by irrigated fields of corn, cotton, sugarcane, grapes, figs, and all manner of plants. Towns press in on the road, and the smell of humanity replaces that of the sea. From roadside stalls vendors offer wine, fruit, bread, sweets, fish, and spicy creole food. A couple of miles farther on, the motor begins to labor as our vehicle carries us up again to the vast stretches of sand, strangely colored by minerals and dried ocean salts. It may be forty or fifty miles to the next oasis canyon.

Abandoned pyramids, towns, and cemeteries lie within sight of the highway, for each one of these small valleys was the home of an ancient civilization—Pachacamac in the first valley south of Lima, Curayacu, the middens of Mala and Asia, Cerro Azul, Cerro del Oro, Tambo de Mora, Paracas, Ica, all familiar to students of South American archaeology.

Traversing a great stretch of rocky desert south of Ica we speed past several small oases. Then, beyond Palpa and Ingenio, unexpectedly we come upon a sign announcing that we are entering an archaeological zone; this one is located *between* oasis valleys. We see no evidence of human activity except a modern steel tower about a half-mile up the road. At the base of the tower a guard stands alongside his motorcycle—although there seems to be nothing to watch.

We climb the tower—and the random undulations in the rocky ground begin to resolve. A plantlike figure appears. Beyond it is a huge trapezoid and in another direction is a curious figure with open hands, five fingers on one and four on the other. Straight narrow lines run off to the horizon, interrupted occasionally by huge geometric figures and representational drawings formed by continuous outlines, light-colored depressions in the dark desert surface. One huge reptilian figure is cut in half by the asphalt ribbon. We are standing among the Nazca ground drawings.

No one knows who first observed these strange markings. Sixteenth-century accounts of the Incas and their provinces do not mention them. They came to the attention of archaeologists only in the 1930s when regular airline flights over the deserts set curious passengers to gossiping about the strange geometric shapes.

In the summer of 1939 Dr. Paul Kosok, an archaeologist from Long Island University who had heard about the drawings, visited Nazca. He mapped a giant drawing of a bird and gained recognition as the discoverer of the Nazca ground art. In 1947 he published the first description of the figures.

But the lines and geometric forms can be detected from the ground if you know what to look for, and drawings on hillsides or adjacent to high land have always been visible. It is likely that local people were aware of the markings long before Kosok's formal discovery.

Markings on the Nazca desert fall into five classes. Most common are the long straight lines. Thousands of these crisscross the desert in every direction. They range from as narrow as 16 centimeters (6.25 inches) to over five meters (16.4 feet) wide and some run for a distance of 10 kilometers (6.2 miles). Sometimes the lines turn back on themselves to form elaborate geometric complexes with zigzags or long parallel sets of oscillating lines.

Second are the large geometric figures—elongated trapezoids or triangles—which were first noticed from the air. They range from a yard or two to several hundred yards wide and from ten or fifteen yards to more than a half-mile in length.

Third are representational drawings of animal and plant forms accomplished with curving lines. As in a contour drawing, the outline generally runs around the entire figure without a break and without crossing itself. These depictions, which range from as small as three yards to more than 200 yards in length, were only discovered by ground survey.

Frequently these three types of markings are combined in a single layout. A line originates from a large trapezoid, turns on itself to form a geometric complex, continues across the desert to outline a representational drawing, and eventually returns to the trapezoid.

A fourth class of ground marking incorporates several kinds of rock piles. The piles of stones, sometimes large groups of them, are probably rocks cleared from trapezoidal areas. Some of the stones moved off the surfaces were heaped along the edges of figures, and others apparently were accumulated in piles. Most of these piles have been carried away, but some remain in place. Piles of stone also occur at one or both ends of some of the trapezoids, and their central positions suggest that they were put there intentionally. Finally, some stone piles are centers from which lines radiate in various directions. Some of these are natural rocky outcrops but others obviously were created artificially.

The fifth class of ground art consists of figures on steep hillsides. These were composed with many short lines rather than one continuous outline. They include the only representations of the human figure on the Nazca deserts; they are more primitive in appearance than the contour drawings; and they compare stylistically with early pottery designs.

In 1946 Kosok was joined by another scholar, Maria Reiche, a German mathematician who has since dedicated her life to investigating the Nazca markings. The early studies of this pair led them to conclusions that have slowly been confirmed and expanded by newer research techniques which employ carbon-14 dating, computerized analysis of line directions and astronomical alignments, infrared photography, soil analysis, photogrammetric mapping, serration of archaeological remains, and stylistic studies of ceramic and textile designs from local prehistoric cultures.

Although Kosok's interest in ancient irrigation first drew his attention to Nazca, in 1947 he wrote that the markings could not he canals or roads: "The people sometimes refer to them as Inca roads, but their very nature, size, and position indicate that they could never have been used for ordinary purposes of transportation. The possibility that they are the remains of ancient irrigation canals must also be ruled out, for they are often found running over hillocks. And where this is not the case, they have no possible physical connection with the river, which would be the primary requisite for irrigation canals."

Kosok also recorded the impressions of airline passengers and pilots who knew the markings only from high above: "When first viewed from the air, [the markings] were nicknamed prehistoric landing fields and jokingly compared with the so-called canals on Mars."

It is ironic that twenty years later Erich von Däniken totally ignored the conclusions of Kosok, Reiche, and others when he constructed an hypothesis whose popular appeal depends on the misrepresentation of the hypothesis scholars reject. Von Däniken sets up archaeologists as ignorant, blind straw men, easily outwitted. He states, incorrectly: "The archaeologists say that the markings are Inca roads." Obviously this is preposterous, so he offers the old impressions of airline passengers as his own new theory: "Seen from the air, the clear-cut impression that the thirty-seven-mile-long plain of Nazca made on me was that of an airfield!"

Von Däniken insists that the enormous drawings were meant as signals for beings floating in the air, for "what other purpose could they have served?" He hypothesizes the lines were laid out according to instructions from an aircraft preparing landing sites for space-traveler "gods."

Since von Däniken bases his interpretations almost exclusively on Nazca markings looking like airfields, let us look a bit closer. From five to ten thousand feet above the ground, the huge elongated trapezoids look remarkably like the multiple-runway airfields we all know from our own experience. But from the top of the tower next to the Pan American highway, we can see that the large trapezoids have soft sand surfaces and are not level. All were made by clearing dark rocks off the light desert, and these rocks are stacked along the edges of the figures. Where trapezoidal, runway-like figures intersect, suggesting airports, it is clear that the trapezoids were built at different times. The stacks of rocks along the edges of later figures form walls across the earlier ones, effectively separating the two. Consequently, any attempt to use the trapezoids as runways would have resulted in collision with rocks, impact with surface irregularities, and bogging down in sand.

A walk around the desert also reveals many small trapezoids that cannot be seen from more than a few hundred feet above. Some are no more than a yard wide and ten or fifteen yards long. Must we conclude, by von Däniken's logic, that these were built for teeny aircraft carrying insect-sized astronaut gods? "What other purpose could they have served?"

No, the elongated trapezoidal figures on the Nazca deserts are not landing fields for aircraft. Any similarity to airports is only superficial.

Some von Däniken enthusiasts believe that desert ground drawings that cannot be seen in their entirety from the ground demonstrate that their builders had to have used aircraft. The ancient astronaut hypothesis argues that laying out such figures required a view from above and the figures have to be seen from above. This logic is obviously faulty.

Are we to believe that the large mosaic jaguar masks the ancient Olmec constructed in deep pits at La Venta, Mexico and then covered over were built to be viewed by mole people tunneling through the ground? Must we assume that the architectural embellishment in unseen parts of dark vaults in medieval European churches were designed for flashlight-toting trapeze artists? Does the cross-shaped layout of many of these same churches mean that medieval Europeans also flew? Was Johann Sebastian Bach composing for computers when he used thirty-nine chords to allude to the thirty-ninth Psalm or twenty-two notes for the twenty-second Psalm in religious vocal works? Clearly listeners could not perceive the structure of this music. The assumption that such art is therefore without purpose ignores the importance of the act of producing art and the fact that many senses can be involved in appreciating art. What is more, shared knowledge of hidden symbols unites those initiated into the secrets. (Witness secret handshakes of modern fraternal societies.)

Ground art is hardly unique to Nazca either. Less elaborate markings are known elsewhere on the coast of Peru. The Incas laid out their capital Cuzco in the form of a feline profile. In North America the Indians of southern California made representational drawings such as the huge figure on the desert near Blythe. Great Serpent Mound in Ohio and other effigy mounds were erected. In southern England monumental white horses were drawn on the chalk downs, while in Japan tumuli were constructed in precise geometric shapes.

The abstract order of the formal European garden or the Zen garden can be perceived only from the air, but is either one any less an expression of human order that can also be appreciated from the ground? And what of modern earth artists such as Robert Smithson, creator of the *Spiral Jetty*? Are we to believe that earth art, which is a nearly universal form of human expression, was produced only under the influence of viewers suspended in the air?

Maria Reiche, using scale models, has made major advances toward demonstrating how Nazca ground art was produced. Although more research needs to be done, the prehistoric engineering skills are no longer completely unknown.

Then what accounts for von Däniken's remarkable appeal? There seem to be two factors. First, Europeans and North Americans are greatly impressed by their civilization and technology. They view much of the rest of the world as "underdeveloped" and assume that technological advance will come to those areas only when the natives are instructed in the technology and civilization of the west. Given this premise, the great engineering feats of the ancient non-Western world are considered mysteries that defy explanation. Westerners need little to convince them that ancient "underdeveloped natives" must have been instructed by Westernlike peoples. This prejudice finds expression in popular myths of lost continents whose tall, blond, bearded, and very European-type populations instructed ancient cultures just as Westerners see themselves instructing the Third World. So von Däniken trades on a popular predisposition to doubt the capacity of native peoples and to believe in lost civilizations.

He also had a second aid. He was writing just as a manned landing on the moon made the space age a reality and as exploration of the Earth's seas made belief in sunken continents progressively less tenable. Von Däniken pushed the lost mother civilization from Atlantis and Mu into unexplored space. Westerners could retain their conviction of supremacy while believing that space visitors instructed ancient natives in the development of civilizational arts.

Of course the real tragedy of the idea is that in supporting Western superiority, von Däniken robs non-Western people of their cultural heritage. He fails to appreciate the true message of prehistoric monuments: the marvelous ingenuity of all races and cultures throughout human time.

If we climb down from our steel perch high above the controversial Nazca drawings and continue south along the Pan American highway, we quickly come to another narrow valley, this one named Nazca. Here dirt roads leading westward toward the sea mark the edges of hundreds of fields, each carefully watered from a tiny trickle which is the Nazca River. The volume of water varies with the seasons, but even when rainfall in the Andean headwaters is heaviest, the little river disappears into desert sand before reaching the coast. Life in the oasis depends on hard agricultural labor, the construction and maintenance of a complex series of canals, and precise timing in planting so that crops may be harvested before river waters drop below the level they require.

Before our dirt road enters the ruined plazas bordered by terraced pyramids that define the ancient capital of Cahuachi, we come upon huge holes in the sand near the valley's edge. Scattered around are human bones, skulls with hair still preserved, broken pieces of pottery, and tattered fragments of cloth. These are cemeteries containing the remains of tens of thousands of Indians who lived and farmed the Nazca Valley in the past. Their success with irrigation farming is attested by the size of the cemeteries and by the beautiful polychrome pottery and superb textiles that accompanied the dead.

Archaeologists arrived here very late, but their studies show that by 1000 B.C. the Nazca Valley was inhabited by successful farmers who already understood the technology of irrigation. Over the next 1,500 or 1,600 years they perfected weaving and pottery to almost unequaled heights, extended cultivated areas, improved their crops, built terraced pyramids, influenced the politics and religion of neighboring valleys (partially through warfare), and experienced the pressure of population growth on their tiny valley oases. During this same 1,500 years, ground art was developed and perfected.

The culture that occupied the area is called Paracas, but from about 200 B.C. until A.D. 600 the name *Nazca* is used, taken from the Nazca Valley itself. However, it is clear that Nazca culture evolved directly from Paracas antecedents, the most striking distinction between the two being the adoption of slip paint for decorating pottery at the beginning of the Nazca period.

Late Paracas pottery is decorated with some of the same designs that appear in the ground art. Most striking is a human figure with broad-brimmed hat, outstretched arms, and a staff in one hand. Another example is an anthropo-morphic form with grossly exaggerated eyes. Since these ground figures are especially primitive, occur on steep hill-sides where they can be viewed easily, and are not composed of a single outline, it is likely that they are the earliest exam-ples of representational ground drawings. About 300 B.C. would be a reasonable estimate of their antiquity.

Early Nazca ceramic designs also occur in ground draw-ings. One of the most obvious examples is the killer whale. The pottery style suggests a date just about the time of Christ and this ground drawing was done with the single outline technique. Many of the birds and other ground figures also have parallels in early Nazca pottery and this period—Christ's time—may have seen the greatest ground art production. One figure of a monkey has a parallel in early Nazca pottery and also in very late pottery, and several of the flowerlike or geometric ground drawings may also date to the end of the Nazca style, approximately A.D. 500.

When ceramic fragments were collected from the desert surface in the vicinity of the ground drawings, early Nazca pottery was by far the most common. Second most frequent was from the late Nazca period. Finally, a wooden stake was found in the ground within one of the markings. Carbon-14 dating produced A.D. 525 plus or minus eighty years—a late Nazca date. There is little question that the years 200 B.C. through A.D. 600 witnessed most of the ground art construction. It probably began slightly earlier, at the end of the Paracas period, became an important activity during the first centuries of the Nazca culture, declined, and then revived for a short time before the Nazca people were conquered by a highland state about A.D. 600. If ground drawing continued after the highlanders' intrusion it must have been a minor activity.

Most of the lines on the Nazca deserts are straight—as if laid out with a transit. Of course straight lines can be produced without sophisticated equipment; it just takes longer. A person sighting over a tall post can look down a row of stakes and see even slight deviations. Instructing a crew in the movement of the stakes, the observer can progressively move the observation position until a line of the desired length is achieved.

How were the perfectly proportioned representational figures made? We know that Paracas and Nazca peoples were among the finest weavers in the world, and they employed a great many structural techniques for a wide range of designs. The loom establishes a natural grid within which a figure is placed. Thicker threads in the warp and weft will yield a larger figure. On the basis of their weaving experience, they could produce a drawing in any size from a scale model by simply enlarging the grid.

The Incas used a decimal system in their mathematics, and Maria Reiche has suggested that Nazca drawings were one hundred or two hundred times the size of the models.

She has also shown that the continuous curves of the outlines were drawn as segments of arcs intersecting on precise tangents. The minimal unit of measurement was 32.5 centimeters (12.68 inches), and standard arcs were employed in multiples of that figure. Arc centers had to be carefully plotted in advance, and Reiche has found that many of these centers are still marked with special stones. Finally, stakes were placed in the centers, strings of desired lengths were attached, and the outlines of drawings were produced.

Slow and laborious, yes. Beyond the technological capacity of the Nazca people? No.

Demonstrating that the ground drawings were made by peoples of the late Paracas and the Nazca cultures and discovering the engineering skills employed still fail to explain why the ground markings were made and in such great numbers.

When Kosok first discovered the markings, he also noted that some were aligned with rising and setting positions of the solstice sun. He proposed that ancient Nazca peoples observed the solar year with the aid of the long lines and were able to predict the seasonal rise and fall of their little rivers.

In recent years Maria Reiche has found many other lines that indicate the rising and setting positions of astronomical bodies and may have been part of an elaborate calendar. Lunar extremes are frequently reflected, and the lines radiating from one rock-pile center seem to be a solar calendar which marks two solstice positions, two equinox positions, and the days April 6, May 6, and November 25. Some lines mark the ancient rising or setting positions of important stars whose heliacal rising or setting (near the sun) may have signaled major seasonal changes.

Astronomer Gerald Hawkins' computer-assisted study of the line orientations shows that twice as many lines align with solar and lunar solstices and equinoxes as would be expected by chance. This supports the findings of Kosok and Reiche, but it demonstrates that we still do not understand how the ancient Nazcans used their lines for making calendrical observations—nor do we know what astronomical phenomena they observed.

The Incas observed the zenith and nadir sun as well as the rising and setting of the Milky Way from the tropical southern latitudes of Cuzco. These were never significant calendrically for Western observers in the northern hemisphere.

Furthermore, anthropologist Gary Urton's recent studies of modern descendants of the Incas show that ancient Peruvians saw the sky quite differently from Europeans. Bright stars are grouped into constellations, but all of these are geometric shapes. However, the Incas' descendants recognize animal forms in dark places in the sky where there are no stars. As we learn more, it may turn out that the geometric and representational shapes on the Nazca deserts are some kind of star chart that has been invisible to a world whose astronomy is rooted in ancient Mesopotamian and Greek perception of the sky.

Maria Reiche has suggested that information may be coded in the representational drawings as well. If the standardized arc segments have meaning—numerical values, for example—the ground drawings could record important sums and cycles, possibly even planetary movements. And we must not dismiss the probability that lines and figures functioned in rituals involving sacred processions and recognition of earthly shrines. It is unlikely that astronomical concerns can account for all of the Nazca ground markings.

Finally, we must consider the value which the labor invested in line construction might have had on the economy of ancient Nazca. It is curious that on the Peruvian coast both ground art and pyramid building were important activities until the evolution of centralized state governments about A.D. 600. After that, surplus labor more frequently went into governmental administrative centers, huge storage complexes, improvement of roads and bridges, and similar public works. The early emphasis on ceremonial construction shows that chiefs were more able to control community labor than goods, and the lack of large storage complexes means that the population was subject to feast or famine, depending on the quality of the harvest.

One of the earliest stories in Western history records this problem: The Jews were obliged to move into Egypt where a state government had accumulated surplus stores for lean years. By extracting surplus food during good years the government prevented energy from going into population growth. The stored food could be released when supplies were insufficient to feed the population.

Ancient Peruvian chiefdoms apparently placed a value on labor-intensive ceremonial activities. If ceremonial construction provided some incentive for individual kin groups to store food that could be contributed for supporting laborers, this would help buffer the population against bad times. After several good years, if stored supplies became substantial and were used to feast all the young men while they were away making ground drawings and pyramids, this surplus energy would not be invested in population growth. The smaller population, in turn, would better survive lean agricultural years.

Thus it is likely that the Nazca ground markings were employed in ritualized observations of calendrical events. An accurate solar calendar enabled farmers to anticipate important seasonal changes. And it also seems that surplus energy was invested in ground drawing when production was high. Young men consumed vast quantities of food as they picked up and carried dark stones off the light sandy subsurface of the Nazca desert to produce the figures carefully planned, probably by priests. Population grew little during the good years so starvation was unlikely during poor years. The energy invested in ground drawing buffered

Nazcans from a boom-or-bust economy that is typical of farming without large-scale storage facilities and efficient long-range exchange.

We are a long way from fully understanding the Nazca ground markings. But scientific research is gradually revealing who made them, when, how, and even why. What is more, the scientific explanations are more exciting than unfounded speculations about ancient space voyagers, and the real explanations place the credit where it should be. Native peoples have achieved marvels in adapting to their special environments. You cannot visit the stark Nazca desert without realizing this.   ■

Editor's note: In 1998, the designs on the Nazca plains suffered irrevocable damage. El Nino's torrents pelted the desert that normally sees only a few inches of rain a year. But worse, vandalous tourists drove their van over the designs, leaving egg shells and fruit peels behind. Since the Nazca designs' self-appointed guardian, Maria Reiche, died in May 1998, trucks have been driving carelessly over the earth art. Archaeologists are concerned that if something isn't done soon, this precious monument will disappear within a few years.

Medicine Wheel Mystery

Jim Miles
May 1984

Scattered across the slopes of North America are enigmatic circular structures of indeterminate age and unknown purpose.

One of America's foremost archaeological mysteries is Wyoming's Medicine Wheel, a huge prehistoric construction above the timberline at the 10,000-foot level in the Big Horn Mountains.

As the name implies, the main body of the structure resembles a huge wheel. It is eighty feet in diameter and 245 feet in circumference and is composed of thousands of loosely piled stones. In the center of this large circle is a mound made of stone slabs three feet in diameter, and from this "hub" radiate twenty-eight irregularly spaced "spokes." Along the rim of the wheel are five stone mounds, smaller than the central one, which are the terminations of five spokes. The other spokes, except for one renegade, end at the rim. The exception extends nine feet beyond the rim of the wheel and terminates at a sixth stone mound.

All of the outer stone mounds are circular except one on the east which is square. This one was formerly covered with stone slabs, and the coffinlike enclosure, large enough for a person to lie down in, could be entered only through a small opening. It faced out of the circle toward the rising sun.

The Big Horn Mountains were sacred to the various nomadic tribes that historically inhabited this region, among them the Cheyenne, Crow, Sioux, Arapaho, and Shoshone. A well-known and heavily traveled trading route passed near the Medicine Wheel, but as late as the 1800s the Indians could not explain who had built the circle. They simply said it was erected by "people who had no iron"—which dates it at least three hundred years ago, before the first Europeans arrived in the area.

Archaeologists fare no better in estimating the age of the circle. Conflicting data gathered by such diverse dating techniques as carbon-14, counting tree rings on timber found in the wheel, and comparing artifacts found nearby with accurately dated similar ones, produced ages ranging from three hundred to two thousand years.

For more than a hundred years, after the wheel was first noticed by white prospectors in the mid-1800s, speculation ran riot as to who had built the mysterious structure. Everyone agreed that the primitive, barbaric Indians could not have built it, so credit was given to such ancient seagoing European and Eastern cultures as the Phoenicians, Chinese, Vikings, and Celts—even those legendary culprits, the Atlanteans. In recent years some authors have unscrupulously attempted to name "ancient astronauts" as the originators of the wheel.

Then, in the 1920s, archaeological excavation turned up fairly recent Indian artifacts (and a few early European trade goods) dispersed throughout the strata of the stone ruin, so scientists assumed that the nomadic Plains Indians had built the wheel only a few hundred years ago—although these American natives never built anything else of a permanent nature. Next, archaeological inquiry turned to identifying the reasons for the erection of the curious configuration.

The first generally accepted explanation was postulated in 1922 by G. B. Grinnell in an article for *American Anthropology*. He believed the wheel was a stone representation of a wooden ceremonial building used in historic times by the Crow Indians. In their Medicine (magic) or Sun Dance Lodge they celebrated the year's most important religious rite in June. The lodge had twenty-eight rafters which, Grinnell naturally assumed, the twenty-eight stone spokes represented. For more than fifty years his idea was believed to explain Wyoming's Medicine Wheel.

In the early 1970s astronomer John A. Eddy (on the staff of the High Altitude Observatory, National Center for Atmospheric Research in Boulder, Colorado) decided to examine the circle for evidence of an astronomical purpose. He thought that the Medicine Wheel might have had a use similar to that of England's Stonehenge.

Significantly, the wheel resembles the sun symbol frequently found in Indian art all across the Americas. Scientists assumed for many years that a wooden pole had been positioned in the center cairn and used to sight over the other six stone piles to mark the rising of the sun on important astronomical or ceremonial dates. This assumption was strengthened by the discovery of a three-foot-deep hole carved into bedrock under the central mound.

The Crow Indian name for the giant artifact gave further credence to the idea that it was used for marking significant sunrises. They called it Sun's Tipi and claimed that it had been "built before the light came." Astronomer Eddy freely translated this to mean "to mark the sunrise." His pioneering research proved him to be correct.

Prehistoric peoples the world over have long recognized that the sun reaches its farthest point north of the equator on June 21 and 22 and its farthest point south of the equator on December 21 and 22. They used this knowledge to establish important religious ceremonies and also for maintaining planting schedules.

Big Horn Mountain is completely snow-covered all winter and often as late as June 21. How could the prehistoric astronomers have used the wheel to mark the solstices? Researchers discovered that the wheel's location, a shoulder of Medicine Mountain, is swept clear of snow by high winds. The Indians must have purposely selected this site. Moreover, the wheel is above the timberline so trees do not interfere with the line of sight. Also, even if the ground is snow-covered, the stone mounds rise above the snow level.

Eddy believes the spokes were not important. They might have been added later for decoration or to count days.

Naturally the astronomer wanted to know if weather conditions would have allowed the ancient Americans to use the wheel at the summer solstice, given fog, clouds, and mist at the high altitude. He found that clear days prevailed at least one-third of the time and since the sun seems to stand still for about four days when measured by such primitive instruments as this one, the observers could wait for a clear viewing day—although they might be uncomfortable in the prevailing bad weather.

In 1972 and 1973 Eddy watched the summer solstice by sighting over the central cairn across to the extended mound. He designated the center mound "O" and concluded that it had been used as a common foresight. "EO," a line of sight over the center mound to the cairn he designated "E," indicated the summer solstice sunrise. Sighting over "O" to a cairn designated "C," he watched the sun set that same day.

"These alignments are convincingly confirmed by observation of the rising and setting solstice sun," Eddy wrote in an article for *National Geographic*.

From point "O" the Indians could determine where the first rays of the morning sun and the last rays of the setting sun would appear. Watching the sun's cycles over a period of years, they would mark the relevant locations, then build the mounds over them. Since each outlying mound covers several feet, Eddy believes a pole stood in each one to indicate the precise rising and setting points.

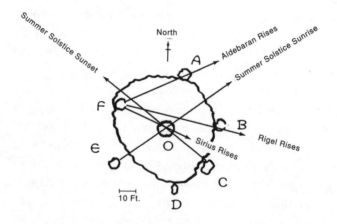

Through careful observation, astronomer John A. Eddy discovered significant astronomical correlations in the Wyoming Medicine Wheel.

In 1902, when ethnologist S. C. Simms visited the Medicine Wheel, he found a bleached buffalo skull resting on the outer stone mound that marked the rising of the summer solstice sun. It faced the sun, an indication that less ancient Indians realized the purpose of this monument. Further investigation of the remaining cairns led to confusion, however. The mounds "A," "B" and "D," sighted over "O," marked nothing. Significantly "FO" marked the position of the rise of the brightest star, Sirius.

The next step was to learn whether any significant astronomical events were marked by sighting over one perimeter mound to another outer mound. One might be a common backsight for the rest of the mounds, or one might relate to another.

Patient research revealed that "F" served as a common backsight and "O" had been used only to mark solar events. "FA" marked the rise of the star Aldebaran, as did "EB," and

Historians have continued to be perplexed about the origin and purpose of the medicine wheels found across North America.

"FB" saw the rise of Rigel. These two stars and Sirius are the brightest near the sun's path in the summer sky in this part of the world. All rise on the horizon at dawn. Aldebaran, for example, rises an hour before the sun on June 20, one day before the summer solstice. It may have been marked twice, by "FA" and "EB," because of its importance in revealing the immediacy of the summer solstice.

The relationship between the marked stars may have something to do with the wheel's twenty-eight spokes.

Rigel rises one lunar month (twenty-eight days) after Aldebaran, and Sirius rises exactly one lunar month later than that. The spokes may have been used to count the days between star risings.

Archaeologists and astronomers now believe that the wheel was built in stages, probably as the builders' astronomical knowledge increased or was refined. The mounds designated "O," "E," and "C" were created first, to mark the summer solstice, and "B", "A" and "F" came later for the star risings. The twenty-eight spokes were added last, possibly to mark the lunar days between star risings.

It is significant that the age of this ancient computer was determined by astronomers, not by archaeologists. The date of its construction was determined by studying the star Aldebaran, whose position in relation to the Earth changes slightly but perceptibly every year. When incorporated into the Wyoming Medicine Wheel, Aldebaran rose in the early morning darkness, well before sunrise, and was thus a good indicator of the imminent solstice sunrise. But today it has lost its usefulness. It rises after the sun and cannot be seen through the glare. By discovering the years of the star's greatest usefulness, Eddy has determined that the wheel was built between A.D. 1400 and 1700.

The Plains Indians were nomads, but that does not mean they were simple barbarians. They lived totally out of doors, and the sky presented more interesting and more readily visible features than the land they traveled. Naturally they noticed the yearly progression of the sun from north to south, the point at which it "paused," and the fact that it retraced its path. They gave this cycle ceremonial or religious connotations, and they marked these points so that they could hold ceremonies to assist the sun on its journey and assure that it would return on time. The Indians surely associated movement of the sun with the seasons. As followers of game, at the mercy of the bitter winters, they needed to know in advance of dramatic changes in their environment so that they could prepare for survival. At some point they decided to invent a system that would accurately mark these important events.

Eddy believes there is a relationship between the wheel and the Sun Dance held in June when, according to an Indian legend recorded in the 1932 book *Black Elk Speaks*, the "sun is highest and the growing power of the Earth is strongest." The ceremonial dance was probably held on the solstice, and the wheel was used for an accurate determination of that date.

No doubt the process of aligning the cairns was a secret known only to a few priests, and the mountain became a holy place. With the passage of time the secret of its workings was lost, its purpose became unclear, and hence the Crow named it Sun's Tipi.

The knowledge of the wheel's purpose was lost after the first contact with European traders, which dramatically changed the Indians' lifestyle. With horses for fast transportation, rifles instead of bows for hunting, and the white man's calendars, the Medicine Wheel fell into disuse and ruin only years before whites first found the enigma. Archaeologists found seventeenth-century Venetian beads among the stones, and these must mark its last days.

The Big Horn Medicine Wheel is not the only such structure. Perhaps fifty more were scattered across the eastern slopes of the Rocky Mountains and plains of the United States and Canada.

A wheel was found in 1963 at an altitude of 11,400 feet in the Rocky Mountain National Park in northern Colorado. It is a small stone mound on a hill with only two rock spokes. These extend downhill an equal distance (fifty feet) in each direction, and both terminate at other stone mounds. The rocks, covered with lichens, have sunk into the ground, an indication of their antiquity. An old Ute Indian trail passes nearby. Eddy's investigation in 1973 revealed that a sighting along one of the spokes through the center mound marked the summer solstice sunrise.

A wheel on the Crow Indian Reservation in Montana, the Fort Smith Medicine Wheel, has six spokes radiating downhill from a central mound located on a prominence. By sighting along the longest line through the central hub, one could watch the summer solstice sunrise.

With a grant from the National Geographic Society, Eddy studied forty medicine wheels in Canada with archaeologist Dick Forbis of the University of Calgary. They found the wheels scattered across the Rockies and prairies of Alberta and Saskatchewan. Few are comparable to Wyoming's Medicine Wheel; some are merely stone mounds with or without rings and spokes and other cairns. Each was different, varying in diameter from several feet to several hundred feet, and if they had spokes the number of these varied. Only one of the Canadian sites had twenty-eight spokes.

Most of the wheels had center mounds and these were often immense. One in Alberta had a central mound thirty feet in diameter and six feet high, containing one hundred tons of rock. The Big Horn wheel has only a half ton of rocks in its center mound.

In cases where a definite orientation of spokes, rings, or outlying mounds could be discovered, it was to the southwest, toward the summer solstice sunrise as seen from the central mound. About half of the wheels had this orientation, and Eddy also found a "tendency" among the devices to mark the places on the horizon where Aldebaran, Rigel, and Sirius rise.

All of the sites were on the highest elevations in the area and free of hillocks or timber which would obstruct the view to the horizon. Many had "tipi" rings nearby which were used to hold down the perimeters of Indian tents. These are evidence of Indian occupation and their use of the wheels.

The Moose Mountain Wheel in Saskatchewan, located 425 miles north of Wyoming, is structurally a twin of the Big Horn wheel, except that it has only five spokes. It is twice as large as any other Canadian wheel, two hundred feet in diameter, with a huge central stone mound nearly twenty feet across and containing sixty tons of stone. Five long spokes extend to an oval outer ring and end at smaller sunken stone mounds. These five spokes exactly match the five important ones at Big Horn.

One, extending beyond the ring as at Big Horn and ending at a larger mound, points to the horizon where the sun rises on the summer solstice. The cairns are in the same position as at Big Horn and mark the rising of the same stars, Aldebaran, Rigel, and Sirius. As it was built 1,700 years ago, the alignments are way off today.

It came as a surprise to the scientists to learn that the Wyoming Medicine Wheel is probably the most recent one to be built for astronomical purposes. The Majorville Wheel, found on the barren plains of Alberta, has a large central cairn and spokes. Its first components were built an incredible 4,000 to 5,000 years ago.

The true purpose and age of America's once-mysterious Medicine Wheel and some knowledge of its builders were revealed when archaeologists and astronomers merged their scientific expertise and experimented with new ideas. This unusual move on the part of two conservative disciplines has produced a revolutionary new field of scientific study called "archaecoastronomy" or "astroarchaeology." Combining their talents, these scientists have greatly advanced our knowledge of the native Americans and helped to dispel the long-held image of Indians as savage barbarians.   ■

The Little People of Skara Brae

Charles Alva Hoyt
February 1998

*The legendary "wee folk" of Northern Europe
may have their origin in historical fact.*

As I hiked through Ireland recently, I strayed farther than I had planned and stopped to rest by a cottage gate. The woman who lived there spotted me and asked me in to tea. As we talked, the subject turned to her country's infamous "little people."

"Ah well," she said, "maybe there were such creatures once, but perhaps they've all died out."

Her elderly mother had been listening quietly, but suddenly she spoke up. "And maybe what was once, could still be," she said.

With that, she told of an incident in her childhood, when she was cutting peat with her brother. As she hurried to finish her work so she could go to a dance, she suddenly spotted a little man, dressed in green and wearing a red pointed hat. With all her might she called for her brother, but he didn't come. At last she thought she heard him, and distracted, looked away for an instant. When she looked back, the man was gone.

"Oh, why didn't you come?" she asked her brother. His response puzzles the old woman to this day. "Why didn't you call?" he replied.

The region's history is filled with accounts of mysterious encounters with little people—alternately known as leprechauns, fairies, "good folk," or "the gentry." They reportedly dance on the lawn in the late-night hours, dressed in red and green, with peaked hats and pointed shoes. They live underground in grassy mounds, raise cattle, and have the power to bewitch and imprison mortal men.

For the most part, we think of such creatures as cute and cuddly—just inches tall and very pretty, like adorable animated figurines. The old fairies, however—the ones with whom people had to deal on a day-to-day basis in the Middle Ages, were a much different order of beings. They were not much smaller than ordinary people—in fact, some were distinctly taller—and they were undeniably dangerous.

Fairy lore is often connected to the Celts, the Scottish Highlanders, the Welsh, the Bretons, the Manx, the Cornish, and the Irish. The popular explanation is that those groups are peculiarly given to fantasy and dreams. Now it turns out those old fairy tales could actually have their foundation in historical fact. Some scholars believe that a race of Neolithic and Bronze Age people populated most of Northern Europe much longer than most of us realize.

Margaret Murray, author of *The God of the Witches*, theorized that they lived in isolated communities for centuries before being absorbed by a more advanced Iron Age culture. Since then, she writes, "This strange and interesting people and their primitive civilization have degenerated into the diminutive gossamer-winged sprites of legend and fancy."

The explanation is plausible, especially from a geographic perspective. Celtic people typically inhabit peripheral areas—peninsulas, mountains, and islands far from urban centers. When the Iron Age Celts entered the British Isles somewhere around 500 B.C., they may have driven aboriginal islanders before them. Successive invasions, particularly those of the Germanic tribes about a thousand years later, pushed the Celts in turn to the periphery—to the unwanted lands of the north and west, the mountains of Wales and Scotland, the peninsulas, the islands, Skye, Orkney, Lewis, Shetland, and Ireland itself.

The Celts were elbowed into the very same areas where they had driven their old enemies and from which they carried on a spirited and unceasing warfare against the Anglo-Saxons. The two races, Celts and "fairies," would have been in close, unwilling proximity for generations.

Some support for this theory may be adduced from the fact that although certain areas, like Orkney, were successively overrun by new populations—in this case, Scandinavian—there was no falling-off of fairy lore.

Orkney is a particularly important site. Far from the mainstream of British culture, it offers enormous archeological wealth. Great numbers of grassy mounds dot the countryside, and most of them have never been opened. But during a severe storm in the winter of 1850, part of the grass covering the mound known as Skara Brae, by the Bay of Skaill, was torn off.

Inside, curious area residents discovered the ruins of a number of small-scale buildings—in fact, a whole town in miniature. Energetic excavations brought to light the remains of a seaside settlement which is generally thought of today as the most notable Stone Age site in Northern Europe. The Skara Brae settlement was always an underground community, deliberately packed in midden—refuse, shells, bones, ashes, and sand—and turfed over. Seven self-contained huts were connected to each other by passageways.

There was good reason to live underground.While seafood was abundant and the grassy shore was perfect pasturage for flocks, the weather was tempestuous and cold for much of the year.

The huts are as tight and compact as space modules. They vary from twenty-one by twenty feet to fourteen by thirteen. Some walls are as tall as eight feet, but most are smaller, and no entrance is taller than four feet.

At the center of each hut was a square fireplace, set in a stone framework. Against each wall facing it were the beds, pen-like structures four or five feet long, formed by stone slabs set on edge. The beds probably were filled with heather or some similar material; their edges provided seats conveniently close to the fire, and there are indications that they were canopied.

Little recesses in the wall above each bed served as cupboards, although special treasures were certainly kept in the beds themselves. Archaeologists found necklaces in them, and well-chewed bones as well.

The community, which evidently was an old one, was abandoned suddenly, in great haste. Excavators found the beads of a broken necklace trailing to one of the exits, where they had been dropped in flight. But there was no pillage: Storerooms, cupboards, and furniture were left intact. Archaeologists carried away a rich collection of jewelry, tools, weapons, and household implements. What could have driven the Skara Brae people from their centuries-old home?

Dr. V. Gordon Childe, a principal investigator of the site, thought nature could be to blame. "We found the huts and passages choked with sand," he wrote. "A great storm setting the sand dunes in motion is most likely to have driven the villagers from their homes, as has happened to far better-equipped folk at Culbin and elsewhere during historical times."

For students of fairy lore, however, there is another possible explanation. The place could have been forcibly emptied of all its inhabitants, and yet not pillaged or even entered by a victorious enemy. For it would have been a brave man indeed who would have actually entered a fairy rath: Stories about such attempts are almost unanimous in their fatal outcomes. Usually, the intruder dies a lingering death, like the victim of Keats' "Belle Dame Sans Merci." Or, as he gets off his horse, he crumbles to dust. Or, after seeing a companion crumble, a fellow invader stays on his mount and rides on forever in despair. At the very least, an intruder finds that what he supposed to be a night's revel has actually taken years—perhaps even a century—and he is doomed to live out his life among strangers.

The origin of such stories is understandable. To outsiders, the Skara Brae people and their contemporaries were odd and frightening. They lived in the ground, under a great green mound into which they probably seemed to vanish or emerge in a heartbeat. They were less than four or five feet tall, and well armed with knives and axes fashioned entirely from stone and bone. (The fairies' antipathy to iron is famous.)

There are no records of any collision between such a people and our own Celtic or Germanic ancestors. The only accounts we have are oral ones: myth, folklore, and tales told from the chimney corner. Many have been gathered into books, like the collection by J. T. Smith Leask, *A Peculiar People*. Leask describes persistent reports of fairies from the district known as Orphi, ten miles southeast of the Bay of Skaill.

In one story, an Orphi man said he had been carried off by the fairies and compelled to work for them. When the fairies freed him, they paid him a magic sixpence that always found its way back to his pocket.

In another, a second Orphi man was kept dancing with the fairies for a whole year, in a mound called the Hillock of Howe, six or seven miles south of Skara Brae. Like others in his situation, he paid no heed to the time, until he found that he had danced the soles off his shoes.

A strange boy and girl were said to emerge from underground near Bury St. Edmonds, in the reign of King Stephen (1135–1154). The children were of normal size, but of a curious greenish complexion, and they spoke an uncouth tongue. There was considerable difficulty in getting them to eat, but when beans were produced they fell to eagerly. Even so, the boy sickened and soon died, but the girl survived, lost her green color, was baptized, and eventually married—although her behavior always retained something of the outlandish. She said that she and her brother had lived in a dim country underground.

When children were born in Orkney, their parents placed a Bible and a piece of iron on a shelf in the bed, to protect them from the little people who might otherwise steal them, and leave one of their own babies—a changeling—in the human infant's place. The superstition persisted for hundreds of years. In fact, at the turn of this century, there was an Orkney woman who was believed to be a changeling. As an infant, she had barely escaped the horrible ordeal prescribed for changelings: She would have been roasted on a red-hot griddle if a neighbor had not intervened.

There are people still alive in the British Isles who have seen creatures they can't explain. Few discuss their experiences publicly, for fear of looking foolish. But after hearing from the old woman at tea, and reviewing the evidence, I wonder: What—or who—is in the rest of those mounds? ∎

The Chinese Roswell

Hartwig Hausdorf
August 1998

Stone discs, UFO legends, and Chinese dwarfs point to a spaceship crash millennia ago.

For thirty-five years, a story has circulated about an alleged UFO crash that happened some 12,000 years ago in a remote mountain area in China. When I first heard of this, I took it to be science fiction. But new developments in this story have made it worth another look.

It begins at the turn of the years 1937 and 1938, when an expedition led by archaeologist Chi Pu-Tei came across the pathless Bayan-Kara-Ula mountains in the modern-day Chinese province of Qinghai. The group discovered some caves in which numerous strange-looking skeletons were entombed. All of the skeletons had abnormally big heads and small, thin, fragile bodies.

There were no epitaphs at the graves, but the explorers did find 716 stone discs with bizarre hieroglyphs on them. From a hole in the center of each disc, a groove spiraled out to the rim. The archaeologists had no idea what kind of information was encoded in the hieroglyphs. Not until the early 1960s did Beijing Academy of Sciences professor Tsum

Um Nui succeed in translating a few passages of the inscriptions on the stone discs. But upon completing his report, the scientist ran into a problem: The Academy banned the publication of his work. This is not surprising when one considers the unusual conclusions that Tsum Um Nui and four assistants drew. They were certain that the hieroglyphs on the stone discs told of the crash of an alien spacecraft in the mountains 12,000 years ago!

After an extended quarrel, the professor obtained permission to publish his report. He introduced amazed readers to the story of alien beings called the *Dropa*, who had crashed in the Bayan-Kara-Ula Mountains after a long space flight. A great number of these beings died, and the survivors could not repair their ship, said Tsum Um Nui. Of course, the scientific establishment considered the story to be nonsense, and Tsum Um Nui was derided as a fool.

What skeptics ignored was that in the Qinghai province, ancient traditions told of small, skinny, ugly beings, with big, clumsy heads and weak extremities, who came down from the sky long ago. Locals have always been afraid of the strange-looking invaders from the clouds.

Shortly after publishing his report, Tsum Um Nui emigrated to Japan. Embittered by the reactions of other scientists, he died shortly after he completed a final manuscript about the stone-disc mystery. My book *Satelliten der Goetter* (*Satellites of the Gods*) was published in Japan in 1996, and I hope the book's Japanese readers may be able to provide new information on Tsum Um Nui and his fate. Where was he buried? What library contains his report on the translation of the hieroglyphs on the stone plates?

Nobody knows what became of the 716 discs. Their existence was last documented in 1974, when Austrian engineer Ernest Wegerer came across two of the discs in Banpo Museum in Xi'an. The discs matched the descriptions from Tsum

Um Nui's 1962 report. Wegerer could even recognize hieroglyphs in the discs' spiral grooves, but by this time they were partly crumbled away.

Knowing the artifacts' background, Wegerer asked the former manager of the Banpo Museum for more details on the objects. Surprisingly, the woman could tell stories about all the other clay artifacts there, but all she could say of the stone discs was that they were unimportant "cult objects." This is also how they were labeled in the museum showcase.

Nevertheless, the Austrian was allowed to hold one of the discs and take the only known photographs of both of them. Wegerer estimated them to weigh two pounds each and to measure a foot in diameter. They both featured the strange hieroglyphs and a hole in the center. Regrettably, the spiral grooves cannot be seen in the photographs, partly because they had crumbled away and also because Wegerer used a Polaroid camera with an integrated flash.

This was more or less the status of the research when *Satellites of the Gods* co-author Peter Krassa and I tried to pick up the trail of this mystery of the century. It would not be easy. China had suffered through its Proletarian Cultural Revolution from 1966 to 1976. Many people lost their lives, and innumerable precious objects fell victim to the unrest. During this time, many artifacts were taken from Beijing into the provinces.

In March 1994, Prof. Wang Zhijun, director of the Banpo Museum, welcomed Krassa and me for a discussion of the stone discs. At first, he seemed unwilling to give details, but soon he revealed that the manager of the museum had been called away from her job just a few days after Wegerer had visited the museum in 1974. Both the woman and the discs had disappeared without a trace. I had the distinct feeling that Wang Zhijun was uncomfortable during our inquiry. When asked for the artifacts' present location, he told us: "The stone discs you have mentioned do not exist, but being extraneous elements in this museum for pottery ware, they have been dislocated."

Isn't it fascinating to witness such a U-turn in one sentence?

For objects that do not officially exist, the Bayan-Kara-Ula stone platters are surprisingly concrete. Prof. Wang Zhijun showed us a book about archeology in which we found a sketch of a stone disc.

Nearly unknown in most of the world is the subject of the book *Sungods in Exile* by David Agamon, published in the United Kingdom in 1978. The book purports to be a documentary based on the 1947 expedition of the British scientist Dr. Karyl Robin-Evans. He allegedly succeeded in reaching the Bayan-Kara-Ula mountains in the Qinghai province via Tibet, where he discovered a group of dwarfish people he introduced as the *Dzopa*. According to Agamon, Robin-Evans found a few hundred of the Dzopa, with an average height of four feet, living in a remote mountain valley. Robin-Evans stayed there for half a year, allegedly made a young woman pregnant, and learned the language, history, and traditions of the Dzopa tribe. They told him that their ancestors came from a planet in the Sirius system and crashed in this mountain area a long time ago. Many of them were killed, but the survivors adapted to living on this rough planet far away from home.

Not long ago, I received a letter from Ukrainian scientist Dr. Vladimir Rubtsov, a member of the Ancient Astronaut Society. He wrote that *Sungods in Exile* was but a science fiction story woven around rumors and legends that would fool only the gullible.

Rumors. Legends. Weird tales and science fiction stories—so I'm told. But in this special case, these uncanny legends seem to be more than a myth, and since late 1995 events have escalated.

It began with news leaking from China and published by the Associated Press in November 1995, just a week after I was fiercely attacked by a skeptic on a German television talk show. The report stated that in the Sichuan province, located east of the Bayan-Kara-Ula mountains in central China, a community of 120 dwarfish beings was discovered. The tallest among them was three feet ten inches tall, and the smallest adult was only two feet one inch!

The thrilling news introduced a new era in the research of the Bayan-Kara-Ula mystery. Could these people be the last living descendants of the survivors of the legendary UFO crash—the "Chinese Roswell?"

A community of 120 dwarfs could never come into existence by chance, as the odds for stunted growth are only 1 to 20,000. In January 1997, a new theory emerged from Chinese ethnologists. They attributed the dwarfism to a very high concentration of mercury in the soil, absorbed by the dwarfs from their drinking water over many generations.

Dr. Norbert Felgenhauer from the Munich Institute for Toxic Surgery called this theory absolute nonsense. Mercury is a malicious poison, harmful to any organs in the body. But mercury does not change human DNA, Felgenhauer said, nor is it able to cause hereditary diseases—because the victims would have died long before!

It is significant that the Chinese authorities for once did not deny the existence of the "Village of the Dwarfs," which is named Huilong, or that this village is located only a few hundred kilometers east of the Bayan-Kara-Ula range. This fact may indicate that the Dropa/Dzopa tribe had migrated into the lowlands, and that they might have done so only recently—perhaps in 1995 or a bit earlier. These little beings must have been isolated for a very long time before their discovery; otherwise, interbreeding with other tribes would have led to an increase in their stature.

So the discovery of these dwarfish people is the culmination of a story haunting our literature for more than thirty years.

There is yet more evidence. Joerg Dendl, a Ph.D. student in history at Berlin University, found a report from 1911 that told of repeated sightings of tiny beings in Tibet and its Central Asian neighborhood.

And while lecturing in Australia in June 1996, I was contacted by a young couple one evening in Brisbane. They told me about their grandfather, who was stationed in central China with the Allied forces during World War II. Until the old man died, he never ceased to talk about several strange encounters he had had with members of an extremely dwarfish tribe in central China. According to his account, these folks were far smaller than the pygmies of Africa, who usually grow between four feet eight inches and five feet tall.

This startling news cries out for intensive research. I have resolved to clear up the mysterious evidence pertaining to a spaceship crash thousands of years ago—a "Chinese Roswell" incident that demands investigation! ■

Ancient Astronauts from Japan?

Simon Peter Groebner
March 1998

Six-thousand-year-old clay figurines in Japan bear a telling resemblance to space-suit technology.

Their ancient Japanese sculptors called them *Dogu*, meaning "tool." The strange, distorted humanoid figures are made of clay and stand three to twelve inches high. Excavators have found three thousand of them in Japan, and radiocarbon dating shows that they range from three thousand to more than ten thousand years old. Dogu are among the oldest clay models known to humanity, but no mainstream archaeologist has a comprehensive theory of what they represent.

Vaughn M. Greene, a researcher of Japanese mythology, ancient mysteries, and UFOs, believes he knows the answer. Dogu, he says, are irrefutable proof that ancient people were witness to extraterrestrial visitation on Earth thousands of years ago. For years, Greene has put forth one major theory: Dogu statues are ancient models of deep-sea diving suits—and space suits.

On first look, the concept seems too far out to take seriously. But study the Dogu photos on this page. The statues show meticulous detail—consistent over thousands of years—that neither matches the human body nor welcomes conventional interpretation. Anthropologists vaguely and predictably suggest that Dogu are "Venus" figures or funeral objects. By contrast, Greene's space-suit argument is airtight.

Photos courtesy of Vaughan Greene

Space suits or ancient gods?

For example, consider the most striking part of the Dogu statue: its head. Greene notes that its features closely resemble those of a modern deep-sea or space helmet.

There are usually two large, round "lenses," too disproportionate to be human eyes. A few Dogu show only one lens instead of two, and others have the "visor" removed, showing humanoid eyes inside. The Dogu's apparent eye slits resemble modern space suit anti-glare shields.

Greene points out rear windows on some helmets, similar to those on deep-sea helmets. And most impressively, the mouth and cheek area of the model usually shows three round, textured features that clearly resemble the modern speaker vents that astronauts breathe and speak through while on the ground.

The statues often display no hands or feet, meaning perhaps that the suit is not being worn; and some Dogu appear with the helmets "removed," sometimes revealing a humanoid head, sometimes not. Greene believes that the artfully decorated Dogu clearly show where the various parts would be clamped and seamed together.

The Dogu were made by a peaceful Stone Age people known as the Jomon, who lived in Japan for 10,000 to 20,000 years with little in the way of technology, agriculture, or even religion. Their culture has been compared to that of early Native American peoples of California. But the Jomon did innovate the world's oldest known ceramic art, and some Jomon pottery has been found dating from 12,700 years ago—well before the dawn of written history.

The stock explanation of Dogu is that they were created as female sexual objects, based on the large hips and apparent breasts. Greene scoffs at the idea, pointing out that the figures are too disproportionate to represent a female body, and that the small "breasts" in question are actually control knobs similar to those used on modern suits.

"Dogu showed the same thing for a period of at least 6,000 years," he adds. "And they did make clay figurines that were obviously human," showing realistic human features. "That means Dogu were designed to look like something else."

That's just the beginning of Greene's observations. His lifetime study of the matter has led to two books: *Astronauts of Ancient Japan* (Maverick, 1985) and *The Six-Thousand-Year-Old Space Suit* (Maverick, rev. ed. 1997), which includes endorsements from notable ancient astronaut advocates Zecharia Sitchin and Erich von Däniken. In *The Six-Thousand-Year-Old Space Suit*, Greene lays out his intriguing Dogu hypothesis in painstaking and impressive detail, invoking mythology, naval and space aeronautics, and archeological fact to support his claims.

If Greene is even close to right, it would mean a complete revision of the way we understand the evolution of civilization and our place in the universe. And the Space Suit concept would lead to much speculation about the related meanings of UFO phenomena today.

But Greene remains a rogue. Indeed, in his penultimate book, *The Demon-Haunted World*, the late Carl Sagan deems ancient-astronaut studies the prime "pseudoscience" vexing serious archeology.

Curiously, the Dogu/astronaut hypothesis seems to enjoy some popularity, or at least familiarity, in the popular culture of Russia. But Greene laments that his work is rarely considered in cliquish ufology circles, to say nothing of the conservative glass dome of archeology. And Greene confesses that in the decades before his book was published, he couldn't even get an article on the subject printed in FATE.

The Six-Thousand-Year-Old Space Suit is a milestone for Greene, who has researched unexplained phenomena since before the dawn of modern American ufology. In 1944, a teenaged Greene became intrigued with the Shaver Mystery, which proposed that flying saucers originated from inside the Earth. When Kenneth Arnold reported the first famous saucer sighting in June 1947, Greene got excited.

"I wrote Arnold a letter, and he was very paranoid," Greene recalls. "I couldn't understand what was bothering him. He accused me of being a war-monger. I was just writing to ask him about his UFO experiences. A couple of months later, a couple of FBI guys came and interviewed me and people I knew, and said I shouldn't have written the letter."

Of course, rather than being turned off, Greene was hooked. He was later asked to volunteer for the U.S. Counter Intelligence Corps, but he was rejected shortly thereafter—a fact he now attributes to his FBI run-in.

Greene entered the Army in 1951 and was stationed in Japan during the Korean War. There, he studied Japanese mythology and Shinto legends and had his first exposure to the Dogu statuettes. With his background in deep-sea excavation and the aircraft industry, Greene automatically noted that the figures bore a strong resemblance to pressurized body suits. When Russians and Americans began to develop human space suits, the Dogu correlations were too strong for him to ignore. The impetus for *The Six-Thousand-Year-Old Space Suit* was born.

Greene has even identified an eerily compatible story of supernatural contact in ancient lore. "In Japanese mythology," he says, "there's a lot of stuff about beings flying in the sky. In particular, there's a group of mischievous gods they called *Kappa*. These people had swim fins and could swim underwater, and the natives were scared of them because they could grab a person, drag them under, and drown them if they wanted. But by the same token, these Kappa people helped them out, showing them how to do agriculture, weaving, and pottery."

"Of course, a lot of people say that's just nonsense," Greene adds. "But I think a lot of 'mythology' is a lot truer and more literal than they think."

The Kappa legend is not merely lost folklore; in Japan today the story remains popular, as evidenced by an ongoing comic called *Kappa*. And the story takes on a new significance combined with recent discoveries of underwater ruins off Japan, thought by some to be ancient Lemuria.

Even more impressive are the correlations found around the world. According to *The Six-Thousand-Year-Old Space Suit*, an ancient Mali tribe known as the Dogon (note the resemblance to "Dogu") passed down a legend similar to Japan's Kappa myth.

Five thousand years ago, the Dogon were contacted by a race of fishlike people they called *Nommo*, who identified their home as a dwarf star near Sirius. The zinger? Modern scientists did not discover such a star until 1862. Meanwhile, Greene has found that *Dogon* is also the name of the oldest hot spring in Japan.

The Kappa/Nommo story is echoed in the lore of both the ancient Babylonians and the ancient Merovingian kings of France. In almost every case, the amphibious beings described are marked by a bald spot on the top of their heads.

And finally, Jomon pottery fragments have inexplicably been discovered in faraway Ecuador, dating at 3,000 years old. Those are just some of the possible worldwide connections that Greene has discovered.

Coincidences, or mountains of evidence? Perhaps ancient devices like statues and mythology are not the stuff of bedtime stories, but reflective of real human history. After all, even mainstream science is becoming more aware of a "missing link" in human evolution—that the birth of civilization is not perfectly explained by all of the accepted facts. Whatever you believe, the Dogu enigma, like other evidence of extraterrestrial intervention on Earth, clearly exposes the possibility that there is more to the past than we currently understand. ■

Is this figurine, discovered in Acambaro, Mexico,
evidence that humans interacted with
prehistoric creatures? (*See p. 163*)

Out of Time and Place

It is a piece of jewelry in gold containing a huge green gemstone .
. . . It is four and a half inches long and described [by some experts]
as a jaguar. It is covered, however, with mechanical devices, including two cogwheels . . . .

A jaguar indeed! Did you ever see a large spotted cat without spots but with a straight tail, rectangular in section and
bearing two cogwheels? Did you ever see any cat with two rock-
er arms sticking out of its rump and holding triangular "mud-
guards" behind its heels? Did you ever see a jaguar or any other
cat with a row . . . of even matched teeth, all shovel-shaped and
slightly recurved?

— Ivan Sanderson, "The Little Gold 'Dozer," FATE, August 1972

In the quotation above, the renowned naturalist and
Fortean researcher, Ivan Sanderson, is describing a golden
artifact discovered in an archaeological site in the Coclé
province of Panama. The artifact is a minimum of a thousand years old, far older, say archaeologists, than any American civilization that knew anything about cogwheels.
Sanderson was convinced the pendant represented not a
jaguar but a very modern-looking bulldozer—centuries before historians think such a machine was possible!

This artifact, while unusual, is only one of thousands of anomalous artifacts scattered around the world. From gigantic manufactured stone spheres found buried six feet underground in Costa Rica, to a 1,500-year-old Carthaginian coin dug up by an Arkansas farmer; from the cocaine and tobacco, known to be indigenous New World products, found in ancient Egyptian mummies, to druid-style stone monuments in New England, objects that are out of time and place have been found all over the world. What do they mean?

The articles in the following chapter explore many of these perplexing mysteries.

The Impossible Fossils

Henry Winfred Splitter
January 1954

*The frog was found completely embedded in a
lump of coal. When placed in a pail of water,
it stirred and was able to swim.*

Several prospectors, one day in the summer of 1877, were exploring a series of barren hills at the head of Spring Valley near Eureka, Nevada. One of the men noticed a strange object protruding from a high ledge of rock nearby. He investigated and was amazed to find embedded about halfway in the smooth surface of the quartzite what appeared to be the leg-bone of a human being, broken off just above the knee.

With the aid of his companions he dislodged the portion of rock that enclosed the bone. Carefully, with their mining tools, they removed the upper part of the encasement. The rock was as hard as flint and the bones were solidly set in it. The quartzite was a dark red in color while the bones were almost black. When the last of the rocky covering had been removed, the leg bone and those of the attached foot stood out perfectly, complete with all the toes, part of the femur, the

131

patella or knee joint, the tarsus metatarsus, and the pha-langes, the joint of each bone being traced precisely.

The length from the fracture just above the knee to the end of the toes was just thirty-nine inches. Clearly the bone structure had once been part of a person of extraordinary size. This unusual object, lying exposed to view on its quartzite bed was brought to Eureka and there inspected by large crowds. All who saw it agreed that the bones were of human origin. A fruitless search was later made for the remainder of the skeleton.

In a letter to the editor of the Zanesville, Ohio, *Courier* in 1853, a certain John G. F. Holston declared that, with Charles Robbins and Dr. Ball, he had recently investigated a phenom-enal object taken from the rock of a quarry at Cusick's Mill, six miles from the city. It was nothing less than the bones of an adult human female, found in a cavity of the solid sand-stone rock perfectly closed and having no communication whatever with any fissure or crack in the rock.

Most extraordinary was the fact that the cavity repre-sented the shape of the body when invested with flesh—the leg, the thigh, the hip, and part of the back being moulded with remarkable exactness. Holston said that if the cavity were filled with plaster of Paris, a mould of the entire figure would result.

In its original position, the body lay on its right side, the head east toward the hill, the feet west toward what was known as Jonathan's Creek. The waters of this creek at high flood swept the base of the hill some ten feet below the level of the body. The identical block of stone containing these remains also held the perfect mold of a pair of human hands, generally believed by those who inspected it not to be those of the enclosed body. This find was made about fifty feet below the surface level of the ground and fifteen feet from the cliff edge of Jonathan's Creek.

Objects apparently of human manufacture have also been found in rock strata. Charles Fort (*Books*, 133) mentions the bell-shaped vessel blasted out of solid pudding-stone rock at Dorchester, Massachusetts, in 1851. A contemporary describes the find as made on the south side of Dorchester's Meeting-House Hill, fifteen feet below the surface.

Among the rock fragments thrown out by the blast was a piece of thin metal, and near this was another quite similar piece. On being joined together the two were found to fit exactly, forming a bell-shaped vessel four and a half inches high, two and a half inches wide at the top, and six and a half inches at the base. It was one-eighth of an inch thick, of metallic composition, dominantly silver.

Near the top of the vessel was a hole about an inch and a half in diameter, where apparently a handle had been broken off. In line with this hole was another at the bottom, covered with a plating resembling lead. Says a contemporary observer: "Whether it was placed in the ground before the rock was formed or was thrown into its position by a volcanic eruption is a matter of conjecture."

On exhibition at the Miner's Saloon in Treasure City, Nevada, during the early winter of 1869 was a piece of feldspar from the local Abbey mine. In this rock was embedded something resembling an ordinary two-inch screw, so perfectly outlined with its regular curve and sharp cut, that many who saw it contended it was of iron and a real screw, which by some mysterious means had become fixed in the rock. This screw is reminiscent of the nail found in a piece of quartz from a North Britain quarry, reported by Fort (*Books*, 133).

The gold thread that Fort says was found in Scotch quarry rock in 1844 (*Books*, 132) is paralleled by the curious find at Morrisonville, Illinois, in 1891. A Mrs. S. W. Culp was breaking a lump of coal preparatory to putting it into the scuttle. When the lump fell apart, she was startled to find embedded in ring fashion a small gold chain about ten inches long and of quaint workmanship.

Her first thought was that the chain had been accidentally dropped in the coal, but as she tried to pick it up she discovered that it was firmly fixed in the lump. Tugging at the middle portion, she succeeded in detaching it, but the ends, being set more deeply, required additional effort before being freed.

The imprint that remained was clear, the two ends being close together as in a necklace. The lump of coal was believed to have been taken from the local Taylorville or Pana mines. Upon further examination the chain was discovered to be of eight carat gold and to weigh eight pennyweights.

An odd exhumation was made in the strip-vein coal bank of Captain Lacy at Hammondsville, Ohio, in the autumn of 1868. A man named James Parsons was digging in the excavation with his two sons when a huge mass of coal fell down, disclosing a large, smooth, slate wall, upon the surface of which were carved in bold relief several lines of hieroglyphics. The lines were spaced about three inches apart, and contained about twenty-five hieroglyphics or words apiece.

The news soon spread, and crowds surged to the mine to see the marvel. Several scholars viewed the carved characters but were unable to identify them. An attempt was made to remove the slate wall from the mine, but as it was feared that the hieroglyphics would be destroyed in the process, this plan was abandoned.

When tapped, the wall gave forth a hollow sound, leading many to believe that a cavern or chamber existed beyond it. Dr. Hartshorn of Mt. Union College was sent for to examine the writing. No further reports seem available on the matter.

Perhaps the most striking, and certainly the most

numerous, of the mysterious objects that have been found underground are animal and insect fossils. Many entombed animals and insects have been found still alive.

One afternoon in 1877 some workers blasting rock forty feet down in a quarry west of Eureka, Nevada, noticed the curious formation of one of the pieces that had been split off. An examination revealed that embedded in the rock was a wasp nest, the texture and cells of which, although turned to stone, were plainly visible. On breaking open some of the cells, larvae and two perfectly formed wasps were found within, in the same petrified condition as the rest.

Both the nest and the wasps were preserved in natural shape and size, not crushed or flattened. There was no visible crack or other inlet by which the insects could have penetrated the rock. The rock was a granitic sandstone of sedimentary orgin. The specimen was carefully cut out and forwarded to the Smithsonian Institution in Washington, D.C.

Near Ruby Hill, Nevada, in 1881, a miner named Joe Molino made a find in the Wide West mine at a depth of about sixty feet. It was a solid piece of limestone in the very center of which was a small cavity containing six or eight large worms resembling maggots. The worms were alive and crawling when the rock was split, and, says the reporter, "the mystery is how they managed to get into the solid rock in this manner."

From the Longfellow mine, near Clifton, Arizona, was taken in 1892 what was declared at the time to be the most interesting insect and mineral specimen in existence. It was presented to Z. T. White of El Paso, Texas. When the specimen was fractured by Mr. White, a dull reddish-gray beetle was disclosed, surrounded by a close-fitting mold of iron ore.

The beetle in its iron sarcophagus lay as perfect as in life. Much impressed, White wrapped it in a piece of cloth. While carrying it home to his curio cabinet, he unfolded the cloth and glanced once more at the beetle. To his astonishment, he saw a small young beetle slowly emerging from its dead parent's body.

The young beetle was placed under a glass where it thrived and grew. It lived for a period of five months. Finally the mineral specimen, the maternal beetle in its cyst of ore, and the extraordinary younger insect were brought to the editorial office of the El Paso *Bullion*, where they were presented by Judge J. F. Crosby, with the compliments of the owner, to a prominent scientific association of the Atlantic coast. The *Bullion* editor was deeply impressed by the find and, though granting its authenticity, declared it almost beyond belief.

Live frogs have been found in coal and in rock strata. Two Welsh miners breaking coal in a pit near Bathgate, Linlithgowshire, in 1846, were astonished on splitting a large fragment to see a frog leap from it. The cavity in which it had lived was perfectly smooth, of the exact shape of the frog, and to all appearances without an opening by which to obtain air or food. The hind legs of the creature were at least twice as long as those of an ordinary frog, while the forelegs were barely perceptible.

In 1848 four young miners were digging coal in No. 8 pit at Gartlee, near Airdrie, Scotland. They had just broken off a mass of coal about four feet in diameter and were chopping it into smaller pieces, when near its center they came upon a kind of petrification. Suspecting that this might contain something of value, they worked at it carefully with the points of their picks.

Soon they saw a brown spot, which upon further examination turned out to be a frog, not fossilized, but apparently alive. It began to stir and before long awakened from its dormant state. When the miners turned it over several times, its movements became more vigorous. One of the men placed the creature in a pail of water. It proved able to swim but seemed to be in great pain and it changed color.

The men preserved the matrix of coal in which the frog had been embedded, there being impressed upon it a delicate mould of the animal's body. This, together with the frog itself, was placed in the museum of the Andersonian University of Glasgow.

Among the many persons who inspected the objects was a Mr. Craig, lecturer on geology in that institution. Craig became greatly interested and went to Airdrie where he investigated the circumstances surrounding the discovery. He obtained a written statement from the four young miners, whom he found to be intelligent and of good character.

Craig commnicated about the matter with the well-known geologist, Dr. Buckland, who on the basis of some experiments he had made insisted that there must have been some aperture, however slight, through which the animal entered and whereby insects and air could be obtained. He had found that toads he had imprisoned invariably got lean and died where such an opening did not exist. The circumstances of the present case, however, Craig found, definitely excluded the possibility of any opening.

Craig cited the corroboration of a friend, R. Jamieson, who with several others had some time before enclosed a toad in clay, and after putting it into a broken bottle had buried it about eighteen inches underground. At the end of twelve months the toad was dug up and found to be still alive and in fair condition. If, declared Craig, an animal can survive for twelve months without food, water, or air, there seemed to be no reason why it should not survive even longer, perhaps for ages.

Coal is a strange enough place in which to find a living animal, but a live frog was found 172 feet below the surface, embedded in solid sandstone, by some workers engaged in sinking a vertical shaft at the Black Diamond Coal Company's mine on Mount Diablo, near San Francisco, in 1873.

The partial imprint of its form upon the rock where it had lain was perfect in outline. The animal lived for twelve hours after its extraction, having very possibly been injured in the process. The president of the coal company was said to have later presented the remains to the San Francisco Academy of Sciences.

From Farmington, Maine, in 1868, comes a similar story. A well digger, in the course of his work, struck some scaly rock two feet below the surface of the ground. He blasted four feet farther through this stratum, at which depth he found three frogs completely embedded in the stone.

These frogs were from three to four inches in length, but only about an eighth of an inch thick, seemingly flattened by pressure. At first they appeared lifeless, but ten minutes later they moved slightly. They commenced inflating themselves, and by the end of half an hour they had resumed their natural shape and size and hopped off. Their color was almost identical with that of the ledge in which they were found.

Perhaps the most detailed description of a rock-imprisoned frog is one published in a Tuscarora, Nevada, newspaper in 1879. Five hundred feet down in the Grand Prize mine near that town a blast released a tiny frog from the rock. It was immediately brought to the surface and placed in a glass jar in F. H. Phelps's drug store on Weed Street.

At first it was almost white in color and nearly transparent, but after a week its back changed to a dingy mottled green. It had no mouth and consequently was unable to eat. Its eyes, which never closed even to wink, resembled two small, black, glass beads. They evidently were sightless, since objects brought even within a hair's breadth of them failed to effect any change in them whatever. The frog's general shape was not unlike that of other frogs, except that its forelegs and toes were disproportionately long. Its sense of feeling and hearing appeared normally acute, and it was nearly as lively as the general run of its surface-bred brethren. Concludes the editor: "While we will not venture any surmise regarding its history prior to its liberation, we will vouch for the truth of the above narrative and description."

Toads, like frogs, seem able to defy scientific dictums and live for ages encased in solid earth and rock. Reports came from Acton, Ontario, in 1893, about a wonderful discovery made at the local Brown & Hall sawmill, while a large pine log was being worked up.

After some outside slabs had been cut off, a large toad was seen to poke its head out of a hole in which it was embedded, having barely escaped being cut in two by the saw. It was declared a mystery how the creature got there, being perfectly encased in the wood, with no possible means of ingress or egress. As that particular log was the fourth or fifth up from the butt of the tree, the toad was located, before the tree was cut, at least fifty or sixty feet from the ground. The only possible conclusion seemed to be that the toad had been imprisoned in the infancy of the tree and had grown up with it and was consequently hundreds of years old.

Local naturalists declared the toad to be of a species unknown to the area. The cavity in which it was found was perfectly sound and as smooth within as though carefully rubbed and polished, The creature was surrounded originally with solid wood from forty-one and a half to thirty inches thick.

A dispatch came from Tacoma, Washington, in August 1893, stating that a toad with curious cat-like claws was found embedded under seventeen feet of hardpan in that city. Some men were digging a cistern when one of them drove a pick into the hard earth, finding at the pick's end a smooth hole in which was the toad, apparently dead.

Ten minutes in the open air, however, revived it. It ate several flies that were captured for it and lived for two weeks in a bottle, where it was furnished with water and pulverized earth.

Hundreds of people inspected the toad, which surprised the members of the local Academy of Sciences by the fact that it did not die after such sudden exposure to the air. The toad escaped from its jar and a few days later was found, pulseless, rigid, and cold in a neighboring house. Pronounced dead, it was just about to be buried when it regained animation. Sometime later the toad again went into a trance, suggesting that it was able to suspend animation indefinitely either at will or by accident. It is described as having been about the size of an egg, of the same grayish color as the hardpan, and somewhat resembling a tree toad.

In the museum of Hartlepool, England, visitors in 1865 stared at the active toad that had been found in a slab of magnesium limestone by some quarry laborers. It was generally supposed to be 6,000 years old.

A tiny toad in 1846 hopped out of a large block of ironstone four or five feet square when this was broken up. The toad was not much bigger than a bee and was very black, like the ironstone. It proved an agile swimmer. The ironstone was located thirty feet below the surface of the Lugar Iron Company's mine near Glasgow, Scotland.

A toad about two inches long was exhumed from the rock by a blast in the shaft of the Metacom mine near Austin, Nevada, in 1866. Its lively habits amused and astounded the local miners. In appearance it seemed not at all different from ordinary toads of the vicinity.

Some investigators believe that toads are found exclusively in rocks belonging to the carboniferous era. If this be true, how can we explain the live toad found in granite, a metamorphic or volcanic rock?

A quantity of granite was used in 1829 to repair the walls and steps of George's Dock Basin, Liverpool, England. A reporter was attracted by a crowd of persons around a block of granite that had been cut apart by the workers. He was informed that a toad had been found in a cavity laid open by the cutting instruments. He observed both the cavity and the toad.

To extricate the creature, one of the men cut away a portion of the stone from the edges of the cell. The toad was removed and for a time exhibited signs of life. All those present seemed to agree that no deception could have been practiced, and most of them, including the reporter, came to believe the toad had been enclosed "from the era of granitic infancy." ■

The Unbelievable Columns of Aksum

Andrew E. Rothovius
May 1977

A centuries-old Ethiopian mystery continues to confound the experts.

Sited in no particular pattern among the numerous ruined structures of Aksum, Ethiopia's former capital, are some of the world's most puzzling archaeological mysteries—about a dozen tall narrow columns, each hewn from a solid block of granite, towering up to seventy feet in height but only three to five feet across at the base.

All of these monoliths bear carved representations of windows, as many as ten stories on the tallest columns, resembling those that admit light and air into the multi-storied clay-built "skyscrapers" of Yemen across the Red Sea. In Yemen people have lived in these whitewashed mud buildings for more than twenty centuries; they are the world's earliest high-rise apartments. Whoever carved and raised the stone pillars of Aksum must have intended to imitate the Yemenite builders—but how and why did they

Into granite so hard it can hardly be chipped by any but power tools, the ancient builders carved "windows" with decorative framing so realistic in appearance that from a short distance away they appear to be real apertures. What was the purpose of this labor? Were the monoliths objects of worship? How long ago were they raised, and by whom?

Archaeology has no satisfactory answers to any of these questions despite extensive excavations begun at Aksum in 1954 by a joint team of French and Ethiopian scientists. They have learned that the city existed at least 500 years before the Christian era and that it was built by Semitic immigrants from Arabia, but it is not old enough to have been the Queen of Sheba's capital city, as Ethiopian tradition holds.

None of their discoveries sheds any light on the origin of the carved monoliths other than to indicate that the Aksumite builders were familiar with the Yemenite style of tall windowed buildings. According to most archaeologists, Yemen was the real Sheba from which the Queen went to visit King Solomon in Jerusalem 3,000 years ago. But if the Aksumites raised these columns, by what technique did they copy the Yemenite facades in granite?

Ethiopian folklore, still current in the Aksum area, claims that in dim antiquity, even before the time of Solomon and the Queen of Sheba, people knew how to "boil" stone to make it soft and plastic. In this state, the legends say, the stone columns with their fake windows were molded inside huge wooden frames and then propped into position. After the stone solidified, the frames were knocked away. Of course science does not recognize such a far-fetched process and can only shake its collective head at the enigma of the Aksum monoliths.

Another puzzle is why the columns were not mentioned by travelers to Aksum when it was still a flourishing city. An anonymous Greek who wrote a first-century *Guide to the Red Sea* tells us of Aksum's extensive maritime trade with Roman Egypt but says nothing about the columns, nor does the Byzantine monk Cosmas who visited Aksum about A.D. 500. It was then ruled by a Coptic Christian monarch, and Cosmas described its points of interest, including a massive marble throne erected a couple of centuries earlier to commemorate the Aksumite conquest of most of today's Ethiopia.

When the rise of Islam in the seventh century cut off Ethiopia from contact with the Christian West, Aksum declined—but the city was still inhabited when the first Portuguese traders and Jesuit missionaries reached it in the sixteenth century. An invasion by the Moslem Galla tribes soon drove out these Europeans. On their return to Lisbon and Rome, they told of the imposing cathedrals built in Aksum during its centuries of isolation, and the even more venerable monuments of crumbling antiquity on every hand—but not a word about the columns can be found in their accounts.

Yet they must have been there. Perhaps because the monoliths were not associated with the legendary Christian kingdom of "Prester John," as Ethiopia was known to Europe during the Middle Ages, they did not attract the attention of these first Western visitors.

The next European to reach Aksum was the remarkable eighteenth-century Scots traveler, James Bruce of Kinnaird, who as British consul in Algiers had become fascinated by Africa and the Middle East. He taught himself Arabic and Ethiopian preparatory to setting out on a single-handed search for the fabled sources of the Nile.

When he arrived in Ethiopia in 1770 the Moslems had only recently been driven out of the major part of the kingdom; it was still remote and unknown to Westerners.

Intellectuals such as the renowned Samuel Johnson, however, persistently visualized Ethiopia as a sequestered realm of happy philosophers—as in Boswell's classic *Rasselas*. They were so shocked by Bruce's account on his return to England of the barbarity and near savagery he had found that they labeled him a liar who probably had never been to Ethiopia at all.

Especially they hooted at the description—which he was the first to give—of the great granite monoliths of Aksum. If these columns existed at all, London's armchair explorers opined, they must be Egyptian obelisks and hence covered with hieroglyphic carvings from top to bottom. Why, this fellow Bruce could not even relate his tall tales with a semblance of plausibility! The windows he insisted were carved on the shafts had to be something else—if he hadn't imagined the whole thing.

Bruce himself did not realize how ancient Aksum was. By his time the city had fallen into decay and its once magnificent structures were mounded with earth and overgrown by tropical brushwood. He conjectured that the columns were the work of Egyptians who had found their way that far into unknown Africa, but he could offer no explanation for the carved windows.

Bruce was so angered by the incredulity he encountered when he had expected acclaim and honors for his discoveries, that it took more than fifteen years for friends who believed in him to persuade him to publish the full story of his journey. It finally appeared in five volumes in 1790, and for the first time the world at large came to know of the Aksum columns.

Skepticism still dogged Bruce despite the fullness of detail in his published account. His was the first book to name and picture giraffes, and since it was not until a generation later that they were understood to be the same animal as the cameleopards of the ancient Greeks and Romans, Bruce was again attacked as an inventor of imaginary creatures.

His blustery scornful temper did nothing to help him gain acceptance, and he died in 1794 at the age of 64, embittered and disappointed. Although later travelers confirmed practically all of Bruce's statements, this first great modern explorer of Africa was soon forgotten. To this day he remains almost unknown.

Thus few persons recalled what he had written about the Aksum monoliths when in 1814, Henry Salt, a semiofficial envoy of the British goverment (which had become interested in East Africa as a waystation to India) published an account of his visit to Ethiopia in 1809–10 and included a description and drawings of the stone columns. He dismissed the idea of their Egyptian origin, but at the same time he could offer no explanation of his own.

From that time on the Aksum columns have been generally known to Westerners. The monoliths have been studied, measured, sketched, and photographed, but still they have not yielded the secret of who carved and raised them or when or how.

In today's Ethiopia, ravaged by civil strife, few tourists visit Aksum to stand enthralled and puzzled by the sight of these needle-like stone columns fretted with false windows towering over the mounded ruins of the ancient capital. Long after peace is restored, it is likely they will still be there to mystify future generations of visitors.   ■

ᴑystery of the fairy Crosses

John P. Bessor
June 1952

What produced these tiny cross-shaped stones?
Are they the work of a race no larger than pickles?

At the point where the Allegheny and Blue Ridge Mountains unite, in the northern section of Patrick County, Virginia, lies a quiet and charming valley noted for its quarry of remarkable little stones. These stones are shaped like crosses and their exact origin has never been satisfactorily explained. Because of their tiny size and their singular design, they are popularly known as "Fairy" or "Lucky" stones.

These "fairy crosses" vary in size from a quarter of an inch to an inch and a half in length and are of three varieties: Roman, Maltese, and St. Andrews. They have been found in two other states, but those of Virginia all are from the vicinity of Bull Mountain.

The United States Geographical Survey issued a bulletin concerning these crosses on September 18, 1925, which states:

Perhaps the most curious mineral found in the United States is Staurolite, otherwise known as 'Fairy Stone.' Staurolite is an iron aluminum silicate, found in Virginia, the reddish-brown and brownish-black crystals occurring in well-defined crosses. There is a commercial demand for the crosses as curios, which are worn as watch charms on one's chains in the manner of a locket or lavaliere—a demand stimulated by the quaint legend which is told of their origin.

Charles Fort, in his monumental *The Books of Charles Fort*, says about the crosses:

Conceivably there might be a mineral that would have a diversity of geometric forms, at the same time restricted to some expression of the cross, because snowflakes, for instance, have diversity but restriction to the hexagon, but the guilty geologists, cold-blooded as astronomers and chemists and all the other deep-sea fishes—though less profoundly of the pseudo-saved than the wretched anthropologists—disregarded the very datum—that it was wise to disregard: That the 'fairy crosses' are not all made of the same material.

It's the same old disregard, or it's the same old psychotropism, or process of assimilation. Crystals are geometric forms. Crystals are included in the System. So then 'fairy crosses' are crystals. But that different minerals should, in a few different regions, be inspired to turn into different forms of the cross—is the kind of resistance that we call less nearly real than our own acceptances.

Fort was inclined to correlate the tiny "fairy crosses" with the minute pigmy flints, a quarter of an inch in size, that have been found in England, France, India, and South Africa. He believed the tiny arrowheads to be the artifacts of a race no larger than pickles. "So fine is the chipping that to see the workmanship a magnifying glass is necessary," he says.

Similarly with the "fairy crosses," it is interesting to observe that each cross looks exactly as though it were cut into shape by a hand-file, the "teeth" marks being clearly discernible except at the end surfaces, which are smooth and perfectly flat.

The crosses have been quarried commercially for more than seventy years by the L. C. Clarke Company of Virginia, which mounts the stones with gold caps and gold plated eyes. They print a little leaflet carrying the legend of the "fairy crosses." This legend is as follows:

> Hundreds of years before King Powhatan's dynasty came into power, long before the woods breathed the gentle spirit of the lovely Pocahontas, the fairies were dancing around a spring of limpid water, playing with the naiads and wood nymphs, when an elfin messenger arrived from a strange city far, far away in the land of the dawn, bearing the sad tidings of the death of Christ, and when they heard the terrible story of the crucifixion, they wept. And as their tears fell upon the Earth they crystallized into little pebbles, one each of which was formed a beautiful cross. When the fairies had disappeared from the enchanted spot the ground about the spring and the adjacent valleys was strewn with these unique mementoes of that melancholy event.

■

Pottery Puzzle

William W. Jenna
May 1989

*Archaeologists say the pre-Columbian artifact is
1,600 years old—but it seems to depict
a twentieth-century machine.*

The year was A.D. 300 and the Roman regions under Claudius Maximus had just completed the conquest of England. Transportation in those days was slow and primitive, carried on as it had been since the dawn of recorded history when humans first harnessed an animal to a wagon. Sixteen centuries would pass before the beginning of the Industrial Revolution and the invention of the steam engine.

Yet in that same year halfway around the world in a remote village in Peru, a simple Indian peasant sat making a strange clay object to be fired into pottery. It was a double-bodied vessel for water, fashioned, as were all of the double-bodied water vessels of that particular tribe, after something from nature or anything at all which the pottery-maker had seen and remembered.

This particular tribe or culture, known as the Vicus people, produced a variety of these jugs in the shape of birds, animals, people and fish. On this occasion, however, the subject was in the shape of a modern twentieth-century steam-roller complete with a smokestack on the front and a cab on the back and with a driver inside seated at the controls.

Amazingly, this was 1,600 years before the steamroller was invented, and the object was sculpted from a culture that did not even make use of the wheel. Everything they moved was either carried or dragged from place to place. The Vicus were a simple people whose greatest achievements were the making of pottery and the weaving of cloth.

Did fourth-century Peruvian Indians have the technological knowledge to build a steamroller?

This piece has been authenticated by the foremost museums of Pre-Columbian art in the United States and positively dated no later than A.D. 300. With these facts confronting us, we are forced to face the possibility that either this simple Indian potter had a vision of things to come, or else he had seen something from a technologically advanced culture of which the world has no knowledge whatsoever, a vanished race that perhaps visited this Earth briefly, never to return.

The piece was unearthed in the ruins of a village near the plains of Nazca, with their great flat geometric designs and long stright lines that some say were landing strips for early spacecraft. This little eight-inch model of a steamroller, positively dated by scientists back at least 1,600 years, is a puzzle shrouded in mystery. ■

The Ancients Had Airplanes

Ivan T. Sanderson
May 1975

Modern reexamination of an ancient Egyptian model of a "bird" suggests that gliders were known more than 200 years before Christ.

Evidence that there were sophisticated gliders and possibly even powered aircraft in ancient times is forcing us to take an entirely new view of history. Many cultural anthropologists, archaeologists, and historians are coming to believe that there was a highly advanced worldwide technological civilization on Earth before 4,000 B.C. In fact, the evidence may force us to reconsider history as far back as 20,000 B.C.

The most astonishing and convincing evidence for ancient flight came to light only a few years ago. In 1969 Dr. Khalil Messiha, a medical doctor and also a recognized Egyptologist and archaeologist, discovered an object in the basement of the famous Cairo Museum in a box marked "bird models." For many years Dr. Messiha's principal line of research has been the identification of ancient Egyptian artifacts. He has brought to light thousands of pieces, mostly from storage basements to which they were relegated over the years because they could not be explained and so were not tabbed for exhibition.

Coming upon this box marked "bird models," Messiha noted that the contents had been found in a tomb at Saqqara in 1895 and had been in storage ever since. The contents, except for one item, were quite plainly and clearly bird figurines, easily identified because the ancient Egyptians were such consummate animal artists.

This one, which is in two parts—a fuselage and a single wing that fitted into a slot—most definitely is not a bird, since no bird has an upright or vertical tail.

In his youth Dr. Messiha was an enthusiastic builder of model airplanes and spotted these divergencies immediately. As a biologist I can assure you this device is not any kind of model of any kind of bird, not only because of its vertical tail but because of its general configuration and proportions; nor is it a "dummy" or "block" forming the basis for constructing a bird. There is no other known winged animal that it resembles.

And there is no use suggesting that someone "planted" it there; it bears its original number, Special Register No. 6347, Room 22, and the 1895 date of its discovery precedes the modern invention of the airplanes.

So convincing were Dr. Messiha's analyses of this artifact that the Egyptian Ministry of Culture, through its Undersecretary Dr. Mohammed Gamal-El-Din Moukhtar, set up a committee of top-notch scientists to study the matter. These included Dr. Henry Riad, director of the Egyptian Museum of Antiquities; Dr. Abdul Qader Selim, deputy director of the Egyptian Museum of Antiquities; Dr. Hishmat Messiha, director of inspectorates at the Egyptian Department of Antiquities; and Miss Nagwa Mohammed El-Nahry, keeper at the Egyptian Museum of Antiquities; with Mr. Kamal

Naguib, chairman of the International Aviation Committee, and Dr. Kahlil Messiha as consultants.

The committee recommended that a special exhibit of models "as might have been originally designed as specimens of airworthiness rather than as bird models" be mounted in the central hall of the museum and this little model airplane be made its centerpiece. This was done in 1971.

Now, professional scientists, especially archaeologists in museums, are not given to sticking their necks out in the case of "unexplaineds," particularly when they upset established historical chronological beliefs. But these men went so far as to identify it as an aircraft in the explanatory label under the model in the exhibit. Moreover, they dated the object as having been entombed in the year 200 B.C.!

As Dr. Messiha explains, the ancient Egyptians always made extremely precise scale models of everything before they built the first full-sized prototype. They made them for pyramids, other buildings, obelisks, irrigation works, and all manner of smaller things. In commenting upon this airplane, Dr. Messiha also noted that we have known of precise scale models of ships for many years, but not until the last decade was a full-sized Egyptian ship found in its own tomb—built on the multiple scale of a known model. If a ship, why not an airplane?

When I first received the photographs, drawings, and necessary measurements in centimeters and millimeters, I set to work to draw diagrams of the model precisely to that scale. The artifact is carved from sycamore wood, and, as seen from above, the fuselage was warped, slightly to the right from behind the wings. We straightened this out, and Messiha conjectures the presence of a horizontal slotted tail unit that may have been meant to push onto the vertical tail unit. The model may have been made to be adjustable (up and down) for the engineers who tested its flight potential and patterns.

I sent the scale drawings I had made to a number of designers, aerodynamics engineers, and professional pilots and glider experts, making no comment and giving no background information, simply asking each one what he felt it might represent. All but one labeled it a glider. One technician working with big wind tunnels for a company under contract to NASA got excited because, he said, it precisely configured an advanced design still on the drawing boards for an extremely low-powered supercargo plane meant to carry huge loads at extremely slow speeds—below sixty mph.

The gimmick is the counter-dihedral wings that curve down at the tips. Dr. Messiha and I carved scale models. He used sycamore and I used heavy balsa wood. Unlike the paper darts we used to make at school that had to be launched with real force because they were delta-winged, these little things need only a slight push and they go sailing away, losing altitude very slowly. However, they do have to be launched. This could have been done with a catapult; certainly the ancients knew about catapults.

An unexpected fact emerged from our analysis of the blueprint we had made from the photographs. Every measurement is either one-third or one-half of all the others. The ancient Egyptians, of course, did not use our metric system—it was unknown in their day—but they must have had an extremely precise calibration of some unit; it looks very much as if they employed a duodecimal system, because of the precision of the divisions into thirds as well as fourths. This object is both aerodynamically and mathematically perfect, and it looks as if the designers first worked it all out on the drafting board and then built the model. While we have known the ancient Egyptians were advanced in mathematics, geometry, and solid geometry, to have designed this thing to do a specific job took more knowledge than we suspected they had.

But assuming this was a glider, which it manifestly is, what would be its use? In warfare or commerce? Can we conceive of the Egyptians staging mass invasions behind enemy lines such as we put on in Normandy in World War II? I think not, unless we have missed, overlooked, or otherwise misinterpreted papyri, tomb paintings, and other sources. It seems more likely these planes were few in number and available only to the priesthood and the semidivinity of the pharaoh. In this case, they would have been even more valuable if they did not have to rely on mere gliding but could be powered. What kind of power could the ancients have had? They did not have the propeller. But could they have had jet engines?

This outrageous suggestion is offered because the pre-Aryan Indians might have had jet engines and used them in flying machines. Such devices are described in a number of Sanskrit texts of varying probity. The best of these texts was translated and published in 1956 in a long paper titled "Yantras or Mechanical Contrivances in Ancient India" by V. Raghavan. After comparing the authenticity and reliability of the text—originally written by one Bhoja—he says:

> The most curious of the yantras described by Bhoja in this chapter is, of course, the one that rises and travels in the air. From the previous notices of this aerial machine, only the barest details of its makeup could be gleaned. . . .
> Firstly, Bhoja mentions the main material of its body as light wood, laghu-daru; its shape is that of a huge bird, mahavinhanga, with a wing on each side.
> The motive force is then explained: In the bowels of the structure, below, is to be a fire-chamber with mercury placed over a flame. The power generated by the heated mercury, helped by the concurrent action of the wings which are flapped by a rider inside, makes the yantra go up and travel far (dura).

A heavier (alaghu) Daruvimana is then described; it contains, not one as in the previous case, but four pitchers of mercury over iron ovens. The boiling mercury ovens produce a terrific noise which is put to use in battle to scare away elephants; by strengthening the mercury chambers, the roar could be increased so that by it elephants are thrown completely out of control. This specific military use of aircraft against elephants tempts one to suggest that the Hasti-yantra advocated by Kautilya against elephants was something like the heavier Daruvimana described by Bhoja.

Raghaven also states that is is clear that

> ... mercury vapor ought not to be confused as providing any lifting power; it was evidently converted into mechanical power, and the machine must have risen ... by the flapping of the wings, and further movement must have been due to the manipulation of the wings and the flow of air itself, on the analogy of the flight of birds.

At first reading this sounds quite unacceptable, but in 1969 two scientists published an enlightening paper in the respectable journal *Science* (January 3, 1969) describing the behavior of mercury in a dish over an open revolving flame. They reported that the mercury revolves in a direction contrary to the movement of the flame below, and that its speed of rotation increases while that of the flame remains steady, and that apparently it will continue to gather speed indefinitely. Presumably it eventually would become so hot that it would begin to vaporize, but this is not necessarily so, for its energy could be collected before that very dangerous (mercury vapor is deadly poison) point was reached.

The problem then is how to transfer this or a similar energy to some kind of mechanical device. Or could it somehow have been converted to act as a form of jet? After all, a Roman in A.D. 200 states that he made a model "plane" in the form of a dove and "flew it with compressed air." We may well ask who was compressing air at that time. The fact, however, remains that a lot of ancient Indians said they had flying machines and that they were propelled by mercury engines. We may never know just how they achieved the propulsion.

The ancients had two major trade routes, one by sea and the other overland from the eastern Mediterranean to India and beyond. Egypt and India traded goods constantly by sea from very early times, and there is no reason to think they did not also exchange information mathematical, scientific, and technological. It is possible, therefore, that knowledge of some form of power unit, possibly without moving parts, could have reached Egypt in very early times. And if we are to interpret the legend of Icarus as being a description of a glider or sailplane with waxed fabric stretched over a light wood framework—the wax on one occasion melting in the hot sunlight and presumably causing the fabric to rupture—it seems gliders were known in Crete at an early date.

Now comes this Egyptian "bird model"!

We have shown that this model is obviously not just a one-shot effort, but the end product of a lot of computation and experimentation, much more than would have been put into the carving of a toy. However, if it were to be powered by some form of jet engine, we have to know where the nozzle or exhaust might be. It is interesting to note, in this context, that the lower portion of the tail is raggedly broken, and we can speculate that this was originally hollow and contained an exhaust nozzle. On the other hand, assuming it existed at all, we don't know how the mercury engine worked or how it imparted its energy in order to cause the early yantras to rise and fly.

In summary, then, the knowledge of gliders appears to be extremely ancient, since what we take to be exact depictions of monoplanes also have been found among the countless gold plaques or seals unearthed from the ancient cities of Harappa and Mohenjo-Daro in the Indus Valley. We do not know that they were powered, nor do we know whether this Egyptian monoplane-artifact of a much later date was powered, but it definitely was designed to be airborne and we do have written descriptions of engines used for powered flight from India at a date historically about halfway (2000 B.C.) between the Indus Valley civilization (4000 B.C.) and the Egyptian culture that produced our model (200 B.C.).

The Indians say their "planes" were devised for war; there is no evidence that the Egyptian model plane was; perhaps it was used to transport important persons or valuable freight. However, further speculation, while intriguing, will lead us nowhere until a great deal more is known on this subject.

The concrete evidence that the ancients knew of flight was forced upon us only a few years ago. Now, we have to explain it. And when we do we will have to rearrange a great many of our concepts of ancient history. ■

Ancient Electric Battery

H. C. Goble
March 1958

A two-millennia-old object unearthed by the archaeologists is peculiar: It strongly resembles a certain "modern" invention.

The Parthians, who lived as an independent nation southeast of the Caspian Sea until A.D. 226, used, if they did not invent, a practical electric battery at least two hundred years before the birth of Christ.

Twenty years ago, Wilhelm Konig, a German archaeologist at the Iraq Museum, began excavations in a hill near Baghdad. A Parthian village had been discovered there by accident. During these excavations a peculiar object turned up. It strongly resembled a modern dry-cell battery. Konig learned that four similar objects, plus rods suggesting present-day bus bars, had been found in a magician's hut at Seleucia, some miles downriver.

Konig's search took him to Berlin. There he found in a museum ten more dry cells like the one from his original digging—except these were broken down into their component

160

parts—as though someone had been interrupted before assembling the pieces into a working battery.

Konig described his findings in a book published in German, *The Lost Paradise*. And that famous astronomer, rocketeer, historian, archaeologist, and student of all knowledge, Willy Ley, reported the find in some American journals.

Here it came to the attention of Willard F. M. Gray, of the General Electric High Voltage Laboratory in Pittsfield, Massachusetts. He volunteered to build a duplicate of the Parthian battery. Ley gave him dimensions, diagrams, and a metallurgical analysis. The duplicate battery, in which Gray used copper sulphate instead of an electrolyte that is still unknown, works perfectly and is in the Berkshire Museum at Pittsfield at the present time.

My information does not give its output, but it seems logical to assume 1.5 or 2.0 volts per cell, unless the long-vanished electrolyte of the Parthians was vastly more efficient than any known today—which, of course, it might have been.

The cell consisted of a cylinder of sheet-copper, about the same length and width as two modern flashlight cells placed end to end, or about one-half inch long and 1.5 inches in diameter. The edges of the copper cylinder were soldered with a 60-40 lead tin alloy (comparable to the best of modern solders.) A copper disc was crimped into the bottom of the cylinder, and on top of this was a layer of pitch or bitumen to insulate it from the electrode.

The electrode was an iron rod placed in an asphalt stopper that was shoved into the top of the copper cylinder. The unknown electrolyte, of which no traces have been found, filled the space between iron rod and copper cylinder walls.

Gray proved that copper sulphate would work very well as an electrolyte, but it could equally well have been acetic or citric acid, both well-known in Parthian times. Or it could have been an unknown compound far more powerful than anything known today.

It is assumed, although no reason is given for this assumption in the material thus far published, that the current from these batteries was used for electroplating by Parthian metal workers. Since the Parthians never showed any remarkable abilities except in military tactics, it is thought that they got the secret of the battery from the Sumerians or the Babylonians. It was not much before 250 B.C. that this nomadic, warrior race got out of the saddle to settle down and build cities, so it seems unlikely they invented the battery.

But obviously someone invented it—and it wasn't Volta in the early 1800s. Again, we are face to face with the idea that nothing is new under the sun—that we only rediscover knowledge familiar to the ancients milleniums before our time. ∎

Mystery in Acambaro

Charles H. Hapgood
January and February 1974

A unique collection of Mexican artifacts of
surprisingly great age may represent
America's oldest culture.

Part I

During the past one hundred years archaeological research has brought to light a great deal of evidence regarding the Indian cultures that existed in Mexico, Central America, and northern South America from about the beginning of the Christian Era to the Spanish conquest. Within the present boundaries of the United States these include the Mound Builders and the Pueblo Indians; in Central Mexico they are the Tarascan, Toltec, Aztec, Totonac, and Olmec cultures. Continuing southward from the old Mayan empire on the Pacific Coast and the new Mayan empire in Yucatan, these Indian cultures include the Chorotega, Chiriqui, Coclé, and other cultures in Guatemala and Panama. In South America they include the Chibcha, Mochica, Chimu, Nazca, and all other cultures whose territories ultimately became parts of the great Inca Empire. Modern archaeological research has been able to tell us a great deal about the individual culture patterns of these civilized Indian people who developed their ways of life and styles of art independently of each other although they shared basic life and thought patterns.

Perhaps the leading problem of Americanist studies during the last century has been the problem of origins. Where did the Indians come from? (The immigration of all the Indian peoples from Asia via the Bering Strait is increasingly in doubt.) Where did the common characteristics of their cultures originate? How, in detail, did they exert cultural influence on each other? Additional information has been produced in recent years through the technique of radiocarbon dating. It has been found, for example, that the Mayan culture is much older than formerly thought. It now has been traced back to 1000 B.C. and may be much older.

From radiocarbon dating we know that separate Indian peoples established different culture patterns in Middle America some 10,000 years ago. This of course totally destroys the myth of a recent Indian immigration from Asia. We even have evidence that men hunted the mammoth on Santa Rosalina Island in California 39,000 years ago.

The evidence suggests that these earliest Middle American cultures were only crude beginnings, but still a great deal of time intervenes between these cultures of 10,000 years ago and the appearance of the civilized Indian peoples of the classical period not very long before the beginning of the Christian Era. What happened in between?

Was there a seminal culture somewhere in this area that existed long before the rise of the classical cultures and that profoundly influenced all of them? Was one original culture, developed very early, responsible for the common traits of all these Indian cultures? It really cannot be doubted that the common features of the Indian cultures were developed in America, for in a survey of East Asia, no people, no culture can be found with any significant similarity to the Indian cultures of America.

Yet logic suggests there must have been a common origin that antedated all the classical cultures and of which they were descendants. Seven or eight thousand years intervened between the first of these recognizable separate cultures of the Indians and the classical period. It is therefore not unreasonable to look for some center, some original source of the major characterstics of later Indian cultures.

This article is an account of the discovery in southern Mexico of what may be evidence of such an original seminal culture. The archaeological evidence consists of about 32,000 artifacts discovered in Acambaro by the late Waldemar Julsrud, a German national, and presently housed in his former residence there. Radiocarbon dates suggest that this culture may have developed between 6,400 and 3,500 years ago. Thermoluminescent tests give ages of 4,500 years for some of the objects in this collection.

One day on horseback Mr. Julsrud was following a trail that ran along a dry ditch on the side of a hill called Bull Mountain on the outskirts of Acambaro, when his eye caught a peculiar object half-buried in the dirt. He dismounted and dug it out. It was a little statuette of baked clay, a ceramic figurine.

In style it was different from anything that he previously had seen. Although he was familiar with Tarascan, Aztec, Toltec, Mayan, Incan, and pre-Incan objects as well as with other Indian cultures, this object did not reflect any culture he knew. He was accompanied by one of his employees, a farmer named Odilon Tanager, and he asked Tanager to dig around in the ditch and bring him any similar objects he could find.

A few days later Tanager came to Mr. Julsrud's house with a wheelbarrow full of small pieces like the one Julsrud had found. Julsrud was fascinated both by their unusual style and their variety of subject. He now suspected he had discovered an unknown Indian culture. There was nothing unreasonable about this speculation. When I went to Mexico many years later I learned that Mexico is covered with unexplored sites. I was told by professional archaeologists that for every site so far excavated at least ten more never have been touched.

Julsrud was a shrewd businessman and he now made a business deal with Tanager that is very important to our story. He told Tanager he would pay him one peso (about twelve cents) for each complete piece he brought in. However, the piece had to be complete. If the digger found it broken or if he broke it in extracting it from the earth he had to mend and wash it before bringing it to Mr. Julsrud's house. Mrs. Julsrud probably had a hand in this last provision. If a figurine could not be mended Tanager was to bring the fragments to Mr. Julsrud, who stored them in wooden boxes in his house. I discovered a great number of these boxes when I reached Acambaro. Mr. Julsrud did not pay for the broken pieces.

At first I was doubtful about the wisdom of Mr. Julsrud's arrangement with Tanager. It seemed to me it would have been better not to try to mend the broken pieces. But I learned Julsrud had a very good reason for his insistence. It was the only way to make Tanager careful in extracting the pieces from the earth. When I interviewed Tanager I discovered he had developed an extremely careful and rather ingenious method of excavation, not learned from books. When he started a hole, he would dig down about four feet, the depth at which he usually found the figurines. Then he would probe carefully with long knives. When he located a cache of figures (they seem deliberately to have been buried in pits, twenty to forty to a pit) he would move a little to one side and dig down farther and undercut the cache so the earth walls would collapse of themselves and the figurines would be revealed.

The method of burial of the figurines was unusual. They had not been discarded as fragments, nor had they been buried in connection with funerals. Only a half-dozen skulls were found in the entire process of excavation. Mr. Julsrud theorized he had found a sacred collection that had been buried to save it from the Spanish. In any case, it was plain the pieces had been buried when they were intact and that they had been packed into the pits with care.

All this information was provided me by Mr. Julsrud, who also confirmed what Tanager told me. However, I found that Mr. Julsrud had an unimpeachable reputation for responsibility and veracity in the city of Acambaro. In my examination of the case from start to finish I never found any reputable and informed person who doubted Mr. Julsrud's honesty or his conscientious accuracy.

Tanager kept coming with loads of figurines. Julsrud's house was a mansion with many rooms and a couple of large patios. First the figurines filled the large reception hall. Then they flowed into the library. Then the upstairs bedrooms were filled. Shelves had to be installed in the hallways. Eventually every nook and cranny in the house was occupied.

When Mrs. Julsrud died Mr. Julsrud filled their bedroom with figurines and thereafter slept in the bathroom. Before the work of excavation stopped, the collection had reached the monstrous total of over 32,000 objects of ceramic, stone, jade, and obsidian. The wooden crates in the house still contain unknown numbers of additional pieces.

The objects are of all sizes, from figures a few inches long to statues three feet high or four or five feet long. A great variety of clays was used in molding them. They all have been baked by the open fire method, a matter of great importance, as we shall see. The richness of the imagination displayed by their creators is incredible, even uncanny; there seems almost a touch of the supernatural to it. All observers have agreed that there is no precedent for it in the annals of archaeology.

An especially important point relates to the different styles of decoration in the collection. There are many different styles of design but each style is consistently carried out on hundreds or thousands of pieces. It is as if the art collections of several different Indian peoples had been combined, perhaps by a conquering people. This would be quite in accordance with Indian custom.

Frank Hamilton Cushing, in his discussion of Zuni culture (*Outlines of Zuni Creation Myths*, 13th Annual Report of the Bureau of Ethnology, 1896), points out that this culture contained two entirely different elements representing the continuing traditions of at least two originally separate peoples:

> There are present and persist among them two distinct types of physique and numerous survivals—inherited, not borrowed—of the arts, customs, myths, and institutions of at least two peoples, unrelated at first, or at least separate and very diversely conditioned for so long a period of their preunited history that their development had progressed unequally and along quite different lines, at the time of their final coalition.
>
> That the Zunis are actually the descendants of two or more peoples and the heirs of two cultures at least is well shown in their legends of ruins and olden times and especially in these myths of creation and migration as interpreted by archaeologic and ethnographic research.

Cultural imperialism was foreign to the Indians. They had not learned the fatal practice of conquerors in the Old

World whose first aim always was and is to destroy, if possible, every trace of the culture of the conquered.

Mr. Julsrud told us that the bulk of the collection was excavated from an area of from six to ten acres on the side of a hill on the outskirts of Acambaro called Toro or Bull Mountain. However, we learned that he sometimes bought pieces brought to him by villagers who presumably had found them in the course of cultivating their fields. We saw for ourselves that fragments of pieces similar to those of the Julsrud Collection were scattered all over the surface of the ground on and near the site. People who had found similar objects might have given or sold them to Tanager. Thus we cannot say that every object in Julsrud's house was excavated from those fields on Bull Mountain.

Mr. Tanager reported, and it is a matter of possible future archaeological interest, that when he was excavating in the fields he often came upon the heavy stone foundations of what may originally have been buildings. I had no opportunity to confirm this report.

Mr. Julsrud wanted to attract the attention of archaeologists to his discovery. He showed the collection to all interested people. He gave interviews to the press and in this manner had the good fortune to interest a young American journalist, William N. Russell of Los Angeles, who made many trips to Acambaro and became Mr. Julsrud's representative in the United States. Through Mr. Russell many people learned about the collection. Mr. Julsrud's interest was purely scientific. He never tried to commercialize his find in any way. He never sold any of the pieces except in one case to a scientific investigator for exhibition purposes. He tried hard to persuade trained archaeologists to visit his collection, to excavate on Bull Mountain themselves. But unfortunately he developed a theory that helped to discredit his find.

Many great reptiles are represented in the collection, some of them in association with people. This association appears to have been sometimes friendly, sometimes not. Mr. Julsrud was not a trained paleontologist, and because some of the creatures resembled dinosaurs, Mr. Julsrud jumped to the conclusion that dinosaurs and people had lived at the same time.

Moreover, he had read books about Atlantis, and he also concluded, without scholarly authority, that humans and dinosaurs had lived together in Atlantis. When articles stressing these opinions were published in the Mexican press, the effect in reputable archaeological circles may be imagined. For many years no archaeologists visited Acambaro. Eventually two or three of them did, only to brand the whole collection a fake.

In 1955 the Foundation for the Study of Consciousness sent me to Mexico where I spent the summer excavating in collaboration with Mrs. Margaret Regler, the widow of the late archaeologist Gustav Regler. Mrs. Regler knew both archaeology and Spanish, and without her I would have been lost. At first, I was overwhelmed by the wealth of the collection. The mere classification of the pieces seemed a superhuman task.

We immediately noticed the numerous different styles and could easily perceive innumerable connections between the artifacts and various aspects of known Indian cultures. Some pieces Mr. Julsrud had identified as pre-Incan, and we saw many that suggested Toltec and Aztec art. Mr. Julsrud told us that some of the statuettes were Sumerian and we found several that indicated a roundabout relationship with ancient Egypt. There also were many pieces that suggested an ancestral relationship to Tarascan culture.

We soon saw, however, that the collection really depicted various aspects of life of one primitive people, indicating their weapons, equipment, arts, methods of procuring food, relationships with nature, and folklore.

The majority of the faces on the figurines are Indian in appearance, but many of them indicate other racial strains. Polynesian, Mongolian, Caucasian, and Negro faces can be seen on the figures.

Waldemar Julsrud and others think these ancient figurines are evidence of a time when humans and prehistoric creatures co-habited.

We made one serious attempt at excavation on Bull Mountain. We knew most of the ground at the site area had been disturbed by Tanager. Detractors also were alleging that all the pieces had been manufactured by Tanager and his sons. Mrs. Regler and I decided the best place to dig would be directly under one of the houses built on or near the site. This would eliminate any possibility of fraud.

We found a house, directly on the site, that belonged to the city's Chief of Police. Mr. Julsrud influenced the chief to give us permission to dig in the house, despite the fact that it was occupied by tenants. We dug in the center of their living room (it had a dirt floor) making a pit about six feet deep. We found many fragments of pieces resembling those in the Julsrud Collection. This satisfied us that the site was genuine.

Returning to the collection, we studied it from the standpoint of the culture it portrays. In many respects this culture was unique, yet not in conflict with the ideas of anthropologists regarding the social life of early peoples. The "Julsrud People," as I call them after the name of the discoverer, appear not to have practiced the custom of human burial. Until the latter part of their existence they evidently did not possess the bow and arrow, and hunted only with spears and clubs or daggers made of wood, stone, or bone. They seem to have known nothing of agriculture, except for raising gourds, and nothing of textiles during the greater part of their history. Yet they did make unpainted pottery. They recorded their culture in ceramic as well as in stone sculpture. It is unusual but not unprecedented to find pottery-making in pre-agricultural societies.

Many indications suggest that these people had close relationships with animals. We see them petting their dogs, riding wild horses or llamas without saddle or bridle, embracing large monkeys or apes, and having loving relationships with reptiles. Some of the figurines suggest that they actually domesticated reptiles as well as anteaters and other mammals. They are shown in friendly relationships with turkeys. They must have identified with animals in a way that we do not.

The collection contains evidence of a vast antiquity. In the first place, it indicates a woodland culture. It becomes clear from the study of the figurines that the climate of the Acambaro region was very different at the time they were fashioned. Instead of the present arid valley with its eroded and dessicated surrounding highlands and sparse rainfall, the collection indicates a well-watered region. Geologists actually have found that the valley was filled by a great lake until sometime after the end of the ice age. The site of the caches of objects was once a beach of this lake. It seems, therefore, that they originally were buried in sand, a matter of some importance, as we shall see.

We found that the fauna represented in the art of the Julsrud People was a woodland and a lakeland fauna and that in many ways their art reflects a forest environment. This by itself indicates a remote antiquity, but far better proof is available.

The collection contains unmistakable representations of the one-humped American camel of the ice age and of ice-age horses, as well as of animals resembling rhinoceroses of extinct species. It contains many figurines of giant monkeys such as actually existed in South America in the Pleistocene epoch. I found some real teeth in the collection and asked Mr. Julsrud about them. He said he thought they might be mammoth teeth, but I considered them too small for that. I had noticed figurines of horses and incised representations of them on pots, but they did not look like modern horses, and Mr. Julsrud himself told me there were no horses in his collection. Dr. George Gaylord Simpson, America's leading paleontologist, at the American Museum of Natural History, later identified these teeth as belonging to *Equus conversidens Owen*, an extinct, ice-age horse.

At first it seemed probable that the reptiles in the collection, despite occasional startling resemblances to dinosaurs, were inspired by the living reptiles of Middle America such as the iguana lizard. When I showed photographs of the reptilian figurines to Professor Alfred S. Romer of Harvard he concurred in this opinion. I knew such monsters figured in many Indian legends and thought the figurines might be visual representations of such mythical animals. However, observation gradually persuaded me that some great reptiles may have survived in the Acambaro region to a very late time.

The idea of a Middle American "lost world"—to use the phrase from Sir Arthur Conan Doyle's novel—may not seem so bizarre if we consider a few examples of so-called "living fossils." The tuatara or *Sphenodon* of New Zealand descends from a Mesozoic group of reptiles which elsewhere became extinct more than 100 million years ago. In 1938 the coelacanth lungfish was discovered in the sea along the African coast, although no fossils of this group of fish are found in rocks more recent than the Cretaceous Period, 85 million years ago. The common horseshoe crab has remained virtually unchanged for 100 million years.

No rule of nature states that because dinosaurs died out in other parts of the world a long time ago they could not have survived in Mexico until quite recently. Possibly Mrs. Regler and I actually witnessed the discovery of the unfossilized bones of one of these reptiles in an extreme state of decay.

Thermoluminescent dating confirms the great antiquity of the mysterious Julsrud culture, perhaps America's oldest.

Part II

One morning a workman came to Mr. Julsrud in a great state of excitement, saying the bones of a monster had been found in a nearby canyon. Mr. Julsrud, who was eighty at the time, grabbed his hat and we all started for the canyon. About a mile from our goal the road gave out and we went the rest of the way on foot. We reached the edge of a ravine that was more than a hundred feet deep, and we had to climb down its vertical wall, holding onto each other and to

Mr. Julsrud. Of course he should not have attempted the descent, but nothing would hold him back.

About ten feet above the bottom of the canyon, the man pointed to a place where some strange forms protruded from the canyon wall. We got them down and found that they were large, porous, and very decayed. They looked as if they might have been bones, but they were not shaped like any bones we knew, and they were not fossilized.

The ascent of the canyon wall proved much more dangerous than the descent. Mr. Julsrud had to be pulled from above and pushed from below, and now for the first time I noticed the whole wall of the canyon was rotted and shook in a menacing fashion with every movement we made. However, we finally reached the top of the canyon safely.

On examination, our unfossilized remains looked a little like the bony flanges on the back of the dinosaur Stegosaurus. I took them to New York with me and showed them to my friend Dr. Harold B. Anthony, Assistant Director of the American Museum of Natural History. He looked at them in complete puzzlement. Rotted bones they could be, but not of any creature alive in the world today. He ended up by calling them "earthy concretions," meaning simply "unexplained." The thought of unfossilized bones of Stegosaurus was too much for him.

When a comparison is made between the figurines and the known fossil species of Mesozoic reptiles, some rather startling facts appear. To be sure, there are few instances of close similarity between one figurine and one extinct species of Mesozoic dinosaur, but there are many cases of figurines that seem to imply some real knowledge of ancient forms of life.

We know, for example, that birds developed from reptiles in the Mesozoic era and that many dinosaurs had bird-like characteristics. These are not, of course, among the well-known dinosaurs. Yet some of Julsrud's reptile figures have birdlike heads. Even more astonishing, some Julsrud figurines seem to suggest the fat-tailed marsupials that are wholly extinct today except for the fat-tailed marsupial mouse of Australia. Only advanced students of paleontology would be likely to have heard of these fat-tailed species.

Also remarkable is a group of figurines that suggest the Mesozoic marine reptiles, the plesiosaurs. This group descended from land reptiles that adapted to an aquatic habitat. The plesiosaur ancestors undoubtedly had legs and a relatively short neck. Typical plesiosaurs had flippers and many had extremely long necks. Some of the Julsrud figurines have the long neck and feet; some have the short neck and feet. None shows the long neck with flippers, although this is the form known to the reading public. It would appear that if a faker produced these figurines, he must have made a great effort to avoid imitating known fossil species. He must have burrowed deep into the recesses of erudite paleontological literature; he must deliberately have sought out little-known forms. Even with these little-known forms he must have made it a point not to imitate any known species exactly, but instead to suggest species that might have existed although we have no record of them!

One notable exception is a very fine jet-black polished figurine about a foot tall. The late Ivan Sanderson considered this figurine a perfect representation of the dinosaur Brachiosaurus, the largest known dinosaur to roam both North America and East Africa. (Not all paleontologists agree with Sanderson, however.)

The Julsrud Collection also contains hundreds of representations of fictitious animals, animals that never could have existed. Here the imagination of the artists was boundless. Some of their productions certainly were inspired by the Indian myths, by the oral literature of the people, but some appear to have been inspired by the forms of dead trees or by hallucinations produced by drugs. Pipes in the collection suggest that their owners may have smoked some drug-containing herb.

In the past few years new evidence that supports a great antiquity for developed Indian cultures in America has come to light. This is connected with the pyramid of Cuilcuilco near Mexico City. Ages ago this pyramid was encircled and nearly swamped by a flood of lava from two volcanoes not far off. The controversy that has raged over the age of this pyramid recently was at least partially resolved when the date of the lava flow was fixed by radiocarbon. The flow occurred between A.D. 200 and 400, and archaeologists now have concluded that the pyramid was built at about the same time as the other pyramids near Mexico City.

However, Mrs. Regler and I visited the pyramid on our way to Acambaro, and she picked up a ceramic fragment which we examined and discarded. Later when we started our study of the Julsrud Collection, we remembered that the piece we had found lying on the ground near the pyramid was very like some of the Julsrud artifacts.

The archaeologist who excavated the pyramid for the Mexican government was Byron S. Cummings, and he made a discovery that has been overlooked by every archaeologist subsequently examining the pyramid. Cummings dug down through the sediment that had accumulated over the lava floor (which has been given the name of the Pedrigal) and very correctly estimated the age of the lava flow at about 2,000 years without the benefit of radiocarbon. Then he dug through the lava flow itself and found artifacts under it representing the early classical period; that is, the cultures flourishing about 2,000 years ago.

Cummings went on digging, until eighteen feet below the lava flow he came upon the platform that had been

built around the pyramid when it was originally constructed. He estimated that the eighteen feet of sediment that
had accumulated over the platform before the lava flow
represented a lapse of about 6,000 years. There were three
"culture horizons" in this sediment.

That is, from bottom to top there was first a layer indicating a very primitive culture, interrupted by a layer of
volcanic ash, then a thick sterile layer indicating no vegetation. Above this was another layer of rich soil containing
the artifacts of a much more advanced culture, which,
however, showed similarities to the earlier primitive culture. This second culture was wiped out in turn by an
eruption that deposited another layer of sterile volcanic
ash. Finally, just under the lava flow, were the artifacts of
the early classical period.

Note that all these three culture horizons had developed
over the basement platform of the pyramid. The accumulation of sediment could begin only after the pyramid had
been abandoned. The evidence therefore indicates, according to Cummings, that the pyramid was abandoned at least
8,000 years ago, which would make the structure twice as
old as the Great Pyramid of Egypt!

Cummings went on to show that the internal evidence
of the structure of the pyramid indicates a long period of
continuous use, thus pushing its possible date of construction back still further. When we consider the Egyptian-
looking artifacts in the Julsrud Collection, we must wonder
whether some of that culture, including pyramid building,
did not originate in America.

Cummings' estimate of the age of the sediments under
the Pedrigal has been modified by radiocarbon dates. If we
accept the four dates from the deepest layers as representing
the earliest deposits over the temple platform, we have an
average date of about 2000 B.C. as the time of its abandon-

ment. If it was in use for a considerable period of time there is no reason to exclude the possibility that its construction takes us back 5,000 years or more.

Compassion for human frailty demands that we put ourselves in the position of the archaeologists who have denounced the Julsrud Collection as a barefaced fraud, even while admitting the honesty of Waldemar Julsrud himself. They have pointed the finger of suspicion at Odilon Tinajero and his sons who, they claim, must have made the figurines. The reasons no archaeologist so far has accepted the collection as genuine may be summed up as follows:

Never in the previous history of archaeology have such vast numbers of artifacts been found in a few acres of ground. This is answered by Julsrud's suggestion that the objects could have been a sacred collection buried to preserve it from the Spanish.

There is no precedent for the almost perfect preservation of so many delicate objects through burial in the earth. This objection is countered by the evidence that the objects were carefully buried while still intact.

The objects conform to no known cultures. We have answered this objection with evidence that the culture in question antedated by many thousands of years the known cultures of Indian America and that it may have been ancestral to them all.

The absence of patina or an accumulation of earth salts on most of the objects is inexplicable. With reference to this we present the consideration that the objects seem to have been buried in a sandy beach on the margin of the former lake. It is known that patina does not form in sand. Moreover, the position of the caches buried at an average depth of about four feet just over a gently sloping surface of volcanic ruff was such that rainwater which usually carries such salts would not accumulate and stand over them.

The reptiles are proof of forgery. We have shown that there were four possible sources of inspiration for the reptiles. One is the living reptiles of Middle America, a second is Indian folklore, a third is inspiration from the forms of dead trees, and a fourth is the very possible survival of some forms of great reptiles in Middle America.

In addition to these five general objections, archaeologist Charles Di Peso claimed to have found proof of fraud. In an article in *American Antiquity* for April 1953, he explained how in a three days' examination of the collection and in an excavation on Bull Mountain he had found proof of fakery. However, his whole case was based on a misunderstanding of Odilon Tinajero's methods of work.

A cluster of small children accompanied Mrs. Regler and me in our excavation on Bull Mountain. They wanted to be in on the dig. They scrambled through the dirt looking for pieces for us and found a good many. Many times Odilon Tinajero would have to stop work for the day when a cache was only half removed from the ground. He did not dare leave the cache open because of the small boys, so he refilled the hole. Then, when Mr. Di Peso wanted to see a dig, Tinajero, not understanding the mistake he was making, did not take him to a new site but simply reopened a site where he already had worked and where he had done a refill. Di Peso saw this and naturally assumed that Tinajero himself had buried the pieces. It was an honest mistake, but disastrous.

Reasoning that a fake is a crime and therefore must follow the laws of criminology, I wrote about this collection to Erle Stanley Gardner, the lawyer who became America's most famous author of detective fiction, and asked him to apply the principles of criminology to its analysis. It was years before he and I were able to visit the site together, but in the meantime, through correspondence, we were able to clarify a good many important points.

In the first place, Gardner agreed with me that if a group of fakers had made all the pieces, their style would be recognizable throughout the whole collection. Every criminal and every criminal gang have their own methods of operating. Police often can identify a criminal or a gang from the method of the crime. From the photographs I sent him, Mr. Gardner said it was obvious that no one individual or group could have made the pieces.

A second consideration is motive. What could have been the motive for faking the objects? Mr. Julsrud did not sell them and therefore had no motive. One peso, amounting to twelve cents in American currency, would never have repaid Tinajero or his sons for the labor involved in making them, for some of them are four feet long or four feet high, and many are extremely intricate in workmanship. Moreover, Julsrud had a theory that the collection was *Atlantean*. He told everybody about this theory, but nothing in the collection suggests Atlantis. As already stated, what is depicted in the collection is a primitive Indian culture.

A third consideration is the competence of Odilon Tinajero. Tinajero left school in the fourth grade and thus could barely read and write. Yet the collection displays profound knowledge of many subjects—Indian social habits, Indian mythology, and rare and exotic extinct animals. It also exhibits extraordinary artistic skill of which neither Tinajero nor his sons ever showed any independent evidence.

A fourth consideration is opportunity. All the ceramic objects have been baked in open fires. This means a fantastic consumption of firewood, a rare and expensive commodity in modern Acambaro. Also it would have involved a great deal of smoke observable by the entire community.

Yet very thorough investigations made to discover the fakers have been fruitless. Several of these were carried out by the municipal authorities, and one was carried out by a local teacher, Prof. Ramon Rivera, who spent weeks searching for the fakers, making use of the whole gossip network of the city. Every effort to find such fakers drew a blank.

Strangely, one of the important points in this problem of fakery has been ignored by everyone concerned: Some of the artifacts are made not of ceramic but of hard stone. These objects, although executed in the same style as many of the ceramic animal figurines, are obviously old, for they have been subjected to the effects of erosion, which cannot be faked without extraordinary expertise.

In 1968 Erle Stanley Gardner asked me to meet him in Acambaro for another examination of the collection, and I prevailed upon Mrs. Regler to join us there. Mr. Gardner, who previously had investigated other archaeological problems, was greatly impressed by the size and variety of Julsrud's collection and the fine quality of many of the pieces. Although he was careful not to pose as an archaeologist, he obviously considered asinine the theory that the artifacts are fakes. He accompanied us to Bull Mountain and himself pried out of the adobe wall of one of the houses on the site a piece of ceramic similar in style to the Julsrud pieces. "Some fakers!" I heard him mutter under his breath.

In 1968 a new technique for the first time made it possible to date ceramics by the radiocarbon method, and I was principally interested on this visit to Acambaro in getting specimens for this test. Mr. Gardner contributed enough money for one test and Mr. Arthur Young for another. We finally had three tests made, with most interesting results.

The radiocarbon method of age determination depends on the rate of decay of the very small percentage of radioactive carbon in the air. Only a few carbon atoms in a million are radioactive. In a period of about 5,000 years half of such atoms lose their extra electrons and become normal carbon atoms. Only living things absorb carbon from the air (or from other living things that have absorbed carbon from the air), and these all contain the same percentage of radiocarbon as the air itself. When they die, they stop taking in carbon, and so gradually the percentage of radiocarbon in them will decline. The measurement of the precise amount of radiocarbon remaining in an object will then give its age.

Ceramic baked clay may contain some radiocarbon, either because the original clay contained vegetable matter or because it absorbed carbon in the process of baking. The open fire method of baking clay, used with the Julsrud figurines, did add organic carbon to them. We faced a difficult problem: how to deal with the possibility that the original clay, taken from some deposit in the earth, might also have contained carbon from decayed vegetable matter. Such carbon would falsify the result since it would mean we would be dating not the figurine but the clay itself.

However, the situation was not as bad as it seemed at first, for clay tends to be deposited in a pure state, and most clay deposits are so old as to have lost any radiocarbon they originally may have had. In practice, most vegetable matter contained in the raw clay would have gotten into the clay when it was collected for molding figurines. Thus the vegetable matter would tend to be about the same age as the wood used to bake the clay.

The first samples I submitted to the laboratory of Isotopes, Inc., in New Jersey, were all from one figurine which had been broken. The pieces were about half an inch thick and showed a dark color due to carbon in their centers. This suggested there had been much decayed vegetable matter mixed with the original clay.

The samples for the second and third tests were selected for the absence of such originally included carbon. For the second test I included some fragments of figurines that seemed to represent extinct animals.

These approximate dates are the results obtained for the three samples: Sample One, 1640 B.C.; Sample Two, 4530 B.C.; and Sample Three, 1110 B.C. Although it would be desirable to have many more tests, I consider these samples properly selected and that the results probably are close to the truth. It is noticeable that the oldest date was found for samples that showed no evidence whatever of the inclusion of carbonaceous matter in the clay.

By 1972 a new and reliable method of dating ceramics had been fully tested in the laboratories of the University of Pennsylvania. Arthur Young submitted two figurines from the Julsrud Collection to Dr. Froelich Rainey, Director of the Pennsylvania Museum, for dating by this new method. Both figurines, and one of the same type submitted by archaeologist Di Peso, were found to date to 2500 B.C. This brings them, it may be noted, within the range of the occupation of the pyramid of Cuilcuilco.

In a letter dated September 13, 1972, addressed to Young, Dr. Rainey wrote:

> When we made the analysis of the first Julsrud figurines in 1969, we were just then perfecting the thermoluminescence method of dating pottery, and I was very cautious about reporting these dates because at that time there were all sorts of possible 'bugs' in the thermoluminescence system. As you know, Di Peso's study of the Julsrud Collection and that area convinced him that these were all fakes, and in view of the uncertainty of the TL method in 1969, I didn't want to put these particular dates on the line publicly.
>
> Now, after we have had years of experimentation both here and at the lab at Oxford, we have no doubt at all about the dependability of the thermoluminescence method. We may have errors of up to 5 to10 percent in absolute dating, but we are no longer concerned about unexpected 'bugs' that might put the whole system in doubt.

I should also point out that we were so concerned about the extraordinarily ancient date of these figurines that Mark Han in our lab made an average of eighteen runs on each one of the four samples. Hence, this is a very substantial bit of research on these particular pieces. Also our lab comments that to give accurate thermoluminescence dates, the pottery would have to be fired above 500 degrees centigrade. The three figurines analyzed might not have been fired to that degree of heat which could explain an error, except that all three figurines give roughly the same age. If they had been fired incompletely, I would expect the TL dates to be extremely variable.

All in all, the lab stands on these dates for the Julsrud material, whatever this means in terms of archaeological dating in Mexico or in terms of fakes versus authentic pieces.

With these tests, then, the case rests. Additional tests undoubtedly will be made, and these may eventually establish the time range during which the people who made the figurines existed as a people. This could have been, and probably was, a very long time, for the collection itself testifies to a development from very crude beginnings to a final level of artistic attainment that in some ways was not equaled by any of the later cultures we know from Indian America.   ■

An Ancient Michigan Mystery

Betty Sodders
June 1993

The accidental unearthing of some unusual statues and a tablet covered with indecipherable symbols confounds archaeological experts.

In the fall of 1896, two local lumberjacks were cutting wood for John McGruer of Newberry, Michigan. Suddenly, a mink darted under the roots of an upturned hemlock. Peering beneath the tree, they saw an almost human face looking up at them.

Believing at first that they had discovered mummified human remains, the men quickly dug the item out. It turned out to be a statue made of a pinkish clay, and in their haste they broke it. The men removed two more idols, completing a family of a man, woman, and child almost life-like in proportion, weighing a total of nearly a thousand pounds. From that time on, the statues were known as McGruer's Gods.

Excavating further, the lumberjacks dislodged a tablet of the same material. Weird as these perplexing artifacts were, it was the tablet that caused rumors to run rampant through this small, turn-of-the-century Lake Superior village. The inscribed tablet became known as the Newberry Stone. It measured eighteen by twenty-four inches. One surface was divided into 140 squares, each containing a strange, undecipherable character. The symbols resembled both Egyptian hieroglyphics and Greek letters.

Where did these perplexing artifacts come from? They were not American Indian finds. Why were they hidden in this remote boreal forest cache? The tree that sheltered them proved to be more than 200 years old. Its root system had grown normally around the statues of the gods and the mysterious tablet, sheltering them before the wind blew the hemlock over.

The Michigan wonders were displayed locally and then, as the excitement waned, McGruer's Gods and the Newberry Stone were stored in an old barn along the Tahquamenon River. At the mercy of the elements, time and vandalism took their toll. The idols and tablet were damaged beyond repair.

When first discovered, photographs of the objects had been taken and forwarded to the Smithsonian Institute in Washington, D.C., for research purposes, but they, too, were lost. My book, *Michigan Prehistory Mysteries* (Avery Color, 1989), first described these ancient anomalies. A sequel soon followed. Both publications delve into my research on the "gods" and the stone, as well as other Michigan prehistory material.

Were the "gods" Pre-Columbian, Egyptian, or Phoenician artifacts? Why were they buried in Michigan? Hints of prehistoric foreign intrusion seem to surface. All I had to work with was a hand-drawn sketch of the male god, plus a blueprint drawing of the tablet's strange characters. This latter sketch was lamp-blacked by an early historian when the artifacts were unearthed in 1896. Searching old newspaper files, I located photographs of both the male and female idols. She was pictured both nude and pregnant, an ancient fertility symbol of the first order.

A reproduction of the Newberry stone. Were its puzzling symbols, similar to those on the equally perplexing Phaistos disk, a 2,000-year-old agricultural omen?

Somewhere down the line, the child god had been lost. Two years later, a researcher turned up the original photographs from the depths of the Smithsonian and we learned the identity of the child statue. These pictures proved that the idol was a boy—the spitting image of his father. The remains of the Newberry artifacts reside at the Fort de Buade Museum at St. Ignace, Michigan. The head and torso of the man and the head of the woman remain, while the Newberry Stone is reduced to clay rubble.

Prof. Barry Fell, President of the Epigraphic Society and author of *America, B.C.*, was able to solve part of the tablet's mystery. The message was written as a magic quadrangle that proved to be an agricultural omen relating to the sowing of seeds. It is written in a text similar to that of the well-known Cypro-Minoan script that also appears on the Phaistos Disk, a terra cotta plate covered with indecipherable hieroglyphs, found on the southern coast of Crete, and dating to 1700 B.C. The language of the text appears to be a creolinized form of Minoan, having a vocabulary similar to that of Hittite, but lacking the formal declensions and conjugations. Hittite was the forerunner of the Greek language, ancient in scope.

Why was a clay tablet relating to early Greece or the Minoan culture discovered in this remote section of Michigan's Upper Peninsula? In early times, people often depicted their gods as man, woman, and child. But where did McGruer's Gods originate? Records, books of mythology, and ancient drawings were searched, but nothing similar turned up. The closest example was the "Sickle God" of the Tisza culture of Szegvar, Hungary, an ancient race of people dating back to 4000 B.C. Their nude goddess predated this figure.

Just before *Michigan Prehistoric Mysteries* was published, I picked up a back copy of *Smithsonian* magazine. In the March 1975 issue, on page 36, was the photograph of a statue with a head that almost perfectly matched our goddess. It had been unearthed at Lepenski Vir in present-day Hungary. It was found in a 1946 archaeological dig and belonged to the ancient Starcevo culture, former neighbors of the above-mentioned Tisza culture. They existed from around 8000 B.C. to A.D. 500. One other fact fits—the ancient script on the Newberry Stone matched writing used in this culture.

While these puzzle pieces fit nicely together, we are right back to square one. Why were the McGruer's Gods and the

Newberry Stone found in Michigan? Perhaps foreign intrusion plays a role. The 5,000-year-old copper culture mining industry discovered on Isle Royale and the Keweenaw Peninsula has never fully been explained either. Documented proof of foreign intrusion is indicated on ancient petroglyphs at Peterborough, Canada, showing Norse ships taking on copper ingots.

I believe that an ancient people did sail across the ocean and arrived on North America's East Coast, then traveled inland for Lake Superior copper, which was in great demand in Europe. These people brought along their mining know-how, plus their customs, which included gods and agricultural omens. With this knowledge they fashioned facsimiles of their gods and a tablet out of local Newberry, Michigan, clay.

Scientific testing of these artifacts proved the hardened clay idols and tablet were manufactured from local material. Perhaps these strange artifacts were hidden for reasons of security during troubled times. When the Jesuits arrived in the 1600s, they found stone statues and altars resembling dolmens of ancient cultures. The Jesuits destroyed these objects, positioned along the Great Lakes shorelines, for religious reasons. The *Jesuit Relations* speaks of a particularly unusual copper statue, depicted with a European-style beard. Indians did not have beards.

Perplexing pictographs and petroglyphs, dolmens, rings of stone, incised discs, mounds, pyramids, earthworks, ancient gardens, stone cairns, engraved rocks in ancient script, copper ox hides, and rock maps are countless signs of foreign intrusion in Michigan's prehistoric past. For now, the riddle of McGruer's Gods and the Newberry Stone remains a Michigan mystery. ∎

Found: The Lost Pyramids of Rock Lake

Frank Joseph
October 1989

Huge objects not created by nature lie beneath the surface of a placid Wisconsin lake.

The yellow anchor line ran straight from a bright, day-lit surface ten feet overhead, disappearing in the opposite direction through the murky depths far below. Following the taut nylon cord down into the green shadows, my body shuddered at twenty feet, as I crossed the thermocline—that barrier separating pleasantly warm from uncomfortably cold temperatures.

Continuing a slow descent, I glanced up to see the silver trail of my air bubbles race toward the surface along a solitary sunbeam twisting through the water. For some moments longer I sank into the buoyant underworld, unable to perceive its bottom, but when my depth gauge read thirty-five feet, the emerald opacity parted like a filmy curtain, revealing the mud floor another twenty feet below. Its brown base, apparently devoid of life, stretched like a surreal desert in all directions.

I knew this submarine wasteland well. In two years of exploration my colleagues and I had criss-crossed its waters numerous times. Always the objects of our search—if they indeed existed—had eluded our persistent efforts to find them. Now, materializing some fifteen feet directly beneath my flippers, a colossal figure reared up out of the mud bottom and stretched across it like a paved highway. Its appearance was so unnatural and unexpectedly huge that I paused momentarily in my descent, surveying the out-sized structure from my hovering vantage-point.

The sides of a gargantuan rectangle ran in straight, parallel lines, the walls sloping steeply and uniformly inward. The apex rose almost to a point, but was flattened at the very top, running the full length of the structure. On its southern end rested our anchor, and I resumed my descent, following its line down for a closer look at the site.

This end formed a blunt triangle rising about ten feet above the silt. From our previous studies, I knew the silt layer to be at least two feet thick. It covered the actual mud strata another four feet deep; beneath lay a clay-like compacted mud strata resting on the rock bottom. The actual height of the structure, then, was about eighteen feet. Its width, judging from the angle of the sloping walls, I estimated at thirty-five feet. Most of the structure was thus buried in mud. The narrow rectangle visible above the silt represented, therefore, only its upper third.

I set out to determine its total length by swimming northward along its flattened apex. As I did so, I could see that the structure was no geologic rock heap, some haphazard remnant from the last Ice Age, but an ordered collection of round, black stones, selected for size, and piled up to form not so much a true pyramid as a kind of elongated tent-like configuration. The stones atop the apex, however, were bigger and seemed mostly square, resembling large cubes. One oversized cube, later referred to as the Altar Stone, was uniformly square, suggesting human influence.

Other strange sights came into view. There was a barbell-shaped stone, and stretching over a long section of the western slope were the remains of a thick, plaster-like substance. Further along, toward the northern half of the structure, I passed over a curious L-shaped object similar to a pelvic bone, encrusted with snails. A further fifteen feet along the apex, I saw another similarly L-shaped object made neither of stone nor bone, but of metal, possibly copper. I was astounded by the prodigious length of the whole structure.

Having counted my kicks, I determined that the site was about one hundred feet long. Perhaps an additional twelve feet were lost in the mud bottom. It was here, at the extreme northern end, that I saw its triangular terminus, identical to its southern counterpart, slope steeply into the silt.

Checking my depth-gauge (fifty-one feet), I swam back and forth over the structure, studying its details, until my air supply began to give out. Carefully re-inflating my bouyancy control jacket, I ascended slowly, pausing for decompression at thirty feet, then I rose back across the thermocline through warmer temperatures and into the sunbeams probing the water around me. Popping to the wavy surface, I tore the regulator from my mouth and yelled to my expectant comrades in the little boat bobbing nearby that we had found the lost pyramid of Rock Lake.

Rock Lake is in the charming Wisconsin town of Lake Mills, located between Milwaukee and Madison, not far over the Illinois border. Three miles east of the lake lies Aztalan, a public archaeological park consisting of two truncated, earthen pyramids partially surrounded by a tall stockade—the modern recreation of a great wall that once encompassed a ceremonial center not unlike the cities built by the Mayas, in far-away Yucatan. Its actual name is unknown. It has been called Aztalan only since its first excavation, in the mid-1800s.

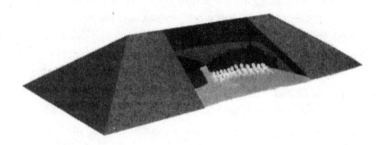

Cut-away view of the pyramid, based on a similar structure at nearby Aztalan, Wisconsin, archaeological park.

Aztalan prospered as late as the early fourteenth century, when its civilized inhabitants finally succumbed to population pressures generated by the indigenous Plains Indians. They torched the Troy-like walls erected to shut them out, then sacked the city, culminating their wild destruction in an orgy of killing and cannibalism. The story of Aztalan seems somehow related to the old legends of pyramids at the bottom of near-by Rock Lake.

The first modern European settlers in Lake Mills, during the 1830s, heard tales of "stone teepees" under the water from the local Winnebago Indians. In subsequent years, in periods of extended drought, when the lake level was low, fishermen sometimes glimpsed what appeared to be large, rectangular structures beneath the surface. During one such period, the future mayor of Lake Mills himself caught sight of a pointed, submerged figure, and the quest for the lost pyramids was on. An imaginative array of search materials soon arose to solve the mystery. Everything from aerial photography and inverted, illuminated periscopes to homemade diving bells and elaborate draglines were enthusiastically put into practice beginning at the turn of the century. But Rock Lake stubbornly refused to share her secrets.

For eight decades, search teams of amateurs and professionals alike scoured the lake, with only fleeting success. Sometimes they stumbled upon a suspicious figure, but when they returned to claim it, the structure was gone. Although less than three miles across at its widest point and perhaps ninety feet at its deepest, the bottom of Rock Lake is composed of high hills and steep trenches that might conceal

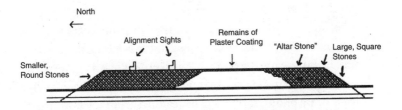

Everything points to the Rock Lake pyramid being of artificial construction, states explorer and author Frank Joseph.

even a large object. While its spring-fed waters are clean, they are normally thick with the bloom of algae, reducing visibility to arm's length. This typically poor clarity is often further reduced by the loose silt bottom which is easily disturbed, billowing into impenetrable clouds of mud. Conditions are no better in the winter. Beneath the ice, millions of thriving micro-organisms make observation very difficult.

By the late 1960s, most professional archaeologists had given up on the credibility of Rock Lake's pyramids. Besides, they argued, the Indians never built in stone on a large scale, especially under water!

But the persistence of a myth often conceals at least some fragmented truth. Thus intrigued, I began scuba-diving in Rock Lake in the spring of 1987—not haphazardly, but only after learning as much as I could about the history and geology of the area and particularly from veteran fishermen, whose lines sometimes snagged on unusual submarine formations. After a dozen dives, however, I had nothing to show for my efforts but a long line of used up air tanks.

Undeterred, my friends and I redoubled our efforts through autumn and into winter—without success. One scheme after another failed, and 1988 was more than half wasted before we finally ran out of ideas. We needed a fresh perspective, so I flew to Loch Ness, Scotland, home of another, better known search. I went there not for Nessie's sake, but to study the equipment used over the years to find her, much of which was displayed at the big Monster Museum. By far the most impressive instrument was an American side-scan sonar, a device that uses sound waves to take highly accurate photographic image readings from the bottom of a loch, a river, or a lake. Resolved to employ such high-tech equipment at the site of our Wisconsin quest, I returned home, contacted a side-scan sonar operator/owner in Muskegon, Michigan, and began preparations for our biggest assault on the pyramids.

On the morning of June 4, 1988, a small flotilla carrying scuba divers, surveyors, reporters, and geophysicists escorted the *Sea Search*—Craig Scott's sonar boat—across Rock Lake. By noon, his towed side-scan torpedo located an enormous structure off the northeast shore in nearly sixty feet of water. Readouts from the graph defined the submerged object as an unnatural formation. Owing to the unprecedentedly superb visibility that day, Doug Cossage, my former diving instructor from Lansing, Illinois, made a clear videotape recording of the site with his underwater video camera. He was, according to plan, the first man down on the target. Other divers later retrieved fragments of the plaster-like substance coating a section of its western wall.

Analyzed at the University of Wisconsin, in Madison, these samples proved to be "unnaturally formed," and further investigation of the compound may help determine the age of construction, which so far is unknown. Not coincidentally, the great stockaded walls surrounding Aztalan were originally covered over entirely with a heavy plaster, the same building material and technique discovered in Rock Lake's structure.

Dr. James Scherz, Professor at the University of Wisconsin in Madison, after viewing the Gossage video tape, said he believes the strange L-shaped objects atop its apex may be devices used to align the structure to True North; Rock Lake site is, after all, oriented due north. Dr. Scherz suspects the sunken structure contains important astronomical correspondences with the earthen pyramids of Aztalan, especially as regards the Polar or North Star.

Even as this report is being written, new revelations from what has come to be called Structure Number 1, or the Limnatis Pyramid, are coming to light. Limnatis was the Roman Goddess, Diana, in her manifestation as protectoress of sacred lakes. After the civilization of which it was a part fell so violently, the pyramid's new name is appropriate, especially in view of its chief function. Although no human remains have yet been brought up from Structure Number 1, there is little doubt regarding its original purpose as a mass-burial mound. Similar, earthen pyramids at Cahokia, in southern Illinois, were charnel houses used to entomb families of the leading aristocracy.

Nor is Limnatis the only such anomaly at the bottom of Rock Lake. At least nine other structures, some of them wildly different from our first discovery, have been identified, and at least two of them have been mapped and photographed.

What, then, do these mysterious buildings represent? How did they arrive in their bizarre location, unique in all the world? Who made them? And why? The answers to at least some of these questions are at last available. The level of Rock Lake, for example, has been gradually rising since it was formed 10,000 years ago. If someone stood on its shore a thousand years ago, at the beginning of the last suspected period of prehistoric civilization here, that person would have seen the tops of hills protruding above the lower water line as little islands. On these the civilizers interred their honored dead, over which they heaped burial mounds of stone covered with thick coatings of pinkish white plaster to give the exterior a smooth surface. During the centuries that followed, the steadily rising waters rose over the structures, eventually hiding them beneath the surface. The drowned pyramids belong to a forgotten necropolis, a sunken city of the dead.

There is no place on Earth like Rock Lake. We found its legendary structures, but who lies under their ancient stones? The answer to that vital question is still a well-kept secret. ∎

Ancient Druid Ruins in New York?

Philip J. Imbrogno
July 1994

Scattered throughout New York state are amazing stone chambers and monoliths that closely resemble Europe's druidic ruins—and they are found in areas with heavy UFO sightings. Is there a connection?

Southern New York state, despite being densely populated, holds great mysteries. From 1983 to 1990, thousands of people from many professions witnessed a boomerang-shaped UFO, with multicolored lights, perhaps larger than a football field. I have encountered a closely related mystery—strange stone monoliths and chambers scattered throughout the New York counties of Westchester, Putnam, and Dutchess.

In the mid-1980s I was investigating UFO sightings in the Hudson River Valley area of New York State. There were so many sightings documented in my book *Night Siege: The Hudson Valley UFO Sightings* (6,000 reports) that I was able to classify and plot them accurately on maps. The reports fell into two categories—UFO sightings from a distance, including many Close Encounters of the First Kind (sightings within 500 feet), Close Encounters of the Second Kind (trace cases, marks in the ground, burns and residue left by the UFO), CE3s (a sighting of a humanoid creature associated with the UFO), and actual cases where people claim to have been abducted by the creatures in the UFO (an abduction or a Close Encounter of the Fourth Kind).

A number of reports had little to do with UFO sightings, but originated from the sighting area. They consisted of strange sounds, sightings of unusual balls of light, globes of energy, electromagnetic phenomena, ghost-like entities, and psychic phenomena. This second category I called High Strangeness Reports (HSR) and kept separate from UFO-related data.

The data was plotted on two maps: one of UFO and UFO-related reports, the other showing the location of the HSR. There seemed to be no direct pattern to the UFO sightings, but the center of all such activity in the Hudson Valley was in the little township of Kent Cliffs. This seemed to be the point of UFO emanation—the first and last sightings were reported there. This was true for reports made during a six-year period.

Plotting the HSR on a second map, I found that 342 occurrences from 1985–1992 occurred in small, concentrated areas less than a half-mile in diameter. The location of these High Strangeness Areas (HSA) also paralleled the UFO reports, especially the close encounters. There was a definite connection between reports of paranormal phenomena and UFO sightings. It was as if the appearance of the UFO triggered these events.

I was curious about these HSAs and organized a search party. I worked with a number of people, a "research team," composed of individuals from many different professions. Equipped with cameras and two-way radios, we combed the back hills of New York. It was quite a task, since some of the locations were very desolate and we had to walk a mile or so into the brush.

At every location we found an array of strange standing stones, carved and arranged in patterns indicating that whoever put them there did so with some idea in mind. The most interesting structures were the stone chambers. Tucked under a wooded knoll or camouflaged behind bushes and wild flowers, they had gloomy stone doorways, and behind them a pitch-black cavity burrowing thirty to forty feet into the earth. The walls and ceilings are typically composed of massive slabs of granite and quartzite, expertly cut and fit together with great precision.

We could walk inside these chambers and do a detailed study on how the stones were cut and placed together. When we first found them, it seemed only a coincidence that they were also located in the HSR, but after finding more at every location, it became clear that there was a connection between these structures and the unusual events reported.

I researched the history of these structures, trying to find a link to UFOs and related phenomena. I spent hours in libraries, museums, and historical societies, talking with people living in the Putnam County area, both long-time residents and professional archaeologists. Still, I could not find out who built the chambers. Everyone I spoke with had their own idea about who the builders were.

There are more than fifty chambers in the Hudson River Valley, and they are found only on the east side of the Hudson. Whoever built the chambers was very particular about the type of stone used. Most chambers are built from fine quartz granite, quartz, and quartzite. Most of the standing stones are carved from limestone, and some larger ones are composed mostly of pink granite that contains the mineral feldspar. This type of stone is common on the east side of the Hudson, but is replaced mostly by shale and some slates and limestone on the west side. That is why chambers were found only on one side of the valley.

There are many theories about the origin of the stone chambers and carved stone structures. They may have been built by ancient Celtic explorers who arrived in the northeast several thousand years ago. Exploring this theory, I found a reference to the structures dating to 1787. The local colonial settlers compared them to similar structures in Ireland built by the Druids and considered evil because they were part of the old religion of northern Europe. The Roman Catholic church outlawed the ancient Druid religion and identified it with the devil. In colonial times people were warned to stay away from these structures by the local priest, so there is hardly any information from this time because colonial people were afraid to talk about them.

It wasn't until the late 1700s, when the witch hunts finally died down, that farmers started using some of the chambers on their property as storage areas, but they were never used as root cellars.

During my research, I was introduced to a ninety-year-old Native American medicine man. He reported that the chambers and stones mark sacred ground, and that the spirits of the Earth live there.

When he was very young, he was told by his great grandfather that the chambers were built by people who came across the sea on long ships. He said "their eyes were as the sky [blue], with horns coming out of their heads [helmets with horns], and their faces were as fire [red beards and hair?]. When they left the stones and chambers, they could only be visited by a high chief or powerful shaman."

The last thing he said was intriguing: "If you are chosen and you listen closely, when you put your ear against the stone you can hear Mother Earth sing."

Much later I understood his meaning. We spent a day together, and although he had never progressed beyond grade school, his knowledge of history, nature, and metaphysics was so vast that, despite my years of college, I felt like a student with much to learn.

What if these structures were built by Druids? Druids worshiped the forces of nature, animals, energy from the Earth, and so on. If they did come to New York, they would surely have built structures to live in and carry on their religion. But why would they have come? Human beings explore for two basic reasons—curiosity and money. Evidence tells us that someone was doing surface mining in the hills of Putnam County long ago. Perhaps these people were looking for metal ores. Putnam County has some of the richest iron ore deposits in the world, which were mined until the first quarter of the twentieth century. It is not mined anymore because of the dense population.

All the chambers and standing stones are built on deposits of magnetite, a high-grade iron ore. There is also an underground stream or pool beneath most of them. All the locations showed a definite deviation in the compass, from three to 180 degrees, depending on the location. Studies with a magnetometer showed a negative magnetic anomaly (a great increase or decrease in the magnetic field of the Earth). This was surprising, since in the past UFO investigators suspected a connection between UFOs and magnetic anomalies. I believed it would be a positive deviation, but all our readings were negative deviations.

The deviations were so drastic that a physicist who looked at the data confirmed that it could only be produced artificially. A large, spherical mass composed of solid, high-grade magnetic iron ore could have been buried at least ten feet deep at each location. The magnetic energy seemed focused at one point. The presence of this anomaly could explain why people and animals have such drastic reactions when they stay too long at a site.

Some forty chambers I investigated over five years were in different states of decay, indicating that they were built over a long period of time and used by many different cultures.

There are two types of chambers—cylindrical and oval. The cylindrical ones seem larger, while the oval ones seem to have the highest ceilings. The stones are massive and are placed and held together without mortar. During my investigation, I brought people from many fields of work to view the chambers. These included a stone mason, a stone cutter, an architect, an engineer, a physicist, an astronomer psychologist, a parapsychologist, and a psychic. All were amazed at how skillfully the chambers were constructed.

Older chambers have a single stone over the doorway, while the more recent ones have two capstones. These doorway capstones are cut from massive slabs of granite and are a major factor in holding the ceiling and walls together. Whoever built these things grew better at it. The single capstone is not as sturdy as the double capstone, since several collapsed chambers were of single capstone construction.

How old are the stone monoliths and chambers of the Hudson Valley? An educated guess, using the available data, indicates that the first chambers were built about 2000 B.C., while the last chamber was constructed around A.D. 500, a long span of time. The people who built the newest chamber probably did not know the people who built the first chambers, but the technique was passed on, and the methods of construction improved. The first chambers may have been constructed by early Celts, while the later chambers were built by ancient Druids. This is not speculation. Convincing evidence suggests that most of the chambers were built by Druid explorers who came from the British Isles and up the Hudson River between 2,000 and 3,000 years ago.

One particular chamber had noticeable markings on the west side of the inside wall. I took a high-resolution photograph of the writing and sent it to a local ancient language expert. This person is a retired professor with an interest in these stone structures. I was told that the writing looked like a very ancient language called Ogham. Ogham writing comes from ancient Ireland and was the written language the Celts used more than 2,000 years ago. It was deciphered as being a prayer or a dedication to the Celtic-Druid god Bel or Beltain.

Several years before that, Dr. Barry Fell, a professor from Princeton University, found markings in a chamber close by that gave a dedication to the Druid goddess of the moon. Fell was convinced that these were ancient structures built by the Scottish-Irish, who came to northeast America more than 3,000 years ago.

On most of the chambers near a wall or on the outside wall are three slashes cut in the rock—the sign of the ancient Druid-Celtic religion. They represent the three forces of nature. Carvings of animals have also been found, including a bison, lions, bears, and turtles. Although most of these animals are no longer found there, they roamed New England around 2000 B.C.

In Fahnstock Park, near Putnam Valley, New York, are two chambers close together. On a flat stone planted into the ground are some interesting markings clearly showing the crescent moon and two bright planets in the western sky. The planets were probably Jupiter and Venus. Was this a record of a celestial event indicating when the chamber was constructed? There were several dates when a conjunction of that type took place: A.D. 1423, 1500 B.C., and 2772 B.C.

One of the best-preserved chambers is located just off Route 301 in Kent Cliffs. On the outside is a carving of an animal resembling a bird of prey. The ceilings are quite high and of magnificent construction. In the west wall I found a piece of limestone about eight inches in height, smoothly carved into a cone. Markings were etched in the rock, and some type of writing was found below.

The markings were small holes shaped like a little dipper, like the Pleiades star cluster. It is often mistaken for the Little Dipper by inexperienced stargazers. The writing below was once again in Ogham, but only a small portion could be translated. The stone praised the spirits of nature during a high holy day. The rest was severely weathered.

The Druids held the Pleiades as sacred. They believed that when this star cluster was directly overhead at midnight, it was a time when the spirits of the Earth and the gods and demi-gods from the other world could enter ours.

This constellation can be seen in that position from October 25 until November 2, peaking from October 30 to 31—on Halloween. The last week of October is when the majority of the paranormal events took place around these HSR. Is this just coincidence, or were the Druids onto something?

The balanced stone in North Salem lies just off Route 116. This road crosses near several reservoirs and has been the scene of a great number of close encounters with UFOs in Westchester County. Near one end of the road lies the stone, and eight miles away at the other end of the road is a chamber. People have reported a number of unusual stories concerning this stone.

In the wee hours of the morning, strange cloaked figures have been seen surrounding the stone, only to disappear into thin air when approached. Some people who have taken photographs of the stone have reported that their photos show globes and lights that appear to circle it. This stone is the location of the largest negative magnetic anomaly in the area. Visitors report an odd sensation when touching one edge. Some have even collapsed. This stone is the focus of all the chambers to the north of it: If you draw a line through all the chambers that are north of the stone, they all align with the huge North Salem Balanced stone. Whatever this stone's purpose is, it is channeling and perhaps focusing some amazing type of energy.

Another unusual spot not far from the Balanced Stone is Magnetic Mine Road, in Croton Falls. Located just off this isolated dirt road is a chamber. The area got its name because at the turn of the century it was mined for iron ore. The mines are extensive, and the area is catacombed with underground caverns. The earth below still contains a considerable amount of iron ore in a very pure form called magnetite. It is not mined anymore because of the high population nearby. Also, New York state and the Federal government bought the land. A large magnetic anomaly occurs there, and the center of the disturbance is just outside the chamber door.

Two couples returning home from a Broadway show in New York City took a shortcut through this area. One man, a lawyer, related the following: "We had been returning from the city in the car and I decided to take a shortcut through the reservoir area. In the car was my wife, my friend (who is also a lawyer), and his wife. As I crossed the bridge toward Magnetic Mine Road, the car began to buck and stop. The headlights went out and everything was dead. It was the summer, and it was hot, so we rolled down the windows.

"My friend, who was sitting in the front seat, looked toward his right and said he heard deer in the woods. He got out after grabbing a flashlight from the glove compartment, walked to the edge of the road, and shined the light. Then he ran back to the car screaming that he saw these people coming toward him. I asked him who they were, and he replied that they looked like they were from outer space.

"We thought he was kidding, trying to make light of the serious situation we were in since it was late at night. We laughed, but I'll never forget the fearful look on his face.

"We heard what sounded like several deer coming up the road from the woods. Then these three little guys came up the hill and started walking toward the car. They were short and wearing some kind of dark, tight-fitting uniform. They had very large heads, and when I shined the light at them, their eyes glowed red in the dark. Suddenly they ran down the side of the hill and it looked like they ran right into a hole in the side of the mountain. Then this object appeared in the sky, just over the location where these guys vanished. It was no more than several hundred feet in the air, and triangular, with very large lights of different colors. The UFO then moved over the road and projected down a number of lights that seemed to be scanning the road in wide circles. The object then moved back over the hill and vanished.

"I started the car again and it ran with no problem, like nothing was wrong. Upset, we drove home and decided not to talk about what had taken place and what we saw."

After investigating the area, I found a chamber where the beings were reported to have run into the "hole in the mountain." It was half-collapsed and one of the oldest stone structures in the Hudson Valley. I have received other reports of beings with glowing eyes and cloaked figures who emerged from the outside wall of the chamber.

A well-preserved chamber found just off Route 301 also has been the scene of some strange reports involving unseen forces and sightings of unusual beings. This chamber is an oval-shaped, double capstone type with a high ceiling, made mostly of granite with fine quartz, with some shale and slate. Although the magnetic anomaly there has the lowest reading, many people have had strange experiences in this chamber. A local resident of Kent named "Mike" related the following:

"I was taking a walk during the late part of the summer of 1992 when I passed by the chamber on 301. I knew about these things . . . but I didn't know too much about them. I had lived in Kent Cliffs for about three years and when I asked people about them, I would get a number of different answers, These things are real spooky, especially at night. It was about eleven P.M. and very dark, a clear sky with no moon.

"I walked by the chamber and noticed a faint red glow coming from inside. I heard a sound . . . like a soft electrical hum. I thought that someone was running some type of generator in there, so I crossed the street and walked through a short section of woods and entered the chamber. As soon as I entered, the red glow vanished along with the sound. I looked around and felt very uneasy, as if someone were watching me. You know the feeling, like you're in a dark cellar with someone down there with you. You can't see them but you know that you are not alone.

"It was no more than thirty seconds when . . . this force hit me, as if someone pushed me. I fell to the ground expecting to see someone standing there, but I saw no one at all.

"As I lay there I felt a presence, like there was someone standing there. I slowly got up and was ready to run out of the damn thing when I was struck again, this time in the face. It felt like some unseen force was slapping me around. I was hit at least four times, and the last time I once again fell to the ground. I looked at the opening and saw the figure of a man standing in the doorway. He was wearing a flowing white robe and had a long black beard with curly hair that hung over his shoulders. His eyes scared me to death. They seemed very dark, but glowed in the dark. In the center of his pupils it looked red. He just stood there looking at me. When my eyes met his, I could feel tingling up and down my spine.

"He raised his hand and pointed his finger at me. The message I got from the look on his face was that I was to leave and not return. Although it was dark, I could see him plainly. It seemed as if he was glowing with a soft white halo around his body.

"The figure then dissolved into a cloud of white mist, and the mist was drawn into a nearby rock just like there was a vacuum. The entire incident lasted about a minute or two, I then got up and ran out the chamber door.

"At night I still see the image of this guy in my sleep. Sometimes I wake up in the middle of the night in a cold sweat because I think he is waiting in the dark to take me away."

Beings of this type have been reported in several nearby chambers. Sometimes the entity is accompanied by Viking-like figures, sometimes by small, dwarf-like figures in hooded robes. Are they ghosts or ultraterrestrial beings, or is there a bridge between time and space at these sites, allowing the past, present, and future to coexist? Reports are too numerous to dismiss, and they are made by people who would rather forget that the entire experience took place.

A new case just occurred among one of the standing stones in Purchase. The witness claims that as he was watching the stone, several hooded entities appeared from nowhere and surrounded him, vanishing after several minutes. The chambers are some type of temple constructed by an ancient race 2,000 to 3,000 years ago. Similar chambers have been found in Massachusetts, New Hampshire, and Vermont. According to archaeologist Sal Trento, they were built around A.D. 500, but he agrees that the Hudson Valley chambers are much older and he is discouraged that no professional archaeologist is studying them.

The stone monoliths and chambers of southern New York are one of the world's great mysteries. They are lost in time. ∎

Ancient Asians in Pennsylvania

Cliff R. Towner
April 1998

*The first navigators on the Susquehanna River
may not have been who you think.*

Did some adventurous Chinese seaman, long before the first Native Americans, sail his rattan junk up the broad waters of the Susquehanna River into the future Keystone State? This seemingly far-fetched idea was once contemplated by a learned and respected archaeologist for the Pennsylvania Historical Commission, based on an exhaustive study of petroglyphs found on islands in the lower river.

The Susquehanna originates in central New York and meanders south through eastern Pennsylvania until it crosses northeast Maryland and finally empties into the Chesapeake Bay. Fed by hundreds of streams and rivers along its path, the small stream becomes a deep, wide waterway long before its final destination.

For centuries Native American tribes from the Iroquois to the Algonquins used the river as a highway to the sea. Like most cultures in the world, the various tribes and nations left written records of their existence, including petroglyphs—carvings on smooth, bare-faced rocks.

The petroglyphs on the lower Susquehanna River islands in Pennsylvania and Maryland have been known to scientists for many years. In 1871 the first accurate reference to them was made by the Anthropological Institute of New York. In 1889, Dr. W. J. Hoffman visited the region, made sketches of the petroglyphs, and declared them to be of Algonquin origin. Of course, by 1889, the first Yankee "graffiti artists" had arrived on the scene, and like most tourists, they left behind mementos of their visits, often carving names, initials, or dates over the original carvings, effectively obliterating any chance of interpretation. Initials dating from 1780 to the present have been found on top of engravings.

In the 1930s, President Roosevelt's New Deal put people to work building new highways, bridges, and, unfortunately for the petroglyphs in the Susquehanna, giant dams across many of the main waterways in the country. When construction began on a new dam at Safe Harbor at the border of York and Lancaster counties in Pennsylvania, the state Historical Commission realized the new facility would eventually inundate the several islands containing the most important petroglyphs.

Realizing that time was of the essence, the commission in 1930 authorized an archaeological survey of the most promising island sites. Archaeologist Donald A. Cadzow was appointed to head the two-year study. Hampered by seasonal rains, snow, and rising waters, the scientific team made rough sketches, took rubbings of several of the figures, and manhandled many of the marked boulders to the mainland in small boats. Cadzow's findings were published by the commission in 1934. The report was less than enthusiastically received by the author's peers in archaeological and epigraphic communities. In fact, because of the controversy, only a limited number of copies was printed. Today, only two copies remain in the archives of the Pennsylvania Historical Commission.

In his report, Cadzow admits that "all eastern archaeologists (agree) that the earliest known Native Americans in the area were Algonquins." However, he contends, the Iroquoian groups found in the area by the first Europeans were invaders. The report states that the Algonquins were the inferior group mentally, and, "We believe they were not capable of developing the complex conventionalized figures found on Walnut Island [one of several islands covered by the survey]."

"To the best of our knowledge," Cadzow continued, "the Walnut Island writing was neither Algonquin nor Iroquoian .... A thin layer of prehistoric culture was discovered in the earth on many of the islands in the area as well as on the mainland. On Walnut Island, however, this culture layer was separated from some of the conventionalized figures by a covering of about eight feet of hard-packed soil!"

To Cadzow, that discovery presented an unusual situation, contrary to the understood progress of human life. It indicated to him that a people "lived and passed away in Pennsylvania previous to its occupation by known Indians. The early group had reached a state of civilization far in advance of their successors, and the highly conventionalized petroglyphs may represent the only intellectual remains of these inhabitants of the lower Susquehanna Valley."

Walnut Island, the site that so excited the usually blasé scientist, was about ten miles above Safe Harbor, near the mouth of Costoga Creek. It was home to twenty-one groups of writings that were unquestionably from an entirely different period than those on the islands downriver.

While shrewdly disclaiming any personal belief in ancient Chinese being on the island, Cadzow did report that "a very close analogy can be made between the writings of the ancient Chinese and those found on Walnut Island." So close, in fact, that the skeptical scientist called on the services of several distinguished scholars of Oriental studies.

The Orientalists were unanimous in identifying nineteen of the twenty-one groups of writing as "identical" to Chinese pictographs, while the other two groups had a random resemblance to Chinese writings, although their interpretation was uncertain.

Some of the interpretations of the apparently Chinese pictographs included symbols for "well of water," "a hill fortress or temporary defense," "mountain or fortress," "stream," "wood or grass," "Sun," "water or lake," the numerals ten and three, "heavy rain," "high or prominent point," "big," and "soil."

"About the antiquity and culture of early man on the American continents much is still to be learned, and occasional bits of evidence of an advanced culture are brought to light in North America," Cadzow concluded. "We think superior groups migrated (or visited) onto this continent from the northwest."

Cadzow's report met with the derision and laughter of his contemporaries in 1934. Six decades later, more and more archaeologists, anthropologists, and epigraphic experts are turning up evidence from Alaska to the tip of South America that Native Americans were not the only immigrant groups that passed this way, left a record of their cultures, and faded into the mists of pre-history. ■

Did legendary lands like Atlantis and
Lemuria ever exist?

Lost Lands

Beyond the pillars of Hercules," Plato wrote in his *Dialogues*, lay the most enchanted land. It was an island continent inhabited by people with advanced knowledge. At the center of the island stood an immense temple to Poseidon, covered with silver and gold. Pavilions, ships, gardens, hot and cold springs, and great beauty, knowledge, and prosperity reigned in this land. Then, "there occurred violent earthquakes and floods," Plato wrote, "and in a single day and night of misfortune, the island of Atlantis disappeared into the depths of the sea."

Plato wrote about this fabled lost continent in the fourth century B.C. Ever since, people have been searching for the ruins of Atlantis. Many claim to have found them. In 1912, Paul Schliemann, grandson of the man who discovered the fabled site of Troy, claimed to have actual Atlantean artifacts in his possession. He had found the lost continent, he wrote in an article for the *New York American*, in the mid-Atlantic, west of Ireland.

Alas, within a short time, Schliemann's claims were proven to be fraudulent.

In 1940, the famed American healer and psychic Edgar Cayce had several visions of Atlantis, a land he said had harnessed nuclear energy, used advanced medical technology, and had mastered flight—more than fifty millennia ago!

Nuclear catastrophes occurring between 50,000 and 10,000 B.C. destroyed the continent, which was in the Caribbean, he said.

Over the centuries, researchers and explorers have identified more than two dozen different areas as the location of fabled Atlantis. The most commonly cited are in the Mediterranean, near Thera or Thesalonika, Greece; in the Caribbean, near Bimini; and in the middle of the Atlantic Ocean, between Europe and North America and south of Greenland. But despite all the claims that have been made, no one knows for sure if Atlantis ever existed.

Other fabled lands, too, have appeared and disappeared in history and in the human imagination. The best-known of these include Mu and Lemuria, generally thought to be located in the Pacific off the coast of Central America; El Dorado, the golden city of the ancient Americans, thought to be located in the Amazon rain forest; and Shangri-La, the earthly paradise someplace in the Himalayan Mountains.

In this chapter, FATE articles explore four fabled lands.

Nan Matol, Lost City of the Pacific

L. Sprague de Camp
January 1957

A startling theory regarding Nan Matol, the huge ruined city on Ponape in the Pacific, emerges from scientific findings.

Of all the world's lost cities—Angkor Wat, Petra, Zimbabwe, Chan Chan, Sijilmassa—none is wrapped in deeper mystery than Nan Matol, on the island of Ponape in the Pacific Ocean. Yet even at Nan Matol science has solved some of the enigmas that shroud this ruined metropolis.

Ponape lies a few degrees north of the equator in the eastern part of the Caroline Islands, between Truk on the west and Kusae on the east. It is the largest of the Carolines, with about 164 square miles. The climate is warm and humid, with much rain and occasional hurricanes. Like the other Micronesian islands, Ponape has plenty of birds and insects but no native land mammals save those, like pigs and rats, brought in by people. This indicates it was never part of a continent.

White people first saw Ponape on the evening of December 23, 1595. An explorer named Mendana had set out from Peru with four ships to hunt for Terra Australis, the Unknown Southland that was thought to fill most of the Southern Hemisphere. He found the Solomon Islands and died there. The surviving ship of the squadron, the *San Jeronimo*, under Pedro Fernandez de Quiros, then tried to reach Manila.

Quiros anchored inside the reef at Ponape to renew his supplies. Grass-skirted natives came out in canoes. They were small, wiry, dark brown men with straight or curly black hair and flattened features that gave them a Mongoloid look. After the natives decided the visitors were not ghosts as they first thought, there was some friendly trade by signage. The Ponapeans later boasted of having stolen one of Quiros's cannon. After eleven days, Quiros sailed on to Guam and eventually got back to Peru. He named the new-found island "Quirosa."

During the following centuries other ships sailed past the coasts of Ponape but did not land; or if they did, it is not recorded.

The next visitor was an Irish sailor, James O'Connell, who arrived with a few fellow survivors from a shipwreck in 1826. O'Connell made a hit with the Ponapeans by dancing an Irish jig and by displaying great fortitude in letting himself be tattooed all over. They rewarded him by marrying him to the fourteen-year-old daughter of the king of Not before he knew what was happening. There he stayed for eleven years, until a passing ship enabled him to escape from the island.

Ponape might be described as an irregular circle, surrounded by a chain of fifty smaller islands and coral reefs.

The interior is covered with thick tropical forest. Nearly all the nine or ten thousand Ponapeans live on the coast and around the six good harbors.

In 1826 the island was divided into five kingdoms: Jokesh in the north, Kiti in the west, Not in the south, Matolenim in the southeast, and U in the northeast. These five kingdoms fought fiercely with one another. (Other regions—Uona, Auak, and Palikir—were independent at various times, but this was the set-up through most of the nineteenth century.)

Nan Matol is a low island or tidal flat at the entrance to a harbor on the east coast in Matolenim.

O'Connell describes it in *The Life of James F. O'Connell, the Pacific Adventurer*, published in 1853:

> The most wonderful adventure made during the excursion, the relation of which will put my credit to a severer test than any other fact detailed, was the discovery of a large uninhabited island, upon which were stupendous ruins of a character of architecture differing altogether from the present style of the islanders', and of an extent truly astonishing. At the extreme eastern extremity of the cluster is a large flat island, which at high tides seems to be divided into thirty or forty small ones by the water which rises and runs over it. It differs from the other islands in its surface, which is entirely level. There are no rocks upon it which appear to be placed there by nature.
>
> Upon some parts of it fruit grows, ripens, and decays unmolested, as the natives can by no persuasion be induced to gather or touch it. My companions at the time of discovering this island were George and a nigurt; the latter having directed our attention to it, promising us a surprise, and a surprise indeed it proved. At a little distance the ruins appeared like some of the fantastic heapings of nature, but upon a nearer approach, George and myself were astonished at the

evident traces of the hand of man in their creation. The tide happened to be high, and our canoe was paddled into a narrow creek, so narrow that in places a canoe could hardly have passed us, while in others, owing to the inequality of the ground, the creek swelled to a basin.

At the entrance, we passed for many yards through two walls, so near each other that, without changing the boat from side to side, we could have touched either of them with a paddle. They were about ten feet high; in some places dilapidated, and in others in very good preservation. Over the tops of the wall coconut trees and occasionally a bread fruit spread their branches making a deep and refreshing shade. It was a deep solitude, not a living thing, except a few birds being discernible.

At the first convenient landing, where the walls left the edge of the creek, we landed; but the poor nigurt, who had seemed struck dumb, with fear, could not be induced to leave the boat. The walls inclosed circular areas, into one of which we entered, but found nothing upon the inside but shrubs and trees. Except for the wall, there was no perceptible trace of the footsteps of man, no token that he had even visited the spot.

We examined the masonry, and found the walls to be composed of stones, varying in size from two to ten feet in length, and from one to eight in breadth, carefully propped in the interstices and cracks with smaller fragments. They were built of the blue stone which abounds upon the inhabited islands, and is, as before stated, of a slatose formation, and were evidently split and adapted for the purpose to which they were applied.

In many places the walls had so fallen down that we climbed over them with ease. Returning to our canoe we plied our nigurt with questions; but the only answer we obtained was 'Animan!' He could give no account of the origin of these piles, of their use, or of their age. Himself satisfied that they were the work of Animan, he desired no further information and dared make no inspection, as he believed them the residence of spirits . . . .

We paid several visits to the ruins, but could find no hieroglyphics or other traces of literature.

The "blue stone" is prismatic basalt, which, crystallizing slowly deep in the Earth from lava, forms big six-sided (and sometimes five or eight-sided) prisms. The best-known formation of this kind is the Giant's Causeway in Ireland. The island of Jokesh, off the north coast of Ponape, is made of prismatic basalt. There is an exposed cliff of these rocks, with heaps of broken prisms at its foot. The builders of Nan Matol had only to haul these prisms down to the shore, put them on rafts, and tow them fifteen miles around the northeast side of Ponape to Nan Matol. Other stones were brought from the coast of U.

The walls of Nan Matol look from a distance as if they were made of logs of black wood, with courses piled alternately parallel to the axis of the wall and then at right angles to it. The "logs," however, are prisms of basalt.

In spite of all that has been written about that wonderful stonework of Nan Matol, it is really very crude, with holes in the walls the size of your head. The stone was not dressed or trimmed. The builders simply hunted through the talus on Jokesh until they found prisms the right size.

Nan Matol has been the subject of many gaudy fancies. For instance, it has been said it was a fortified base built by Spanish pirates; that it was the capital of a once great Pacific empire; that it is a relic of a supposed lost continent. The meager facts that are known about it point to a different answer.

While O'Connell was living on Ponape and fathering two children by his native wife, the Russian bark *Senayin* under Lutke touched at Ponape in 1828. Lutke had a fight with the Ponapeans when he tried to send a longboat into Kiti harbor. In the following years, more and more whites came to Ponape. Whalers stopped there; deserters and beachcombers settled. The Ponapeans massacred a British crew, and the British Navy massacred them in turn.

American and Spanish missionaries came to the South Sea Islands. They undermined the native cultures and replaced the islanders' superstitions and beliefs with their own. They stopped such harmless fun as singing and dancing and forced their own clothing customs and nudity taboo on people to whom clothes merely brought dirt and disease. They helped depopulate the islands by bringing in European diseases.

The missionaries' attitude is shown by the answer one of them gave an anthropologist in the 1920s. The latter objected to the missionary's plan to set up a mission on an island in the Solomons that had had almost no white contact, on the ground that he would take to the islanders diseases that would be fatal to them. The missionary said: "Better that they should die and be saved than live and be damned."

In the last great scramble for colonies, Spain annexed Ponape (renaming it Conception) in 1886. The Spaniards never controlled much of the island. The warlike Ponapeans rose several times against them. The Ponapeans had a stern, Spartan culture that went in for self-mutilation as a sign of bravery. Before missionaries, traders, and adventurers demoralized them, though, they were said to be a notably cheerful and honest people.

During the Spanish-American War the United States took control of the Carolines, but handed them back to Spain after the war. Spain promptly sold them to Germany. The Ponapeans rebelled against the Germans in 1910–1911. The Germans put down the revolt with the help of a bombardment from the famous cruiser *Emden* and hanged the leaders. In the Kaiserian War, the Japanese seized the Carolines and kept them under an ill-observed League of Nations mandate. Now the United States holds them under a United Nations trusteeship.

The mystery of Nan Matol, like that of Easter Island, is mainly a case of human ignorance. Facts were deliberately erased or allowed to lapse from memory without being written down. The missionaries tried to blot out 'heathen' native traditions, and during the long rules by the Germans and the Japanese, nosy foreigners were not encouraged.

Much information on Ponape was gathered by a German Pole, Johann Stanislaus Kubary, who settled in the Carolines in the late nineteenth century and took four native wives. He kept the wives on different islands. Kubary killed himself when one of his wives eloped with another man. His manuscript passed into the hands of a native Ponapean family who kept it as an heirloom until it was accidentally burned in the 1930s. It might have told us much.

The richest modern source on the past of Ponape, however, is the data gathered in 1908–1910 by the Thilenius expedition from Germany to Micronesia. Of this team of scientists, the late Dr. Paul Hambruch made Ponape his target. The results of his visit were published in three large paper-bound volumes in 1932–36. Hambruch devoted his first volume to the history of Ponape; his second to the anthropology of the island—the Ponapeans' physique, culture, and so forth—and his third to the ruins of Nan Matol and the native myths and legends. One of his most helpful informants was Nalaim of Matolenim, a hereditary high priest and tradition bearer.

Because this great work is in German, its information has seeped only slowly into the English-speaking world. Hence Lemurian speculations about Ponape have continued to flourish.

The only story on the building of Nan Matol tells how two young wizards, Shipe and Shaupa, set out from Jokesh to build a great cult center to the gods, demons, and ghosts. There they meant to set up the festival of Pun-en-chap. They tried several places on the coasts of Ponape, but each time the wind and the surf destroyed their handiwork. At last they found their ideal site at Nan Matol. A mighty spell made the basaltic prisms on Jokesh fly through the air and settle down in the right position on Nan Matol.

This tale does not get us very far. The Ponapeans themselves made more of the conquest of Ponape by the king of Kusae. Once upon a time, they said, all Ponape was ruled by a single king whose title was the Shau-telur. A prosaic version of the conquest said that the Shau-telur demanded tributes from the king of Kusae, who replied by conquering Ponape. The invader, Isho-kalakal, started a new dynasty with the title of Nanamariki. The Nanamarikis failed to control the whole island, which split into five kingdoms. The Nanamarikis ruled Matolenim with the title of Ishipau, while other dynasties ruled the other kingdoms with other titles. The Ponapeans were a formal people, with a caste system and a passion for titles. As in Japanese, the language changes according to whether you are talking to a superior, an equal, or an inferior.

The more mythical versions of the conquest run as follows: In the days of the last Shau-telur, the thunder-god Nan-japue came to Pona. There he seduced the wife of Shau-telur. When the king found out, he trapped Nan-japue in one of the buildings of Nan Matol and blocked him up. The god would have died of hunger and thirst had not his screams drawn another man, Ishopau, who turned him loose. Nan-japue went to Kusae, riding on a fish. He sprinkled an old woman with lemon juice, so that she became pregnant and bore a son, the famous Isho-kalakal.

One day Isho-kalakal was out fishing and he sighted Ponape. Back home, he built a great war canoe. With 333 followers he sailed to Ponape. The Shau-telur received him warily but hospitably. A quarrel soon arose between one of Isho-kalakal's followers and the nobleman who was supposed to feed the visitors. War began. After victories on both sides, the Kusaeans prevailed. The Shau-telur fled and turned himself into a fish, and thereafter Isho-kalakal's line reigned in Matolenim.

There are other versions. For instance, some say Isho-kalakal, disheartened by the might of Nan Matol, was about to sail away when a cast-off wife of the Shau-telur showed him a secret way into the stronghold. Isho-kalakal reigned for many years. One day, while on a journey, he looked at his image in a pool and saw that his hair was white. Ashamed of his age, he killed himself in a complicated and gruesome manner.

The Kusaeans also have a legend of their conquest of Ponape. While this tale differs from the Ponapean version, there is little doubt that such a conquest took place.

As for the chronology of these happenings, Hambruch inferred that Nan Matol was built by one of the early Shau-telurs. While such a task would not, as some have said, need the manpower of a vast empire, it would require that all the Ponapeans be working together on the same project, instead of at war with one another.

Hambruch's informants thought there had been twelve Shau-telurs, the first being the nephew of the great wizard Laponga. Then came Ishokalakal, followed by seventeen Nanamarikis. Hambruch estimated that these two dynasties covered about 500 years. As for Nan Matol's having been built by an advanced prehistoric culture, the crudity of the work and the lack of any writing or relics of urban civilization are strong reasons against this idea. Everything points to Nan Matol's having been built as a religious or cult center rather than as a city in our sense.

Other Micronesians built similar centers, though never on so vast a scale. They probably did not duplicate Nan Matol because they did not have a mountain of prismatic basalt, already broken into pieces of handy size, for building material.

Nanpei of Matolenim told Hambruch that until recent times Nanmatol was a center for the worship of the turtle-god Nanushunshap. When they caught a sea turtle they brought it to Nan Matol and kept it in one of the buildings. When the tribe was assembled, the priests anointed the turtle with coconut oil and hung it with ornaments. The priests loaded the turtle into a boat and paddled about the canals of Nan Matol. One priest had to stare at the turtle and blink his eyes every time the turtle blinked. When they arrived at the place where a fire had been lit, a priest killed the turtle by breaking its shell with a club. The turtle was cut up, cooked, and served to the priests and the king, with prayers and ritual.

In the reign of the Nanamariki Luk-en-mueiu, in the late eighteenth or early nineteenth century, this ritual was brought to an end. At one ceremony, a priest got no roast turtle. He walked out in a rage, howling curses, and went off to live by himself in a sand bank and eat eels. The Matolenimans feared he had so profaned the ceremony that they could not hold it any more. Then the missionaries overthrew all the native usages.

Hambruch preserved one myth about the sacred turtle. This is nothing much in itself (the turtle got its head snipped off in a fight with a crab), but Hambruch thought it tied in with the use of Nan Matol as a turtle-cult center.

Another myth told of a dragon (a crocodile or giant lizard in different versions) that lived in Jokesh and gave birth to two girls. When the girls grew up they married the reigning Shau-telur. They asked their husband to let their mother come to live in one of the buildings of Nan Matol. The dragon moved in, excavating the canals of Nan Matol in the process. The next morning, when the Shau-telur brought some food for his mother-in-law, he saw the dragon for the first time. In terror he set fire to the house, burning up house dragon. His wives, seeing what was happening, jumped into the fire. In grief, the Shau-telur did likewise.

Hambruch thought, from this myth, that Nan Matol might once have been the center of a dragon or crocodile cult. This is possible, though the evidence is slender.

What then do we know about Nan Matol?

About 1400, after many migrations and conquests, the population of Ponape was much as it is now. At this time, when Chaucer was finishing his *Canterbury Tales* and Bolingbroke was deposing the feeble Richard II to make himself Henry IV of England, a single chief made himself high king of all Ponape with the title of Shau-telur. He or one of his successors started to build Nan Matol as a cult center. Successive kings added new buildings to take care of more cults.

About 1600, when Shakespeare was writing, the Shau-telur demanded tribute from King Ishokalakal of Kusae. Instead of sending tribute, Isho-kalakal came with his warriors and conquered Ponape. His successors ruled as the Nanamarikis of Matolenim. They continued to use Nan Matol as a cult-center; perhaps they added to it. There were probably several cults but the turtle cult is the only one we know. As the Nanamarikis did not rule the whole island long, but only one of the five kingdoms, Nan Matol was no longer the religious center of all Ponape. Therefore, its importance diminished. The other kingdoms built their own, smaller cult centers. These ruins still exist also.

The last active cult of Nan Matol, the Nanamarikis' own personal cult of the sacred turtle, was interrupted, probably in the early 1800s, when a hot-tempered priest profaned it. Nan Matol was abandoned altogether.

Then the missionaries arrived.

So Nan Matol was left forlorn, to be covered with mangroves, to mock later visitors with its great silent black walls and empty, overgrown courts. ∎

Lemuria Did Exist

Jack Sheppard
May 1950

Are the Tchachilia, a Galapagos people,
the remnants of Lemuria?

While it is not the purpose of this article to dispute the sincere advocates of a lost continent in the Pacific, sometimes referred to as Mu and other times as Lemuria, it cannot well be denied that evidence of a concrete nature has long been wanting. Most claims have been based upon visions, dreams, and hand-me-down reports that will not bear scientific investigation.

Studious readers will recall that Lemuria is presumed to be a hypothetical land which was the original home of the lemurs, a nocturnal animal closely associated with the monkey family.

They are by no means extinct, since they are found today in fairly large numbers on the island of Madagascar. Madagascar is admittedly an island formed by the higher land of a former continent that existed thousands of years ago in the Indian ocean, not the Pacific or Atlantic.

In the old Roman religion, *Lemures* were said to be the souls or spirits of the dead. *Mu* is the twelfth letter of the Greek alphabet. The letter "M" also stands for 1,000, but if you put a line over it, it represents one million. Originally *M* or *Mu* comes from the Phoenicians and may go back to the Egyptians. *Mu* is also an ancient word for "May." Atlantis was mentioned by Plato, Pliny, and other writers of The Golden Age, who wrote of it as an existing land of the Atlantic Ocean, and Bacon represented himself as having been shipwrecked on such an island.

If you boil down all of this and other ancient data, you still fail to have anything really definite on Atlantis, Mu, or Lemuria, but that old adage "Where there's smoke, there's fire" has prompted a great deal of wishful thinking on the part of those who choose to believe that one or more of these fabulous lands did exist at one time or another. Unfortunately, they have done little about it aside from a tremendous amount of day dreaming, which has found its way into books, studies, and articles, most of which conflict with each other, since neither day dreams, night dreams, or visions are apt to coincide.

Yet such a land actually did exist, and I propose to convince you of it through a series of indisputable facts that I have uncovered during the past decade of my researches and investigations. If we've got to have a Mu or Lemuria, let's have a real one and back it up with something better than old records that no one is allowed to see because they do not exist, or fanciful visions that are at variance with each other.

The present day Galapagos islands, 600 miles off the coast of Ecuador, in the Pacific Ocean, are quite obviously the highlands and peaks of what was once a very large island, probably a small continent. This much is an acknowledged fact, and ocean soundings have demonstrated it. The islands are decidedly volcanic, and further, the Galapagos, or as they were formerly called The Enchanted Islands, boast a considerable amount of vegetation, as well as bird, animal, and fish life that is distinctly peculiar to the region.

Much of this is entirely unique and lends itself to no other land or continent on Earth today. These truly "enchanted islands" have their own fauna and flora and are still shrouded in mystery.

Nowhere else in the world do you have plant, bird, animal, and sea life of both the temperate and tropic zones, living side by side. Imagine, if you can, banana groves thriving next to a field of wheat or corn. Visualize tropical birds nesting, reproducing, and living next to penguins, a south polar bird.

Gigantic tropical iguanas of six to ten feet in length are intermingled with animals you may see in the northern part of the United States or even Canada, and the huge Galapagos turtles from which the islands derive their name, are like nothing else on Earth today.

Only those who have spent some time in these strange islands can believe what their eyes show them. The fish life is startling. I have seen fish so thick in the waters of these islands that they interfere with navigation. I have tried to row a boat through "fields" of fish so thick that the oar or paddle pushes against living bodies instead of water. Is it surprising, then, that I smile when I read about the good fishing off the Florida or California coast? You have no conception of what fishing can be until you have fished the waters of the Galapagos.

Torres, Olmedo, the great Darwin, Villamil, the German Wolf, Paez, Moreno, and the millionaire Vanderbilt have cruised these waters and seen and marveled at this land of mystery, which astounds all who view its wonders. As these scientists and explorers have said repeatedly, "It is another world." All investigations point to the fact that once, long ago, this was a vast land that sank beneath the sea, leaving but a few of its high tablelands and peaks, which today form the islands in question: Isabel, Santa Maria Espaniola, Santa Cruz, Salvador, Fernandina, Pinta, and Marchena—to mention the most prominent islands of the group. Many of them are totally uninhabited. This land, this continent that has been lost except for the islands remaining, was known not as Mu or Lemuria, but *Tchachilia.*

How do we know this? Why, just as you know that your forbearers came from England, Germany, France, or Spain— because that information has been passed on down to you through the line of your ancestors. Today's descendants of Tchachilia form two colonies or groups upon the mainland of South America, in what is now the Republic of Ecuador. They have their own language, call themselves "Tchachilias" in their proper tongue, have their own characteristic coloring, stature, body measurements, and distinctive types. Their history has been handed down through their chieftains, and they are as proud of their lineage as you are of yours. They know that they came from Tchachilia and that this land still has its peaks above water in the Pacific and is known as the Galapagos Islands. They are splendid navigators, and in no sense are they either Indians or Negroid. A fair percentage of them have blue eyes and light hair.

Mind you, these are not dream people; there is nothing whatever imaginary about them. Just as I have lived and worked among them, so can you. They are clean, kind, and friendly, but definitely averse to adopting the war-like ways and hectic life of our self-styled civilization.

Heart disease, nervous disorders, and cancer are unknown to them. Money means nothing, and they live for the pleasure of life, rather than monetary gains and the competitive pace of a modern world that has lost its sense of balance. To avoid being drawn into a semi-slave existence of high taxes, long labor hours, conflicting religious beliefs, and the world's incurable ills, the Tchachilias have hidden away in Ecuador's lush green jungles. One group of them live along the banks of the Cayapas River, which empties into the Pacific, north of Esmeraldas, and the other faction resides in the Santo Domingo area close to the White River, which in turn flows into the Esmeraldas and the great ocean.

Tourists, with their ever-gaping cameras, countless foolish questions, and false attitudes of superiority, are not welcomed by the Tchachilias. They offer no violence to such unwarranted visitors, but avoid them and refuse to render the hospitality they show serious-minded persons who accept them for what they are, without question and sans the Christian conversion efforts that are lost upon a people who, unlike ourselves, are totally unfamiliar with wars and the business of mass murder on the modern—or any other scale. Peace, tranquility, and a good life devoid of hustle and rush appears to be today's watchword of these friendly folk.

To connect the present day Tchachilias with those of yesteryear and their sunken land, of which only the island peaks remain, I delved into their ancient burial mounds, known as *tolas*, in Ecuador. Here lies an amazing array of figures and figurines dating back, according to qualified archaeologists, more than 3,000 years. The headdress motif of the human-like figures is somewhat Egyptian—high and curving about the sides of the head. Jewelry is represented by necklaces and bracelets, and, strangest of all, many wore nose pieces that were inserted into the tip of the proboscis and consisted of a half-moon facing straight ahead.

There are many figurines that indicate a form of sun worship, and, of course, the half-moons would tend to show that this heavenly body was also regarded as a deity, probably the sister-wife of the sun. Animals, birds, and fish are shown in their figures, and these closely resemble today's unique biological life of the Galapagos Islands, proving again that the

Tchachilias came from that sunken land. This is another of the positive connections that links the South American mainland and today's Tchachilias people with the sunken tierra of the Pacific.

There is no similarity whatever between the pottery and figures that came out of these mounds and those regarded as Incan or Chan Chan. Further, the Tchachilias' relics are far older than the Incan Quichua discoveries, which date back no more than 800 years, against the approximate 3,000 of the Tchachilias' *tolas*. Perhaps the most striking figurines unearthed from these mounds are those that resemble a zeppelin of sorts or a submarine.

These figures are all in miniature, ranging in size from three inches up to eight or ten inches in over-all length. Some are of hard-baked clay, others of solid stone, hand-carved, and a very few of them are of pure, soft gold.

It has been my pleasure to prepare a rather extensive vocabulary of the Tchachilias' language. Obviously, space prohibits anything like a complete translation of this tongue, but the scientifically inclined reader may derive some interest from a small cross-section of this ancient idiom that goes back thousands of years into the dim past of a land that could well be the Mu or Lemuria so often visualized and speculated upon today. Here, then, is a group of the more common words, phonetically spelled:

house – *ya*	shirt – *juali*
man – *umbela*	trousers – *babara*
woman – *supula*	head – *mis puca*
wife – *shimbu*	face – *cajuro*
boy – *caila*	eye – *ca puca*
son – *ignama*	car – *ji paqui*
daughter – *iguatala*	hair – *achua*
banana – *panda*	foot – *tehapa*

rubber – *sabe*

dog – *cucha*

bog – *cuche*

egg – *napipo*

chicken – *guallapa*

rooster – *ataco*

deer – *mana*

turkey – *limpu*

salt – *teyo*

material – *jali*

hand – *mehapa*

good – *ura*

bad – *jacu*

big – *aba*

small – *achushu*

food – *jinu*

drink – *cuishnu*

cry – *huanu*

meat – *alla*

dance – *relanu*

With a knowledge of the foregoing plus some 300 additional words that were easily learned, I was soon able to converse freely with the Tchachilias. Ethnologists may find some vague similarity in the Tchachilias' idiom with that of the Incas (Quichua). Some years ago I wrote and published the first Quichua or Incan vocabulary translated to both Spanish and English. If there is a resemblance in the two languages it is because the Quichuas acquired many Tchachilias' words. There is some reason to believe that the Quichuas or Incans were originally a part of the Tchachilia empire. Their history, too, is cloaked in mystery and can scarcely be traced back more than eight centuries.

Leaders of the surviving race appoint teachers who, in turn, hold regular classes for the children to instruct them in the history of their people, teach them to count, speak the language fluently, and also learn tropical agriculture. Those who wish to become healers are given special training in the setting of bones, massage, and the use of medicinal herbs. Leadership is inherited from father to son or the nearest male relative, for the function of royalty is like that of Great Britain today, and with little more authority. A group of counselors is elected yearly to supervise such laws or rules as need to be enforced. These, however, are few, because the natural tendency of the Tchachilias people is to observe what we would call the Golden Rule. Theft is entirely unknown to them, while murder, so far as I could determine, has never been committed in the history of the race. In fact, they have no word for murder in their tongue.

No danger whatever is encountered in contact with these people, for if they resent your intrusion they simply avoid you by such elaborate means as to make you sharply aware of your trespass. Unwanted visitors see only the backs of the Tchachilias. They refuse point-blank to face any foreigner whom they wish to have gone from the region. Needless to add, they also abstain from trade, sign language, or any form of conversation with the individual who makes him- or herself obnoxious or unwanted.

An interesting sidelight worthy of notice is one of the Tchachilias fruits that grows on a bush and resembles a small orange with a peach-like fuzz. The inside of this delicious fruit—pulp and juice—is a bright green in color, even when fully ripe, and the flavor seems to combine pineapple, orange, papaya, and a dash of almond. A few of these fruits found their way to the "outside" world and were so enthusiastically received that expeditions were sent to bring out plants and seeds so that the fruit might be propagated elsewhere. Although tens of thousands of seeds, besides hundreds of the living plants, were made available to a score of countries and climates, not one bush has ever produced an edible fruit outside of this region.

The Tchachilias people, whom I consulted regarding this curious fact, claim that pollination is impossible by hand and is accomplished only by a certain species of humming bird which, if removed from the area, will die within a week. They state that not only does this hummer transfer the pollen from one plant to another, but that the bird adds a drop or two of its own saliva when making the transfer. Without that saliva the pollen is sterile—an odd affinity. Botanists have stated that this is a virtual impossibility, but those same botanists have failed utterly when they tried to hand-pollinate the flower of the bush elsewhere.

I brought out about fifteen pounds of these seeds which, being tiny in size, probably total half a million or more. These I have given away freely to all who cared to experiment with them. I have sent packets of the seeds to the near and far east, Africa, various parts of South America, and a few to North America. Most growers report lovely bushes with fragrant and beautiful flowers, but no fruit. On my last visit to the Galapagos I found the same fruit and the same species of humming bird flourishing on one of the uninhabited islands.

I cannot flatly deny that some other continent existed in the Pacific in bygone ages; call it Mu or Lemuria, or call it Smith or Jones. What does it matter? I do claim that Tchachilias was a real land, that its remnants are there today in the Galapagos Islands, and that enough of its people escaped when the land sank to form two colonies that exist today here in nearby Ecuador, close to the Pacific coast.

This was the point of landing of the ancients when they took to their odd craft, as their land, shaken by earthquakes and dropping beneath the blue waters of the great ocean, no longer offered its people a safe refuge from impending disaster. How many died during the upheaval we shall never know, but it may well have run into the millions. Yet a bit of this land remains today and a remnant of its people. It is an interesting subject and one that will occupy much of the remainder of my life with the same fascination that it has given me during the past decade.

A Voyage to Atlantis

Lawrence D. Hill
February 1958

The captain investigated the island that had just risen from the sea. Had he discovered the fabled lost continent of Atlantis?

All voyages to Atlantis must begin with a passage between the Pillars of Hercules. The steam schooner *Jesmond*, 1,456 tons, had no fear of the dread whirlpools of Scylla, which with certain tides can be dangerous to small vessels.

The *Jesmond* was 252 feet of British engineering, launched on the Tyne in 1880, with a steam engine of 150 h.p. to drive the twin screws. The schooner had sails on all three masts to use God's wind as well. A flutter of flags at the mast told Lloyds Agents at Gibraltar that the *Jesmond* left Messina in Sicily on February 24 and was outward bound to New Orleans with a cargo of dried fruit. The year was 1882, and the new, electrical telegraph told the owners, Messrs. Watts, Watts & Co. of London, that their fast, modern freighter was making good time.

Captain David Amory Robson was forty-three. He had held a Masters Certificate (No. 279II) for ten years. His home was in Jarrow, and he had come up the hard way in sail. Just then he was rather pleased with himself, for he was well ahead of his rival ship, *Finsbury*, also owned by Watts, Watts & Co. After arriving at Messina with coal from Newcastle on February 22, he had got the cargo out, holds cleaned, boxes of dried apricots and prunes loaded, and the vessel back to sea by the evening of the twenty-fourth. Modern nautical opinion is that with a crew of twenty-two men this rapid turn around is possible, but Robson must have bribed the foreman stevedore. For in 1882 captains got commission on freights and, with speed, there was a chance of getting a cargo of cotton to take home to Liverpool from New Orleans.

From what is left in memories and the few remaining records (the offices of Watts, Watts & Co. burned in the 1940 blitz), he was a heavily bearded, North Country seaman, with an eye for the "brass" and a still harder eye for dim brasswork. Consequently, the *Jesmond* was as trim as a yacht. It sailed like one, too, and the schooner drove south to pick up the strong trade winds that carried Columbus, for its engine was merely for calms and to save a tug, and its blend of fore and aft canvas and square topsails was meant to give a steamship-passage with a sailing ship's fuel bill. Its job was snatching the best-paying fast freights.

About two hundred miles southwest of Madeira, Captain Robson noticed "the singular appearance of the sea." It was clouded, muddy, and carpeted with dead fish as far as the eyes could see. The date was then about March 1, and a submarine volcanic eruption was reported as a slight shock in both the Azores and the Canaries. Captain Robson was probably the first to see the effect of this slight shock on the fish of the Atlantic, to see the polluted water at beginning of the great Ocean River that ends in the Gulf Stream. The mortality was estimated half-million tons of dead fish covering 7,500 square miles of the Atlantic. On March 14, nearer the east coast of the United States, the sea was covered with the bodies of a species called tile fish, and a Captain Ole Jorgensen reported sailing from six A.M. to five P.M., for sixty-seven sea miles, through the other end of this carpet of dead marine creatures.

To the south, Captain Robson could see the smoke of a steamer on the horizon. This was before radio and he could not exchange views on the fish carpet with that boat's Master, but we now know that it was the *Westbourne* of Hull, a larger but slower steam schooner bound from Marseilles to New York under Captain James Newdick.

Just after dawn the next day Captain Robson was waked by his Second Officer with the news that land was in sight where the Admiralty chart showed 2,000 fathoms of water! The *Jesmond* might have driven onto the unknown shore in the darkness, but dawn had come; now it lay right on her course—an island with lofty peaks wreathed in the smoke of the volcanic eruption that had raised it from the bottom of the sea, as many islands have risen before and many since.

Steam was raised, for the wind was light and Captain Robson was taking no risks on the Canaries Current driving him onto unknown reefs. Moreover, he made up his mind to enjoy some private exploration. His fast turn around gave him time in hand, and it was his duty to investigate an island in the main shipping lane to America for vessels under sail from Mediterranean ports.

He sailed in, sounding as he went, and anchored twelve miles off shore in seven fathoms. The position of the island was Latitude 2.5° N, Longitude 2.3° 40' W. The *Westbourne* passed it in the night, so Captain Newdick saw it astern, but so far as we know did not turn back and land. He made the position Latitude 25° 30' N, Longitude 24° W. If both captains were exactly right that makes the island thirty miles between the two points, with the *Westbourne* away beyond the mountains and increasing her distance as the *Jesmond* came in to anchor.

To find the position approximately on a small-scale atlas, lay a ruler from the most easterly of the Azores (St. Maria) to the most easterly of the Cape Verdes (Bonavista). Put a mark 800 land miles from the Azores and 500 from the Cape Verdes. The nearest land is Ferro in the Canaries, 340 miles away. The African coast is 540 miles due east of the Spanish colony of Rio de Oro.

Captain Robson lowered the yawl—a large boat with sails as well as oars—and set off with his Second Officer and a volunteer crew, leaving the Third Officer in command. They continued sounding and found the bottom depth so varied that the *Jesmond* lay where she was throughout their stay.

The rocky headland with its steep, beachless black basalt cliffs sloped away to the west. As they rowed around, they noticed strata of other rock, and even encrusted marine shells. On the western side they found a beach of breccia or volcanic gravel washed off the surface of the rising land when millions of tons of sea water had swept away the fine ooze of the sea bed to spread it like a mud cloud among the dead fish.

The party scrambled up the lower cliffs at this point to find themselves on land that sloped back to a high plateau which, in turn, stretched away to the bare mountains in the distance from where steam or light smoke still rose. It was a barren, lifeless landscape, and the surface was so cut by fissures and chasms that the party decided to return to the beach and explore where they could hope to make more progress in the time available.

One of the sailors, who carried the boathook for chasm crossing, idly stirred some of the loose gravel where it had swept in fan shape through a gap in the cliffs. He found a flint arrowhead. The whole party began searching with enthusiasm because archeology was then popularly associated with treasure hunting. They found many more arrowheads and some small knives. At dusk Captain Robson decided to return to the ship and excavate the site more thoroughly the next day, when they landed very early with all the tools the *Jesmond* could provide.

Fifteen sailors with stokehold shovels can do a great deal of digging, and they soon discovered a large stone statue. It was a bas relief cut on one side of an oblong rock, squared roughly, rather larger than life-size, and very heavy. Evidently it had lain on the sea bed a long time, for it was encrusted with shells and marine growth, as well as volcanic scoria.

They found, further inland, two walls of unmortared, squared stone set quite closely together. Between them lay a collection of relics rather like those found in a British Bronze Age grave. Besides a straight yellow metal sword with a simple cross hilt, there were spear heads, axe heads, and metal rings, carved stone and pottery figures of birds and animals, and two large, almost spherical, flatbottomed jars containing bone fragments. The *Jesmond* carried no passengers and, therefore, no doctor, but there was an almost intact cranium, which is the easiest part of a skeleton for a layperson to identify as human.

The weather was deteriorating, however, and so Captain Robson ferried the material off to the *Jesmond* and weighed anchor as soon as the heavy statue had been hoisted aboard.

As he looked on the island for the last time (for it sank again beneath the waves) it is highly unlikely that he thought of Plato's Atlantis, which is often cited approximately where the island rose. Before February 17, 1882, only a determined scholar could find references to Atlantis, but on that day Harper Brothers of New York, published

Atlantis, The Antediluvian World, by Ignatius Donnelly. It was an international best-seller that put the lost continent back "on the map." The British first edition by Messrs. Sampson Low appeared in May 1882 and impressed even Mr. Gladstone. But this was before the time of aircraft, and there was no way a copy of the book could have arrived in Messina by February 24, or in Marseilles by February 23—Captain Robson had been reading no books on Atlantis.

The *Jesmond* arrived in New Orleans at twelve noon on March 31. It moored alongside the wharf at the bottom of Erato Street, where the cargo was unloaded into the warehouses of Messrs. A. B. French. Either the pilot or the Port Doctor, or perhaps even a ship chandler's runner, heard the story of the island first and told the New Orleans *Times-Picayune.*

Their reporter arrived on board during the evening, and the next day the news of an island risen from the sea blazed under three-inch headlines.

The reporter added his opinion that the relics were Egyptian, and that the vases had on them either hieroglyphics or Hebrew inscriptions. He added also four noncommittal lines on Atlantis—Donnelly's book was a slow starter; a year later he would have played up that angle.

The story was syndicated to more than a dozen American papers. The New York *Sun* ran it first on April 6. The *Odebolt Reporter* ran it last of all, on April 28. These later versions were cut, and *23°* became *28°*, which gave the *Jesmond* a distance to steam that would tax a modern destroyer. The original articles included an offer to "show the collection to any gentleman who is interested," and also the announcement that Captain Robson would present it to the British Museum when he reached Liverpool, where he hoped to sail shortly.

After two years' investigation this writer cannot see how a hoax is possible. There was no time to collect fake material with that rapid turn around, and the statue, alone weighing over a ton, would have had to be brought from Newcastle. Also, it is incredible that two British captains, from ships that sailed from and arrived at different ports, docked on the same day, to play the same pointless practical joke. Without radio contact it is not possible. Neither man had anything to gain, and the type of third-rate scholar who fakes an archeological find is rarely in command of a ship.

The result of the syndication, which cannot have made more than $100, if that, was a flood of letters from Atlantis fans. Apparently to stop this flood, on April 23, 1882, the newspaper printed the statement that the "whole story was a fake from start to finish." They gave no motive for destroying their own reputation for accuracy. They do not say that they were deceived by a rascally British captain or an imaginative reporter; they just tell their readers they lied to them.

One wonders exactly what any gentleman who accepted Captain Robson's invitation saw when he walked up the *Jesmond*'s gang plank. This could be learned only through old letters or diaries from New Orleans.

The *Jesmond* sailed on April 6. Captain Robson failed to get his cotton cargo. All he could find was a smaller-paying freight from the Coosaw River in South Carolina. There he loaded rock phosphate in bags for London. The *Jesmond* arrived in London on May 19.

Here the real mystery begins! For he did not present the collection to the British Museum, nor to any of the fourteen likely Northern museums whose records I have searched. Atlantis had become a favorite topic, yet not only Captain Robson, but his whole crew kept their mouths tight shut.

There is one possible answer. It hinges on the geological formation of the Cape Verdes and the Canaries, which make tin for bronze unlikely, but gold and copper probable. Let us suppose that one of the visitors to the *Jesmond* was a New

Orleans jeweller, whose shop and whose grandsons may be there still. To him the metal that looked like reddish brass would be *tumbaga*, an alloy of 80 percent gold and 20 percent copper used extensively by the ancient American civilizations. The Spaniards discarded it, but later treasure hunters knew it, and in 1882 a jeweller would know exactly how to separate the two metals. It is not quite as hard as bronze (it is long odds that Captain Robson had never seen prehistoric bronze in his life, but very few people today have seen tumbaga) and does not corrode.

To a jeweller that straight sword in the scales may have meant a considerable sum in dollars, and when the spear and axeheads and rings were added, Captain Robson may have accepted the jeweller's offer. Robson was an honest man, and the result was probably a summoning of all hands aft and a shareout, with strict instructions to keep the news quiet, for there was more where that came from.

The following British ships were all on courses that could have crossed the position given for the newly risen land:

Trinacria, Capt. William Russell, Messina to New York, April 5

Assyria, Capt. James Brown, Valencia to Boston, April 5

Egypt, Capt. Robert Reavey, Beni Saf to Baltimore, April 7

Elysia, Capt. Linquister, Naples to New York, April 10

Huntingtower, Capt. John Peacock, Palermo to New York, April 10

Ashburne, Capt. William Hall, Gibraltar to New York, April 13

Louise H, Capt. Peter Voss, Gibraltar to New York, April 13

James Turpie, Capt. Walter Smith, Beni Saf to Baltimore, April 13

The date in every case is arrival in an American port, and the question, of course, is, what did the captains tell reporters from the local papers? Ship log books, unfortunately, are kept by the British Board of Trade for only seven years, then they are destroyed. Ship owners do not keep records forever either, but other sightings, landings, and perhaps even the date of the final sinking of the island may lie hidden in the files of old newspapers in the seaports of the United States.

We know what happened to the *Jesmond*, for like all the ships in this story, it is in Lloyds Registry of Shipping. The schooner lost its masts and swelling canvas, was fitted with new engines, and cashed in on the freight boom of the First World War. Then when its old-fashioned but lovely and lasting iron hull could no longer earn a living, the *Jesmond* was sold to a Japanese firm, renamed the *Tomashima Maru*, and lost in 1925.

Captain Robson commanded the schooner until April 21, 1884, but the bombed records of Watts, Watts & Co. do not say where he retired and drew his pension.

There are thousands and thousands of Robsons in England, but some day I shall find the son or grandson of the man who found Atlantis. And someday, perhaps, I shall take a ship out along the old sea road that only small yachts use in this age of steam and diesel engines. For this story of Atlantis should end, not with the Dialogues of Plato, but with echo sounders, underwater television, and aqualung divers.   ■

Has Atlantis Been Found?

L. Sprague de Camp
July 1953

*Was ancient Tartessos, engulfed by the mud of the
Guadelupe River, the true city of Atlantis?*

If we assume that Atlantis existed, where would be the
most logical place to look for it? Not down on the bottom
of the Atlantic, for modern geology is convinced, from
movements of the Earth's crust, that no such large area as
Atlantis is supposed to have covered could sink practically
overnight. A continent would take millions of years to disappear, so Atlantis would have had to start sinking back
before the Pleistocene period when our ancestors still sat on
branches.

Why not look for Atlantis on terra firma, among the
ancient cities we know did exist but of which today no
traces remain? The likeliest of these is the mysterious city
of Tartessos or Tarshish, which stood about 200 miles
northwest of Cadiz along the coast of southwestern Spain.
Cadiz is the oldest surviving city in the world. It has exist-

ed under the same name, with continuity of population and culture for the longest time. Older cities, like Babylon and Thebes, have been abandoned and depopulated in the course of their history and so can not count. But Cadiz is still flourishing.

In a sense, Tartessos *was* Atlantis. At least that seems the most rational solution of the double "mystery" of Tartessos and Atlantis.

Some 3,000 years ago a ship crept along the Moroccan coast. On its left rose the brown Riffian hills; on its right sparkled the blue Iberian Sea. Aboard were traders, the greatest of their day: hook-nosed, black-bearded, swarthy men in kilts and jerseys. If you had asked them what manner of men they were, they would have told you, in a Semitic speech full of rasping gutterals, that they were Canaanites of the city of Zor, or, as we should say, Phoenicians of Tyre.

The ship was little more than a large rowboat with a pair of steering oars and a single mast in the waist with one square sail. It could not tack against the wind. When the wind blew the wrong way, the ship sat in harbor, held by a doughnut-shaped anchorstone on the end of a rope. When there was no wind the crew unshipped oars and heaved their way slowly over the glassy sea with mighty grunts.

As the ship was a merchantman and not a war galley, the crew was small even for so tiny a ship: probably less than a dozen men. In the small covered space at the stern, the ship carried a cargo of perfume and spice from Arabia, glassware from Sidon, and Tyrian textiles dyed with the purple pigment of the murex, a spiny sea snail of the eastern Mediterranean.

On the ship sailed, seeing its way by means of the eyes painted on its bow. Now the coast trended northward and then back eastward. The seamen exchanged looks. Had they come to the end of the sea? No; the coast fell away in front and they saw that they were rounding a peninsula with a rugged hill rising from its interior. And then ahead, looming over the sea, the men saw what looked like a tall rounded island of rock.

They sailed north and found that the immense rock, like a monster's egg, was part of a slender point of land that jutted out from a low-lying coast that stretched away on both sides. The two points, with their guardian mountains, looked too regular to be natural. They were more like pillars erected by the gods as a gateway—perhaps by the lion-slaying hero Ba'al-Melkarth.

The Tyrians tied up beside the Rock of Gibraltar in the landlocked harbor of Algeciras. They learned strange things about this new country. The sea behaved oddly. It flowed, but not uniformly like a river. It rose and fell and changed direction twice daily, and in flowing it set up vicious whirlpools. One of these caught the ship and whirled it round and round—until the frantic Phoenicians rowed clear. A crewman with a reputation for diving went down to look for pearl oysters and had the wits scared out of him by an enormous octopus, which fortunately was as frightened as he.

People came to gape, short dark men wrapped in voluminous cloaks of coarse black wool. The eyes of the Phoenicians gleamed at the sight of bangles and bracelets of silver and gold. But though the crew spoke a score of dialects, none could make anything of the landsmen's gabble. At last by sign language and sand pictures, the natives conveyed the news that a great city lay three days' sail to the west and that the king of that city was their ruler also.

The Phoenicians set out again. Their stout hearts sank as the strait opened out into a limitless waste of waters. The sea rose and boomed night and day against the flat beaches. The captain wondered if he had misunderstood, but the sight of other ships of curious design heartened him. There appeared to be a real seaport somewhere along this low coast.

Then they saw a huge walled city rising from a large flat island that blocked the estuary of a broad river, so that the river issued by two mouths, one north and one south of the island.

Cautiously the Phoenicians crept into the port. The people received them cordially and told them the name of their city, which in the Canaanite tongue became "Tarshish." The river was the Baitis or Baetica—the modern Guadalquivir.

The Phoenicians' eyes popped at the extraordinary metallic wealth of the place. The people were loaded down with ornaments of gold and silver, and their temples were adorned with these metals as well as with ivory and bronze. The king kept his wine in silver jars and fed the royal hogs in a silver feeding trough. Tartessian rule extended along the coast for hundreds of miles in each direction. The people were called Turduli and Turdetani—perhaps separate tribes, perhaps different forms of the same name as that of the Tartessians.

The Phoenicians brought out their Sidonian glassware and other trade goods a little at a time to extort the highest prices. Into their ship went ingots of gold and silver. The captain had acquired the largest weight of precious metal that he could safely carry in his cockle-shell before he had exhausted his own goods. How to carry more of the stuff?

"Cast an anchor stone of silver," said a sailor and it was done.

Where, the captain asked, did these folk get all this silver? From the mines of silver mountain, said the men of Tarshish, pointing northwest. The gold and the copper? From other mines. The ivory? From the Berbers across the strait, by trade.

The tin? That came from islands in the sea, many days' sail away. They pointed northwest. One sailed until one came to lands of fog and storm, inhabited by savages who painted themselves blue. With luck one made the round trip in four months.

Had ships from the east ever visited Tarshish before? Yes, they said; in the time of their great-grandfathers ships had come from the east to trade, operated by small, clean-shaven, long-haired fellows in breechclouts who called themselves Minoans.

The captain nodded. Those must have been the men of Crete who had ruled the eastern seas. But Cretan power had vanished. The half-barbarous Achaeans had seized the government both of Crete and of its mainland colonies. Then the wholly barbarous Dorians had overwhelmed the colonies, while in Crete the capital of Knossos had been leveled by an earthquake.

But the Phoenician captain was strictly a businessman and not interested in history. He hoisted his silver anchor stone and sailed away, crawling back along the North African coast and hoping to keep his fabulous cargo secret until he was safe again in the harbor of Zor.

Though the Phoenicians were close-mouthed about their trade routes, news of this amazing city of silver leaked out. Phoenician sailors carried the news to Greece, where civilization was beginning to revive after the Dorian disaster. The Greeks, descendants of those Achaeans and Dorians who had put down the might of Knossos, were not yet a trading or seafaring folk. They raised cows and sheep, lived on roast meat and bread and resinous wine, and butchered each other or anyone who irked them. Some decades previously, a whole war band of them had gone off to sack the old city of Troy in Asia Minor, which had been sacked before and would be again before it vanished.

But the Greeks were beginning to borrow from the Phoenicians the invention of writing, which the Phoenicians had adapted from the Egyptians. They passed around the stories of the wondrous city in the West, and by the time they wrote down these stories they had much distorted the original. The hills of Gibraltar and Ceuta became the Pillars of Hercules, the Greek version of Melkarth. The tides of the Outer Sea were noted. The whirlpools around the Straits were personified as a monster:

> 'Neath it the deep black water is swallowed by mighty Charybdis.
> Thrice in the day she doth swallow it down and thrice she rejects it.

The octopus that terrified the diver became:

> ... Skylla, a howling and horrible monster ...
> Round her a dozen feet she is always waving suspended
> Six long and sinuous necks before her and each one
> Beareth a head terrific with teeth in threefold order ...

About this time (ninth century B.C.) Greek poets began stitching together lays of the Trojan War and the homecomings of the heroes of this war into several major epics. Two of these epics have come down intact to modern times, the *Iliad* and the *Odyssey*. Both are credited to Homer, which may have been the name of one of the poets who compiled these collections, or may have been a name adopted by or applied to a whole school of them.

The authors of the *Odyssey*, in any case, used the story of Tarshish. (In Greek the name became *Tartessos*, with a masculine case ending, as Greek has no *sh*.) They sent their hero, Odysseus, to Tartessos after his escape from the island of the nymph Kalypso, only they called it *Scheria*, the land of the Phaeacians or Phaiakes.

Meanwhile, a flourishing trade had sprung up between Tartessos and Tyre. In 970 B.C. Hiram ascended the Tyrian throne. The more barbarous Canaanites of the interior, twelve tribes who called themselves Hebrews or Israelites after their mythical progenitors Heber and Israel, had banded together into a single kingdom. The shrewd Hiram cultivated good relations with these fierce Bedouin shepherds under their aggressive King David (which was not hard since both spoke dialects of Canaanitish) and even better relations with David's son Solomon. Hiram and Solomon formed a trading syndicate, operating a fleet in the Red Sea and another in the Mediterranean. Hiram furnished the seamen and ships, and Solomon furnished a guard of his warlike subjects.

The Mediterranean fleet sailed to Tartessos, taking three years for the round trip, and returning with "gold and silver, ivory and apes and peacocks." The gold and silver were from mines in the mountains back of Tartessos. The ivory was probably from the Moroccan elephant, a smallish variety of the African elephant later used by the Carthaginians in war and hunted to extinction in Roman times. The monkeys were from Gibraltar or from Africa, while "peacocks," *thukkiyim*, is perhaps an error for *sukkiyim*, "slaves." Tin for making bronze, brought by the Tartessians, from the Scilly Isles off Britain, also figured in this trade.

The Phoenicians did not merely trade with Tartessos. They set up a trading-post of their own twenty miles southeast, on a small island at the mouth of the small Guadalete River. This post, established about 1100 or 1000 B.C. shortly after their discovery of Tartessos, they named *Ha-Gadir*, "the hedge," perhaps meaning that they fortified it with a stockade. The Greeks later called it *Gadeira* or *Gades*, whence modern *Cadiz*.

In the latter half of the ninth century B.C., events in Tyre affected the future of the whole Mediterranean. When King Metten I (or Matgen or Mutton) died about 851 B.C., his son Pygmalion and his daughter Elissar (the latter with the backing of her husband Akerbas) contended for the throne. Pygmalion had Akerbas murdered, and Elissar fled with her followers to Cyprus and thence to the North African coast near some other Phoenician colonies. She bought a tract from the local Berber chief, Iarbas, and founded "New City" or Karthadshat—our Carthage. Carthage grew rapidly and soon extended its authority over Utica and the other neighboring Phoenician cities.

Then in the seventh century the barbarous Gauls or Kelts crossed the Pyrenees and invaded Iberia. They daunted their foes by rushing upon them stark naked, howling and waving long iron swords. In a few decades they conquered most of the tribes of central Spain and set themselves up as a ruling caste. They were probably not very numerous, for they soon mixed with the subjugated peoples, who were thereafter known as Keltiberians.

While the Keltic invasion of Iberia was going on, the Greeks made their first contact with Tartessos. About 631 B.C., according to Herodotos, a ship from Samos bound for Egypt under Kolaios was blown far out of its course by a storm and ended up at Tartessos. The Samians disposed of their trade goods to the Tartessians and made the enormous profit of six talents, or more than $75,000.

The Greeks had now taken to the sea. When the population of a city became uncomfortably large, a band of the younger folk would set out to colonize some distant part of the Mediterranean or the Black Sea. Thus the men from Phokaia in Greek Asia Minor founded Massalia, our Marseilles, about 600 B.C. Soon after, they too arrived at Tartessos, where they found King Arganthonios ("Silverlocks") reigning.

Herodotos says that Arganthonios lived 120 years and ruled eighty of them, which probably means that there was a dynasty of two or three kings of the same name. Garcia thinks the Phokaians reached Tartessos as early as 700 B.C.

Arganthonios was delighted with his visitors and invited their whole nation to settle in his land. When they declined, he gave them money to build a big wall around Phokaia.

Then in 546 B.C. a Persian army appeared before Phokaia. Its general, Harpagus, demanded submission to the all-conquering King of Kings, Kurush or Cyrus. The Phokaians asked for time to think it over. When the Persians withdrew, the Phokaians, despite their fine wall, crowded into their ships and rowed away. Hearing that Arganthonios was dead, they settled in Corsica, and after a hard-fought war with the Etruscans and Carthaginians they moved again to the coast of Italy.

The cities of Phoenicia had now lost their independence, first to the Assyrians, then to the Babylonians, and finally to the Persians. The Phoenicians of Gades, having trouble with the native Iberians, the invading Kelts, the competing Greeks, and perhaps with their Tartessian neighbors, called in the Carthaginians to help. As a result, the Carthaginians began conquering all of Andalucia in the seventh century. They destroyed the Spanish city of Mastia and built "New Carthage" (modern Cartagena) in its place.

About 500 B.C. the Carthaginians reduced Gades itself to subjection. They sent out two great expeditions through the Pillars into the unknown West. One, under Admiral Hanno, sailed down the African coast to a place he called Kernë (probably Cape Arguin) where he set up a trading post. The other fleet, under Himilco, sailed north to the Tin Islands where the Tartessians had been trading, thus opening up direct Phoenician trade with Britain.

And Tartessos disappeared. It may have been abandoned as a result of the silting up of the Guadalquivir estuary, which became a vast malarial marsh, Las Marismas.

But, more likely, Himilco or some other Carthaginian stormed the city, massacred and enslaved its people, pried loose its ornaments of gold and silver and ivory, and leveled and burned the rest. There is no record of the destruction of Tartessos; it simply dropped out of history. But it dropped so thoroughly that later generations were not sure where it had stood (again, evidence that it probably sank). Roman geographers confused it with Gades and with Calpe and Carteia near the Pillars. If the Carthaginians did destroy it, they did as effective a job as the Romans later did on Carthage.

This, however, was not the end of the Tartessian people. Those who did not live in the city struggled under Carthaginian rule for the next three centuries. When the Romans came, after the Second Punic War, the Tartessians, less warlike than most Spaniards, hired Keltiberians to fight for them. But they were conquered again and, like most Iberians, Romanized.

Lost Tartessos had another echo in classical literature. A century and a half after it disappeared, the Greek philosopher Plato started to write a trilogy of dialogues expressing his ideas about ideal government. To make his theories more palatable, he proposed to present them in the form of fiction. He imagined that 9,000 years before there existed an earlier Athens embodying all the perfections that he described in *The Republic,* and that this land of virtuous heroes defeated an invading army from a continent in the Atlantic Ocean, which thereafter had been sunk by Zeus for the pride and avarice of its people. Plato never finished his trilogy; he completed the first dialogue, *Timaios,* and got halfway through the rough draft of the second, *Kritias.* In these dialogues, however, he set forth his tale of Atlantis, taking ideas from various sources.

For instance, the year before his own birth, in 426 B.C., an earthquake had shaken Greece, and the earthquake wave had inundated the little island of Atalantë. Also, the demigod Atlas was connected in legend with the Western Ocean which people were hence beginning to call "Atlantic."

There was said to be a huge, steep, pointed mountain with a perpetual cloudcap out there named after Atlas. This was probably the volcanic Pico de Teyde on Tenerife in the Canary Islands, but it got mixed up with the mountains of Morocco that are still called the Atlas range. There were rumors, false but probably spread by the Phoenicians to frighten away trade competition, of great unnavigable shoals in the Atlantic west of the Pillars. And there was the story of a great walled city glittering with precious metals which stood on an island in the Far West and mysteriously disappeared.

The Atlantis story was a tale of great impressiveness and lasting charm. How much of this is fact and how much fiction?

The part about the first Phoenician ship creeping up to Tartessos is of course pure surmise. Some such ship must have made some such voyage about then, but no record remains. The part about the silver anchor stones and feeding troughs is stated in ancient literature. We do not know whether the Cretans got to Tartessos, *but they might have!* The connection between Tartessos on one hand and Homer's Scheria and Plato's Atlantis on the other are conjectures, but informed conjectures. Tyre and Gades and Carthage and the voyages of Hanno and Himiloco are from ancient history.

It fostered many controversies and speculations; at least 2,000 books and articles have been published on the subject. While there remain many possible alternative explanations of the Atlantis legend, the Tartessian one seems, at least to me, by far the most reasonable.

In ancient Greek and Roman literature there are only about fourteen specific references to Tartessos, plus thirteen (to "Tarshish") in the Bible, some of which may refer to Anatolian Tarsus or even to a port of doubtful identity on the Red Sea. For instance, Jonah was bound for Tarshish when he was given the heave-ho.

We do not know where the Tartessians came from. Though in some ways they were like other ancient Spaniards, they differed in others. They buried their dead instead of burning them, and they sailed the sea when most Iberians were landlubbers. Their language differed from that of other Iberians also, though that tells us little, because we do not know what the Iberians spoke. At one time, probably, there were many people of Berber stock in southern Spain, who therefore spoke a Hamitic tongue, while in the north to this day live the Eskualdunak or Basques whose language is completely unrelated, as far as linguists can tell, to any other on Earth. Presumably much of Iberia spoke languages of the Basque type until the Romans imposed their Indo-European tongue on the whole peninsula except for the Basque-speaking strip in the northeast.

Arrianus, a second-century Greek historian, said: "Tartessos was a colony of the Phoenicians," but this is probably the result of the confusion of Tartessos with Gades. Strabo says: "Ephoros says the Tartessians report that Ethiopians overran Libya as far as Dyris [the Atlas Mountains] and that some of them stayed in Dyris, while others occupied a great part of the seaboard." That sounds as though by "Ethiopians" the Tartessians meant Berbers, which implies that they were not themselves Berbers.

Some recent historians have suggested that the Tartessians were Iberians with a ruling caste of Kelts, but this is impossible because the city was a going concern before 1000 B.C., whereas the Kelts only invaded Spain after 700.

In the 1920s Professor Adolf Schulten of Erlangen University, assisted by the archaeologist Bonsor and the geologist Jessen, dug up what he thought, according to Strabo's directions, was the site of Tartessos. All he found were a few blocks of masonry which, he thought, indicated two former cities, one dating from about 3000 B.C. and the other from 1500 B.C., and a golden ring with inscriptions inside and outside, in an alphabet resembling Etruscan. The inside inscription consists of one word, something like *psonr* or *khonr*, repeated three times as if it were a magical spell.

That was all. They could not dig further because of the water table, so Schulten concluded that the remains of Tartessos had sunk deeply into the mud of the Guadalquivir estuary. Other archaeologists have doubted that he dug at the right site, or even that the city ever existed, despite the statements of classical historians.

If we assume that Tartessos was the prototype of Scheria and Atlantis, we can combine the common features of these fictional cities with what little we do know about Tartessos and ancient Spain to get a pretty good picture of this lost city. It stood on the island at the mouth of the Guadalquivir, surrounded by a great circular wall in which light and dark stone were set in a pattern, like a mosaic. The harbor was crowded with ships, mostly high-sided sailing ships built for the rough Atlantic waters, perhaps with leather sails. The temples and palace were decorated lavishly with gold, silver, ivory, and bronze.

Male Tartessians wore short, hip-length, purple-edged tunics, and over these big black woolen cloaks such as Spaniards continued to wear almost to the present. These cloaks sometimes had hoods and were buckled around the neck. The men wore their hair long or cut short in a bristling black crew cut. Most of them shaved.

The women wore brightly colored, ankle-length dresses and over them mantles with hoods and pointed tails and sleeves. They dressed their hair in elaborate coiffures, sometimes with horned headdresses about which they wound black veils much like the more modern high comb and mantilla. Others went in for crazy hats with fantastic wheel-shaped extensions over the ears. Around their necks they wore several big ropy necklaces with golden pendants.

Spanish soldiers carried shields, either small and round, or larger and rectangular, or eliptical. A poor Spaniard protected his head with a cap of woven sinew; a more prosperous one, with a plain bronze helmet; a rich one, with a bronze helmet with a triple purple crest. The rich warrior might also wear a corselet of overlapping bronze scales. He fought with a bow, a sling, javelins, a spear, or a sword. His sword might be either a straight double-edged broadsword like the Roman *gladius*, or a single-edged double-curved weapon like the Turkish *yataghan* or the Nepalese *kukri*. Spanish armies specialized in fast hit-and-run tactics; "guerrilla" is appropriately a Spanish word.

Early Greeks and Romans in Spain found in the people the same qualities that later visitors have attributed to them: that they were sober, haughty, brave, independent, stoical, and indolent. When besieged, they fought to the end, often committing mass suicide rather than surrender. But they fought each other as grimly as they fought the invaders and so were easily subdued piecemeal.

Today the Tartessian region is inhabited by people a little taller and broader-headed than most Spaniards, but otherwise not very different from them.

The ancient Tartessians seem to have differed in other ways from the Iberians: hospitable to extremes, intrepid mariners and much given to pleasure and luxury. As Homer's Phaiakes say of themselves, they loved "the feast, the lyre, the dance, change of raiment, warm baths, and love." They were a cultured people; as Strabo says: "The Turdetanians are ranked as the wisest of the Iberians; and they make use of an alphabet, and possess records of their ancient history, poems, and laws written in verse that are 6,000 years old."

At least two alphabets, generally similar to the early Latin and Etruscan alphabets, were in use in pre-Roman Iberia. Neither has been deciphered, though an inscription on a vase has recently been given a tentative reading as *gudua deitzdea*, "battle cry."

For centuries the Tartessians worked their fabulous mines, built their temples and palaces, raised cattle and sheep, and sent ships to the Scillies for tin. They worshipped the sun-god Neton at Acci, the dawn-god at Ebura, and moon-gods elsewhere. They ruled the neighboring Elbisini, Ileates, Oretani, and Cilbiceni, and they dominated or were allied with the powerful Mastians on the southeast coast of Spain. And they got a lot of fun out of life. Then the Carthaginians came and it was as if they had never been.

But you can still go to Cadiz, the world's oldest city, and see the narrow streets between the whitewashed houses thronged with people in whose veins still runs the blood of the Phoenicians who sailed to Tartessos 3,000 years ago. ■

Vanishing Islands of the Arctic

Russell W. Gibbons
December 1957

Why has no trace ever been found of the new Arctic lands that famed explorers have reported seeing?

On March 30, 1908, more than 300 miles out into the vast uncharted Arctic Ocean and 400 miles from the nearest Eskimo settlement on the far-off shores of Greenland, three figures, looking like black specks against the endless snow-covered ice fields, struggled northward with their dog teams and sleds.

The, leader, an unkempt, bearded white man, his face bronzed by many years exposure to the polar wastes, was becoming alarmed at the restlessness of his two Eskimo companions. The group had left land eleven days before, when they set out from the desolate tip of Axel Heiberg Land. Nevertheless, Dr. Cook, known and trusted for many years by these Smith Sound tribesmen, assured them they were never more than "two sleeps" from land.

His knowledge of the Eskimos and their superstitions convinced him that they would not venture further out into the unknown sea of ice. They had a traditional fear of the unknown, and the unknown was the miles of never-ending, windswept ice. But also, they were curious about this "Big Nail" that white men had been trying to reach for many years. They knew that many had perished in the search.

Now the two remaining members of Dr. Cook's expedition appeared to be upon the verge of panic. At the very moment they pleaded to return, the doctor later wrote, the darkened western sky cleared, and "my promise of nearness to land was unwittingly made good, as under the western heavens lay, to my surprise, a new land!"

Thus reassured, Cook's Eskimo companions continued with him to his goal, the "Big Nail." Whether Dr. Cook arrived at the North Pole in 1908 has been a subject of bitter controversy—a controversy that splits scientific and geographic groups to this day. And while historians may continue to argue this question, there remains an even greater riddle: What was this "snow-covered, ice-sheeted, and desolate" land that Cook named Bradley Land? And, more important, what became of it?

While many have questioned this discovery of Dr. Cook's (and later he was generally discredited in the eyes of the public in his unfortunate dispute with his contemporary, Peary), Cook's narrative is accepted by leading geographers and polar scientists today. While some question still exists as to who first discovered the Pole, most persons agree that the doctor did see something resembling land more than 100 miles from his goal. He is not alone in his report.

For more than a hundred years explorers from numerous nations, many of them scientists of unimpeachable integrity, as well as Eskimo travelers and hunters, have reported the discovery of new lands and islands in the North Polar regions. Their narratives have been accepted, their diaries have recorded the discoveries, and charts and maps of the

Arctic have included these new lands. Yet in time they have disappeared like the Arctic mist. They have become a part of the phantom lands of the Far North, the vanishing islands of the Arctic. They present an unsolved mystery which, to this day, has not been answered to the satisfaction of science and geography.

Doctor Cook, wrote in his diary in 1908 that "we noted many curious land mirage[s] of cliff[s] and mountains invested of glacial walls and pinnacles, but signs of land of this kind have been seen so often . . . that I did not at this time credit our eyes."

However, later on that same day he recorded:

> At noon, though, we saw actual land to the west. It was an ice-sheeted country about 1,000 feet high and about sixty miles away. What we saw of its coast ran almost in a straight line from north to south for thirty miles, and at both ends the coast line fell off quickly and was lost in steel-coloured haze which soon obscured the entire outline . . .

Delay was hazardous; the threat of flash Arctic storms and the diminishing food supply did not permit Cook to follow his impelling desire to inspect the newfound land. He wrote that they continued their journey Poleward. His Bradley Land was never seen again.

Was Cook's account just a great fabrication? Did "Polar delusion," which comes on Arctic travelers as mirages appear to desert travelers, overtake his party? Or was this new land real, and later, like many others, disappeared to become part of the riddle of the Arctic?

Historians of the Far North have recorded many similar discoveries. Some of them have since been acknowledged to have been floating islands of ice that looked like land from a distance; others were possibly mirages, but still others remain a mystery.

Two years before Cook's disputed journey, his former exploration mate—and later his rival—Commander Peary, reported that he had found a new and fabulous land northwest of Ellesmere Island. He wrote, "North stretched the well-known rugged surface of the polar pack . . . and northwest of it was with a thrill that my glasses revealed the faint white summits of a distant land." Peary called this distant land Crocker Land and recorded his disappointment that he could not explore the "snow clad summits of the distant mystery land" that season.

It was not Peary but his assistant, Donald MacMillian, who set out in search of Crocker Land in 1913. He traveled 150 miles into the frozen, uncharted sea, hunting the white summits that Peary had seen in 1906. He found nothing. Twelve years later MacMillian went back with another expedition still determined to solve, as he wrote, "that one great area in the Polar Sea that remains a mystery." It was on this expedition that Richard E. Byrd, destined to become famous as a polar explorer in his own right, made the first pioneer aerial flights over the vast Arctic basin. Crocker Land was not found from the air and has continued to be a question mark on the maps.

Cook's Bradley Land was destined to remain a mystery also. In 1914 Rudolph Franke, a member of Cook's 1908 polar expedition, planned to hunt the misty land in an attempt to vindicate his former commander's claims. Fate intervened. Plans for the Arctic expedition came to an end when Franke, recently returned from Germany, was interned as an enemy subject by the Canadian authorities.

However, in 1929 another German, a scientist named Dr. H. E. Krueger, took up the search and with a Danish assistant and two Eskimo companions set out on the ice cap toward the reported land to the northwest. They were never seen again.

Cook and Peary were only the last of that long line of hardy polar explorers who charted the north regions by dog team and sled, using Eskimos as guides and living off the land and sea when possible. They followed many illustrious explorers who had contributed to the list of vanishing islands. Always at first, these lands were accepted as fact; then, when subsequent explorers found no trace of them, bitter arguments arose as to the veracity of the discoverers.

Some prefer to catalogue them as imaginary polar islands and to explain them as hallucinations caused by the water, sky, or other Arctic phenomena, or as the unrestrained desire of some explorer to discover a new land. But their discoverers, regardless of scorn and ridicule, continued to maintain that what they saw was real.

In 1871 the American expedition under the command of Captain Charles Francis Hall, who proclaimed a "divine call" to find the lost Franklin expedition and later the North Pole itself, reported one of the first of these discoveries. A large, ice-covered island was seen in the Lincoln Sea and named Presidents Land. Expeditions that followed Hall into the frozen seas found no trace of the land.

Later Captain John Keenan sighted another uncharted land in the Beaufort Sea, in that hazy region north of Alaska and west of the American Archipelago. In 1917 the famous explorer and dean of Arctic scientists, Dr. Stefansson, ventured out onto the ice cap on the Beaufort Sea. Keenan Land was not to be found.

Russian Arctic explorers reported the existence of a vast land mass in the unexplored fringes above Asiatic Siberia. They called it Sannikov Land. Years later when Soviet aerial expeditions covered the eastern Arctic regions, Sannikov Land had vanished into the polar limbo with its predecessors.

Other explorers who reported lands not found later were Captain McClure, Marcus Baker, and Dr. R. A. Harris.

Dr. Harris believed in the existence of a large land mass in the Arctic Ocean where Crocker and Bradley lands had been reported. Observations of ice, tides, and currents in the region, the finding of driftwood on the shores of the western Queen Elizabeth Islands, and the legends of the Eskimos strengthened Dr. Harris' view. Both Dr. Cook and Commander Peary had reported bear and fox tracks 300 miles from known land. Possibly this is the strongest indication that an uncharted land mass exists where many have reported it.

What, then, is the answer to this puzzle of the Arctic? In this day and age is it possible that there are still blank spots in our maps of the top of the world?

When both Cook and Peary announced that they had reached the geographical North Pole in 1909 the stimulus for further Arctic expeditions was gone. Miles and miles of polar waste had been charted in the Arctic during attempts to reach the Pole. Now that that was accomplished the eyes of the nations turned to the bottom of the world, to Antarctica. They left vast, unexplored areas in the Arctic.

For more than fifteen years the windswept ice was almost forgotten. Then, starting in 1925, the explorers of a dozen nations looked down on the North Pole from the aircraft of Byrd, Amundson, Sir Hubert Wilkens, and Nobile. Yet the mysterious polar riddles of Captains Hall, Keenan, Cook, and Peary still remain unsolved. The supposed locations of the phantom lands were not on these direct flight routes to the Pole and back. And no one has explored further on foot.

In 1934 Sir Hubert Wilkens, flying with one companion over the very area where Dr. Cook had reported his Bradley Land some twenty-six years previously, saw something that led many to believe that he had found the lost island. Wilkens reported that a cloud forced them to descend, and, while their altimeter indicated that they were 1,500 feet above sea level, they actually found themselves flying only a few hundred feet above an "ice-sheeted country." Had they been unable to see the surface they might have crashed into the ice. Did Wilkens see Bradley Land?

Since 1946 our Northeast Command, in charge of the ever-increasing defense of the North, has sent out almost daily reconnaissance patrols over the western Arctic. Supposedly, the Soviets do the same on their side of the Pole. With this constant aerial coverage that has continued for more than a decade and with our new instrumentation in navigation and radar, is it still possible that "lost islands" exist?

Colonel Joseph Fletcher, commander of the Air Force task group that surveyed the Polar ice cap over a period of three years, says, "In many respects the region between the Pole and Ellesmere Land is still a mystery. While we have learned a great deal in the last decade our understanding is far from complete."

It is no secret that reconnaissance planes cannot master the topography of the Arctic through the mist and haze which hovers continually above the surface. The fact remains that hundreds, perhaps thousands, of square miles of Arctic vastness remain unexplored. What is to be found there is left up to conjecture and theory.

These fabulous floating islands of ice have been explained as huge break-offs from the Ellesmere glacier. Some authorities suggest this glacier may have been in existence since the last Glacial Age. Air Force observation teams that staffed stations on one of these "ice islands" for several months found that earth and boulders on the ice, having been deposited there by the Ellesmere glacier, gave it the illusion of land. They even found freshwater ponds and mosses.

The "ice islands" travel a circular course in the Arctic basin, affected by winds more than by currents. Some geographers have concluded that this is what Cook and Peary and others saw and called new lands. Further reflection, however, leads one to seriously doubt that this presents the solution.

In all the instances of the vanishing islands the travelers who reported their discovery observed them from a distance of sixty to one hundred miles. The American whaling captain, Keenan, saw his new land more than 150 miles from the northern waters of Alaska. Peary's "snowclad summits of a distant land" is self-descriptive. Cook describes a definite mountainous topography and even supplies a photograph of his land in his book on the polar quest.

All three of these narratives rule out the ice islands as we have to understand them, for few if any ice islands have points 100 feet above sea level. None have "snow-clad summits," nor "glacial walls and cliffs 1,000 feet high."

Cook did refer to "submerged land-ice," as he called it in 1908. He came upon it fifty miles north of his line of march from Bradley Land. There seems little doubt that the doctor passed over an island there; but what did he see 100 miles from the Pole?

No one knows.

Until every square mile of the uncharted Arctic Ocean is explored we will not know. Theoretical supposition will have to suffice. Until they are proven wrong we must credit the narratives of the pioneers of the Polar cap who risked death to explore the top of the world.

Arctic mist still shrouds the top of our globe, wrapping the mystery of the vanishing islands of the Arctic.   ■

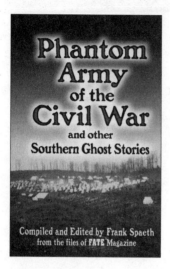

PHANTOM ARMY OF THE CIVIL WAR
and other Southern Ghost Stories
Compiled and edited by Frank Spaeth
from the files of FATE Magazine

Phantom armies from the Civil War and the Creek War still roam the battlefields that claimed their lives so many years ago. Why do these armies struggle through ghostly reenactments of battles long past …

A West Virginia town was named after a poltergeist and his phantom clipping shears. Read how other spirits made an extraordinary impact in Southern history and geography …

Why did a mysterious apparition of a tall woman draped in white leave a red rose as a token of her visits? Fifty years later, the dried rose remains as evidence of her strange presence …

Phantom Army of the Civil War features 35 stories of personal encounters with spirits throughout the South, filled with a flavor and tone that is truly and uniquely Southern. From Tennessee to Texas, and Louisiana to Virginia, these tales represent the best Southern ghost stories ever to appear in *FATE* Magazine during the past forty years. You will meet angry ghosts, still looking for answers as to why they are no longer alive … phantoms roaming the countryside searching for their lost loves … grandmothers protecting their kin from beyond the grave … and many, many more.

1–56718–297–6, 5³⁄₁₆ x 8¼, 256 pp., softcover $9.95

PSYCHIC PETS & SPIRIT ANIMALS
True Stories from the files of *FATE* Magazine
FATE Magazine Editorial Staff

FATE Presents:
Psychic Pets & Spirit Animals

True Stories
from the Files of FATE Magazine

In spite of all our scientific knowledge about animals, important questions remain about the nature of animal intelligence. Now, a large body of personal testimony compels us to raise still deeper questions. Are some animals, like some people, psychic? If human beings survive death, do animals? Do bonds exist between people and animals that are beyond our ability to comprehend?

Psychic Pets & Spirit Animals is a varied collection from the past 50 years of the real-life experiences of ordinary people with creatures great and small. You will encounter psychic pets, ghost animals, animal omens, extraordinary human-animal bonds, pet survival after death, phantom protectors and the weird creatures of cryptozoology. Dogs, cats, birds, horses, wolves, grizzly bears—even insects—are the heroes of shockingly true reports that illustrate just how little we know about the animals we think we know best.

The true stories in *Psychic Pets & Spirit Animals* suggest that animals are, in many ways, more like us than we think—and that they, too, can step into the strange and unknowable realm of the paranormal, where all things are possible.

1–56718–299–2, mass market, 172 pp., softcover $4.99

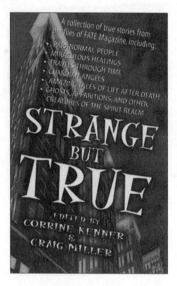

STRANGE BUT TRUE
From the files of
FATE **Magazine**
Corrine Kenner & Craig Miller

Have you had a mystical experience? You're not alone. For almost 50 years, *FATE* readers have been reporting their encounters with the strange and unknown. In this collection, you'll meet loved ones who return from beyond the grave ... mysterious voices warning of danger ... guardian angels ... and miraculous healings by benevolent forces. Every report is a first-hand account, complete with full details and vivid descriptions:

- "*Suddenly, a vision appeared at the foot of my bed. It was a young woman, wearing a sad expression on her strangely familiar face ...*"

- "*Running across the clearing from one thickly wooded area to the other was a thin, hunched creature, covered with light gray hair ...*"

- "*As I got closer to the white light, I heard a loud and forceful voice say, 'No!' ...*"

- "*At that moment I whooshed back into my body and sat up ...*"

Whether you're a true believer or a die-hard skeptic, you'll find Strange but True a book you can't put down.

1–56718–298–4, 5³⁄₁₆ x 8, 256 pp., softcover   **$9.95**

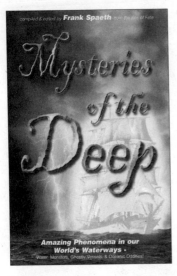

MYSTERIES OF THE DEEP

Amazing Phenomena in Our World's Waterways
compiled and edited by
Frank Spaeth
from the files of
FATE Magazine

I snapped a look out the window. The right wing had simply disappeared from sight! It was an eerie feeling, as though we'd flown into some impossible limbo. I then noticed that what had been blue sky had changed to a creamy yellow, as though we were in the middle of a bottle of eggnog.

— "The Triangle with Four (or More) Sides"

Thinking of going deep sea fishing? You'll think again after you read *Mysteries of the Deep*, a compilation of the best sea stories from the past 50 years of *FATE* Magazine. From Atlantis to the Bermuda Triangle, from the Loch Ness Monster to giant jellyfish, you'll find more than a few reasons to stay out of the water. The reports presented here come from the personal experiences of the average citizen as well as the detailed investigations of well-known authors such as Martin Caidin, Dr. Karl P. N. Shuker, Jerome Clark, and Mark Chorvinsky.

Now, from the safety of your beach chair, you can enjoy the best accounts of sea serpents ... lake monsters ... merfolk ... ghost ships ... mysterious shipwrecks ... the search for ancient vessels ... cities under the sea ... and many other ocean oddities.

1–56718–260–7, 5³⁄₁₆ x 8, 256 pp., illus. $9.95